FAIREST

FAIREST

a memoir

MEREDITH TALUSAN

Meredith Talusan

VIKING

VIKING
An imprint of Penguin Random House LLC
penguinrandomhouse.com

LIBRARY OF CONGRESS CATALOGING-IN-PUBLICATION DATA
Names: Talusan, Meredith, author.
Title: Fairest : a memoir / Meredith Talusan.
Description: [New York] : Viking, [2020]
Identifiers: LCCN 2019031336 (print) | LCCN 2019031337 (ebook) |
ISBN 9780525561309 (hardcover) | ISBN 9780525561316 (ebook)
Subjects: LCSH: Talusan, Meredith—Childhood and youth. |
Harvard University—Students—Biography. | Transgender youth—
United States—Biography. | Transgender women—United States—
Biography. | Filipino American youth—Biography. |
Gay college students—Massachusetts—Biography. |
Immigrant children—United States—Biography. |
Albinos and albinism—United States—Biography. |
Albinos and albinism—Philippines—Biography. |
Gender identity—United States—Psychological aspects.
Classification: LCC HQ77.8.T36 A3 2020 (print) |
LCC HQ77.8.T36 (ebook) | DDC 305.30973—dc23
LC record available at https://lccn.loc.gov/2019031336
LC ebook record available at https://lccn.loc.gov/2019031337

Printed in the United States of America
1 3 5 7 9 10 8 6 4 2

Designed by Amanda Dewey

for Josh

Ang hindi lumingon sa pinanggalingan, hindi makakarating sa paroroonan.

One who does not look back at their origin will never arrive at their destination.

—Tagalog proverb

There are some who, should we intrude upon them in the morning, still in bed, will present to our gaze an admirable female head, so generalised and typical of the entire sex is the expression of the face; the hair itself affirms it, so feminine is its ripple; unbrushed, it falls so naturally in long curls over the cheek that one marvels how the young woman, the girl, the Galatea barely awakened to life in the conscious mass of this male body in which she is imprisoned has contrived so ingeniously, by herself, without instruction from anyone else, to take advantage of the narrowest aperture in her prison wall to find what was necessary to her existence.

—Marcel Proust, *Sodom and Gomorrah*

Beauty is power; longing a disease.

—Stephen Sondheim, *Passion*

BRIDGES OF LIGHT

R ed brick; white tent; green grass. The outlines of prestige at an inner courtyard on a drizzly day. That was what I saw, the same as what I remembered, the specifics fuzzy from afar, my albino eyes only able to render life in scant detail unless I held it close. But I couldn't well squat down to examine those blades of grass under my feet as I entered the cover of that tent, not at a reunion reception for queer students at Harvard, whether at that moment in 2017, or when I graduated in 1997. I couldn't reveal myself a freak, especially not in this crowd, which would damn me for my failure of sight.

I arrived at this reception from New York, passing several bodies of water by train, but somehow the Charles still stood out to me when I took the T from South Station, the vast expanse of it, the first substantial body of water I crossed after the Pacific Ocean, when I left the pain of my childhood and hurtled to a future of great promise. This was a memory I could only vaguely make out from that distance of time, though I was used to the feeling, since my physical vision could never represent anything far except as blurs. My way of seeing had advantages though. Since I couldn't perceive detail from far away, I could more easily associate what I saw with my past, like how those language philosophers say that when a person hears the word "chair," they picture an idealized chair in their mind, drawn from an amalgam of memories. My vision was like that all the time, except it absorbed the few details I could actually see and integrated them with the objects I imagined.

Unable to identify any specific blade of grass on this occasion, I could imagine the blurry mass under my feet as the same uniform stalks of verdant green I'd stepped on twenty years earlier, and so became two people without much effort, the person who arrived today and the young man from the afternoon of my improbable graduation from the most prestigious university in the world. Me, a child from a Philippine province, descendant of peasant farmers, son of derelict immigrants.

Except: I was no longer a son, no longer a man. I became more aware of this as groups of gay men, mostly aging or aged, circulated around me. Their manner of casual evaluation was all too familiar from the countless gay occasions I'd been exposed to—clubs, parties, rallies, meetings—events where official interactions were always tinged with the energy of male desire. Though having such blurry vision made me pay closer attention to what I could perceive, and what I saw was the change in how those men approached and retreated, the way their bodies created invisible patterns in space, the distinction between being observed but found wanting and being dismissed offhand, the difference between being a not-so-hot guy and a woman.

"It's kinda fun to see a bunch of boys who rejected me under the same tent," a droll voice behind me said, whose owner I immediately identified as Kit Clark, a black alum who was several classes ahead of me but had worked at Harvard after graduation and never left. We got back in touch a few years earlier, so he was one of the few people I'd seen since I finished college.

"Haven't snagged one yet?" I asked as I turned to face him.

"It's a lot worse than when you were here," he replied. "The men keep getting younger and I'm only getting uglier."

I would protest if it were anyone else, but Kit's tone had always made it clear that he did not invite praise whenever he said something negative about his appearance. What he invited was empathy, agreement with the injustice of how looks so determined our place in the gay pecking order and how our lack of attractiveness had so much to do with our race and femininity.

Kit's broad, open face, his strong jaw, his wide nose, would not be considered ugly, if not for the kinky hair he kept long. His olive skin would have also been attractive, except that it didn't come with the hypermasculinity that seemed to be a prerequisite for black gay men to be thought hot. Instead, Kit refused to subject his tall, lanky frame to the rigors of a gym regimen and preferred activities like circus silks and modern dance, which he could perform with a lithe grace.

"You can always leave Cambridge," I suggested.

"You're not serious. My life is here. I accept that I'm undesirable."

This struck me as a fundamental difference between us and why I'd kept my friendship with Kit at arm's length over the years, because his self-acceptance rattled me. Kit would not allow himself to butch it up or keep his hair short just to court suitors; he wanted to be wanted, but he wouldn't compromise himself for the sake of another's desire. I, on the other hand, didn't have the same solid sense of self. I'd been more than willing to clamp down on my most undesirable traits, especially two decades ago, when I had such an unclear sense of who I was beyond other people's reflections of me.

At the same time, Kit recognized long before I did how alike we were, that we both occupied liminal places in our white-dominated Harvard gay society. He recognized me as an albino Asian when everyone else thought I was white; he could tell that my workout regimen was cover for a femininity I obscured because it was not attractive. He could also tell that someone needed to see the reality of me even when I took such pains to hide it, and Kit generously gave my inner self a witness, even when I could never settle for long under his glare.

Kit motioned to someone who approached us, and when he got close, I surprised myself when I recognized Sean Chambers, an English lit grad student while I was in college. His appearance had not changed much, just a few more pounds and a widow's peak, his red hair duller than I remembered.

"I'm Meredith," I said.

"I remember you," he replied. I couldn't tell whether he'd learned about my transition through the grapevine or if he was just good at going with the flow. Though the change between old and new me wasn't as drastic as it used to be; I'd cut my hair in a bob and was not wearing makeup, had on a loose gray jumpsuit that could be feasibly worn by a man or a woman.

"Do you recognize anyone else?" I asked.

Sean motioned with his head toward a man passing by in tight jeans and a white shirt under his blazer. The man's tanned skin seemed leathery to me even from a distance, his hair equal parts pepper and salt.

"Vince Parker. I had a crush on him," Sean said. "He was so hot."

"Everyone had a crush on him," Kit rejoined.

As Kit and Sean gossiped about how attractive Vince had been, I reflected on the word "was." I imagined the man would feel hurt to be spoken of like this, his beauty in the past tense.

"Anyway, we all get older and uglier," Kit concluded.

"Except for Meredith," Sean said as he turned to me. "You look the same."

"Isn't it weird," Kit observed, "how she changed genders and looks more like she did twenty years ago than any of us?"

I chuckled then. I used to look really different when I wore heels, dresses, and a full face of makeup nearly every day. But as I put more and more of my thoughts out into the world, I also grew wary of the need to conform to that world's expectations of me. So the heels came off, then the makeup, then the girly clothes, until I was left presenting myself in much the same way I did before transition, except hormones had given me breasts that allowed people to identify me as female. Though I hoped my belief in my own womanhood also came across, regardless of how I looked.

When I noticed a break in the drizzle, I walked away from the Lowell House courtyard where the reception was, across Massachusetts Avenue, and back to Adams House, where Harvard was housing me for the weekend. A concrete gargoyle whose mouth

opened out onto a small fountain, long out of use, greeted me before I opened the heavy, carved door to my old undergrad dorm.
This grandness was a remnant of a time when Adams was known
as the Gold Coast apartments, housing for the richest among Harvard men. I walked down the marble-tiled hallway to the room I'd
been assigned, its door also heavy as I opened it, with a ceiling at
least eleven feet high and a giant fireplace whose marble mantel
reached above my head. It was next door to FDR's old room back
when he himself was a Harvard man, which alumni of the house
had lovingly restored with Persian rugs and period furniture.

My own room was barren except for the same oak table and
dresser from twenty years ago, the same chair upholstered a pale
teal, with legs that connected and curved in the back, the better to
tip it upward in a precarious balance while lost in contemplation,
as I often did when I lived in Adams. I spied the same single mattress from my college days when I opened the door to the bedroom,
on a frame with a headboard made of black metal that vaguely
reminded me of prison bars. A clear plastic bag with sheets and a
towel lay on top of it, which only amplified the prison effect, ironic
given how it was my younger brother who went to jail my senior
year, a fact I barely registered through the haze of classes and fi-
nals. I went in and was about to put sheets on the bed when my
eye caught a white glint, and I turned to face my reflection against
the mirror through the open bathroom door, which I knew was the
same kind of mirror from twenty years ago even when it was
blurry, a shallow vertical rectangle, its corners rounded. As for the
reflection itself, I could only really see the shape of my head from
that distance, the yellow outline of my blond hair, the entire re-

flection brighter on the side closest to the window, receding to near blackness at the lower left corner.

I remembered a game I used to play with myself when I saw my reflection from afar. About twelve feet away, I couldn't make out the details of my face, could only glean the fuzzy outlines of my eyes and lips, the holes of my nostrils, as the rest of my features blended with my skin. From that distance, I could only imagine what my face would really look like when I got closer.

The words "you look the same" lingered in my mind, and I wondered whether I could imagine myself with a man's face, knowing that for many years now, I only saw a woman's face when I looked in the mirror, and it had taken so much sacrifice to bring that reflection into being. I still got plenty of comments online that I looked like a man, insults I brushed off because I trusted my own perception over anyone else's. It felt perverse, even dangerous, to bring my old face back, the man I used to be.

But I wanted to prove to myself that I could recall my old face without shaking my confidence in my womanhood. The more my skin prickled at the thought of imagining myself as a man—instead of a woman like before, or a white American instead of an albino Filipino before that—the more I wanted to play that game again. Being in that room, in that place where I had spent so much time as a man, I wondered if I could recover my old self, at least for a moment.

I faced the mirror and imagined my prominent brow, my angular jaw, my flat chin, the features that made me fear I would always be perceived as a man when I started transition. I took one step toward that mirror, and then another, when I noticed that my jaw was no longer so sharply angled, as fat had settled on that part of my face and turned what was once a line into a shallow curve. Another step and I noticed my rosy cheeks, another the natural pucker of my lips. So by the time I got close and leaned against the sink, I found myself unable to maintain the sensation that this face was a man's, or that I by extension was a man, even when I understood what Sean meant when he said that I looked the same, my essential features more like they were twenty years ago than the other people at that reception. None of the reflections from outside could unmoor my own perception of myself, one that I'd honed and maintained over many years like a delicate, well-tended plant.

I hardened the muscles on my face, furrowed my brow, and clenched my lips into a hard line so I would look more like a man. Though the impression I got was not of a man but of a woman pretending to be a man, and not very well, as my features softened back to their original expression. This reminded me of how after I learned to speak with an American accent, and tried to get back my old Filipino one with its hard consonants and singsong intonation, it always felt like I was making fun of the accent even though it was the one I grew up with. I also couldn't manage to use that accent in daily life because it reminded me too much of being made fun of, being thought less because I came to high school in America speaking that way. Maybe my mind also protected me from my male past, as I gave up and accepted that I could no longer perceive myself as a man or harden my features to look like one. I wondered to what degree the image in front of me conformed to what was real, but as soon as I wondered this, I also reminded myself that there is no single, objective truth, how reality is so much more malleable than people make it out to be, that the first step in making something real is believing that it could be real, that my very presence in front of this mirror, in this school, in the world, was itself proof of the power of belief in a reality that seemed entirely farfetched.

So the mirror was just a mirror now, the reflection of a reality I myself perceived, that I was a woman. But as soon as I understood this, I also understood that the reality of my race was even more embedded, how I imagined myself as a white American for so long that I didn't need to even try to conjure an image of myself as an albino Filipino to know that I could not, because I'd relied on my image as a white person for even longer than I had as a woman. Even though I knew I was albino and lived with the sensory reality of poor vision and the palest skin, I perceived myself to be a white person of European descent when I looked in the mirror; I relied on that perception to bolster my belief that I could do well in America, that I was better than the brown rural peasants I left behind.

For most of my existence, mirrors were not just mirrors to me, but bridges made of light to fantastic destinations, where I would be different than myself and lead a better life. If the other side of the mirror was another world, then my imagination was the vehicle that could take me there. In that dimly lit bathroom, I came to acknowledge that I was no longer at my place of origin but at my destination, the world I'd determined for myself I would someday reach, and that my imagination had successfully taken me there, a place where passing had transformed into being.

But having arrived, it turned out my imagination did not have the fuel to take me back, that the journey to this world I now inhabited was a one-way trip. I touched the mirror and felt the truth of its material surface, how it was a piece of glass with beveled edges, coated in silver that had oxidized in places, creating black spots like little islands on the edges of the frame.

It was eerie to be on the other side of that glass, when I once stared at my reflection in a mirror so much like this one and believed I could never become the beautiful woman in my fantasies. Then I remembered that I'd already crossed one bridge toward whiteness and its advantages, including an education I could have never imagined possible, had I been the color I was meant to be.

It was sophomore year, the Saturday before Halloween, 1994. I ended up on the top floor of the farthest entryway in Adams House, which I didn't mind because the eaves made my room feel like a garret. I'd recently learned that word at a lecture on Virginia Woolf's *A Room of One's Own*, where the professor proposed the garret as an ideal space for writers in search of quiet and contemplation. I felt inspired in that room, even though I occasionally bumped my head when I sat up in bed.

I'd skipped breakfast that day, so it was past noon by the time I shuffled into the dining hall. I hoped to see people I recognized after I got food, but when I didn't, I sat alone at one of the square tables in the middle of that vast space with its dark wood paneling and red velvet curtains, hoping still that someone I knew would come along and join me. I had only lived in the house for six weeks and was slow to make friends.

At the next table, I overheard some juniors I didn't know well talking about Drag Night, an Adams tradition I'd heard about but didn't realize was happening over dinner that evening. They were planning to do a number to "It's Raining Men."

"We need to go to the thrift store to get costumes," a compact blond man named Zach said.

"And he needs to shave," a redheaded girl named Sarah commented. I sneaked a peek to see who she was talking about, someone whose name I didn't know, who had dark curly hair and patches of stubble.

"It'll be funnier if I don't shave," the guy said, who I immediately assumed was straight.

I wondered if I should ask to join their group, but I couldn't rely on them not to laugh in my face or make excuses not to let me in. Anyway, just because I was gay didn't mean I should automatically do drag. I'd never dressed in women's clothes before, not even in private or, for that matter, gone out in costume for Halloween, since we didn't have Halloween in the Philippines. No one at lunch seemed interested in asking me anyway.

I walked over to the mailboxes after my meal and ran into a girl I'd gotten friendly with the day I moved in, another sophomore named Lucy Bisognano.

"So," she began, "what are you doing for Drag Night?"

"Just watching."

"You have to at least dress up. Come over to my room. I have dresses that would probably fit you."

I agreed to meet Lucy later that afternoon. Though I was excited to wear women's clothes for the first time, I was even more thrilled that someone at Harvard cared enough to hang out with me, especially someone as popular as Lucy, small-boned and fine-featured yet unfailingly jovial, like a bird in mid-flight. I was a poor kid who'd gone to a mediocre public school in Chino, California, in the smoggy, working-class part of Los Angeles where my uncle worked as a nurse, so that was where we ended up when my family immigrated four years earlier. My brain and my will got me to Harvard, but I didn't want to be the poor immigrant kid once I got there. I pretended to be like everyone else, did a good enough job with my accent to pass for white and native-born but not a good enough job that I could keep other kids from thinking I was weird. Hardly anyone wanted to be my friend, and the few who did I didn't really care for, not until Lucy came along.

A couple of hours before dinner and the Drag Night festivities, I knocked on the door of Lucy's suite, and she led me through the halogen-lit common room into her bedroom, where Monet and Degas posters livened up the beige walls. Her room barely fit her desk and single bed, which suited me fine because I liked being near her.

"I'm not sure what will fit you so let me just show you what I have."

As I sat on Lucy's bed, on a comforter adorned with tiny pink flowers I couldn't identify—maybe peonies, or gardenias—she opened her closet door and pulled out dresses on hangers one by one, then draped them in front of her. I wanted to examine the details of those garments, admire the lace pattern of one and the pleating of another, but I would have needed to get really close, and it felt too early to expose my poor vision to my new friend. But she must have sensed a heightened reaction when she showed me a sleeveless dress made of black velvet, a fabric I immediately identified because its shade was darker than any other cloth, a depth of color I hadn't known back home.

"I bet this would look great against your skin," Lucy said.

She left the room so I could change. After I stripped down to my white briefs, I stepped into the dress, put my arms through the sleeve holes, and shivered at that forbidden thrill I'd only known about secondhand, of being a man in women's clothes. I'd grown up seeing such men, had even worked with a few when I was a child actor in the Philippines, those bakla a staple of slapstick comedies on TV and in movies. But while my culture tolerated bakla, nobody ever took them seriously, so I wasn't interested in being like them. But maybe because I knew I could dress up as a girl if I wanted to, I also didn't really find the idea particularly exciting, not until I got to America and noticed how men dressing up as women seemed so much more taboo than it did back home.

I was able to zip the dress up most of the way, as it stretched to encompass my back, muscular from pull-ups at the gym. The neckline scooped tastefully in front and was bordered in a shiny material, maybe satin, which I didn't notice from afar. I looked down to observe that the dress ended a couple of inches above my knee and had a slit on one side. I remembered a woman on a talk show say that every girl needs a little black dress in her closet; this was the kind of dress she must have meant.

"I hate you," Lucy said when she came back into the room and helped me zip up the rest of the way. "This looks way better on you than it does on me."

As Lucy looked through her jewelry box to see what might work with my outfit, I recalled the moment a few years earlier, I must have been thirteen, when my cousin Baby walked in on me as I was about to put a shirt on in front of our old wooden house's only mirror, attached to a weathered armoire.

"You have a woman's waist," she observed, as she brushed her palm down my side to demonstrate how my body curved in below my rib cage and then back out toward my hips. I smiled into the mirror at my cousin's compliment and felt an echo of that pleasure with Lucy.

"Your hands are so dainty and small!" my friend marveled as she held one and slipped a gold bangle through my fingers. I looked down and noticed that my hand was indeed smaller than Lucy's, though that was only because I was Asian. My hands weren't particularly small by Filipino standards, but people judged my body differently in America, especially someone like Lucy, who didn't know I was albino.

We sat on the bed as Lucy applied gray eyeshadow to my lids with a tiny, padded brush, then used a stick whose end reminded me of a spider's legs to rub the tops and bottoms of my nearly white lashes with mascara, a cosmetic item I hadn't known existed until that moment. She ordered me not to blink even though my eyes started to water, and I felt the heavy thickness of the substance when she was done. Lucy complimented what she called my "cupid's bow" before she uncapped a black tube of bloodred lipstick and rubbed it against my lips. She stood up and looked under piles of papers on her desk until she found a gold-and-black hair ornament she called a barrette and affixed it to my short hair right above my forehead.

"You're almost ready," she said. "We just need some pumps."

Lucy gave me a pair of narrow black shoes made of plastic that was as shiny as the velvet of my dress was matte, with heels that tapered at the bottom, a couple of inches high. When I stood up after I put them on, pleased that they fit, I also found that I didn't have as much trouble walking in them as I expected. Lucy led me back to her common room, where she opened a closet door. With a flourish of her hands, she motioned me toward the mirror on the other side. When I ambled over, I realized I was looking down because I was afraid to fall, so I tilted my head upward to see myself.

"Not bad," I said. I didn't look nearly as ridiculous as I expected.

"Come on, you look great!" Lucy countered, and I smiled to please her, grateful she took so much effort to get me ready.

Lucy's suite was in an entryway near the dining hall, and as we walked downstairs toward the Gold Room—the vestibule before the main eating area that was literally painted gold—I came upon a few guys wearing dresses. In makeup and wigs, the thick hair on their faces and arms looked out of place, their movements clumsy as they loomed above me despite my heels, which clattered on the emerald tile floor.

"Whoa, you look like a real woman," Kit Clark observed as he greeted me in the Gold Room. "It's almost too convincing."

Kit came dressed in a turquoise medieval gown that swooped to the floor, his curly hair in a low ponytail. He would have made a plausible woman too if not for his stubble, and a chin that was even broader than mine.

"What do you mean, too convincing?" I asked.

"Drag is supposed to be ironic," he replied. "You just look like a girl."

I understood what he meant when Zach and his friends did their "It's Raining Men" number that night and wore ridiculous blond wigs as they sashayed and stomped on a makeshift stage in the middle of the dining hall, fingers splayed and wrists bent. Other men performed classics like "I Will Survive" and more

recent Top 40 hits like "Express Yourself" with that same ludi-
crous air that felt designed to make fun of women.

Still in my outfit, I went clubbing with some gay friends after
dinner, who let me hang around because we were all queer and at
Harvard, even though none of them gave me the time of day ro-
mantically.

There was a Central Square club named ManRay whose Liquid
night on Saturdays catered to a mixed crowd, and, befitting the
name, people were encouraged to gender-bend. I'd gone there a
few times in shiny tops or spandex bell-bottoms, but this was the
first time I'd bent my gender all the way.

It was amusing to see curious looks from men who gave off
straight vibes as I danced to bands like New Order and Pet Shop
Boys throughout the night. Though my feet started to hurt after a
while, I enjoyed the way my heels made my butt wiggle as I walked
out of the club. I didn't have the money to take a cab, so I left
shortly after midnight to catch the T before it closed and ambled
down the brick pavement of Mount Auburn Street toward Adams,
after I got out at Harvard Square.

I hadn't had anything to drink, but even so, I was afraid of tripping
because of the brick, my heels, the tiredness of my feet. I also realized
it had been a mistake not to bring a jacket. It was an unusually warm
fall night, but the temperature had turned chilly over the last several
hours, and I had to hug myself for warmth. I was about a block away
from my dorm entrance when I became aware of a rumbling sound,
unusually close to the sidewalk, then the honk of a horn.

I kept walking, figuring the noise had nothing to do with me.
But as I got closer to my house and the street got quieter, I began
to hear yelling from several young men.

"Turn around!" I heard one of the voices say.

I paused and swiveled my head in their direction, where I saw figures so dimly lit they looked like shadows, crawling by in a giant, early-model American car.

"Hey, beautiful!" someone from inside yelled.

"Come ride with us!" another said. I smiled and shook my head as I rested a hand on my cheek.

"Not tonight," I replied, my voice suddenly breathy and high. I observed my thickened eyelashes bat before I turned around.

It was only when I started walking again that I felt the sting of fear. I consciously pieced together what my instinct had already computed, that these young men had mistaken me for a woman, and I played my part to appease them. I also became aware that if one of these men had decided to get out of the car and examine me more closely, they would realize the mistake they'd made, and that this would make them angry, maybe angry enough to use their fists, and that it would be my body and not just my heels against the bricks. A deep part of me knew that running might incite them to chase me, and the safest choice was to walk at an even pace.

I was just half a block away now, and instead of their shouts, my mind tuned in to the outlines of my world, the rectangles on the ground that were barely red in the darkness of that hour, the thick white lines of a crosswalk in the distance. Lucy had lent me a black beaded clutch, and when I finally got to my dorm entrance, I fumbled for the clasp before I was able to fish out my keys, the ones I had a hard time getting in the keyhole because of my weak eyes. I had learned to unlock the door by feel rather than sight.

I brushed the hole with a trembling finger then tried to fit my key into the slot for seconds when each gust of wind felt like a man's breath, every failed jiggle like a trap I couldn't get out of. I turned myself into a ghost like I did as a child, without a body and free of fear, when my mother beat me or left me locked in my room overnight. The voices of those men, so loud only a few seconds before, sounded as if they came from the other end of a long tunnel, slippery as I tried to crawl out. Finally, my key found the hole and I clicked the latch above the handle with my thumb, then opened the heavy door as fast as I could.

I ran into a wall of fluorescent light and was suddenly afraid my broad shoulders would give me away. I hurried down the hallway and out of sight, started the climb up to my room as my heels made an almost clanging sound when they reverberated on the circular stairway. I only felt safe once I closed the door to my suite, as physical sensation returned to my limbs and I realized how much my feet hurt. I went to my bedroom to take off my shoes, relieved that my roommates weren't there to see me. I felt ashamed somehow, to have attracted attention and then gotten so scared. I would turn the incident into a good story at brunch the next day, how some straight guys followed me home because they thought I was a hot girl. But that night, I just wanted to live with the fear and shame on my own, without the need to transform my experience into a witty anecdote.

I sat on the bed and took off my heels, rubbed my feet as I reflected on how tired they were, how nervous I still was, as my palm gripped my chest and I felt my heartbeat slow to a normal pace before my fingers relaxed. Yet as I recalled my fear, there also grew in me a surprising, pleasant sensation, and I smiled despite myself, fascinated at the sudden feeling that the experience had been worth it. Those men were convinced I was a woman, and I became curious about what they saw.

I left my bed and crossed our empty common room to look at myself in the bathroom mirror. But my face was too hard, the fluorescent light too harsh up close. So I took a step back, and then another, and then a few more, until I only saw my face as a sketch whose details my imagination could fill. The colors were more pronounced than I was used to, my eyes and lips outlined in smoke and red. I noticed the pleasant semicircle of my dress's neckline against my chest and imagined graceful clavicles I couldn't see. Though I did see that my neck was thin and long, something I'd never paid attention to before. All evening, people had told me I looked like a real girl, and those anonymous men had given me proof, but it was only then, in that bathroom mirror, that I perceived a glimmer of what they saw.

From afar, I felt like a girl to myself, even a beautiful girl. I gazed at that reflection and imagined my face as a woman's face, holding features in my mind that others had told me were feminine—my high cheekbones, pouty lips, small nose. I grinned to myself at the thought of my nose, which I'd pulled on since childhood, hoping it would grow, since Filipinos preferred sharp, protruding noses. But I realized that my nose was dainty on a white woman's face, as I also became conscious that of course it was a white woman's face I imagined in that reflection, one of those vivacious ballerinas who thrilled audiences night after night, or the heroine of a nineteenth-century novel.

Though as I began to walk toward my reflection, more and more of my masculine features came into focus, my broad shoulders and strong jaw, my prominent brow and high hairline, receding slightly at the corners. By the time my hands touched the sink's cold porcelain again, I couldn't help but perceive myself as a man dressed as a woman, a fool who would have been laughed at and beaten up had those men looked at me close in the light and found out the truth. I felt the immediate urge to rub off the makeup, but something stopped me, and instead, I leaned even closer toward my reflection. I suddenly remembered that I didn't always think of my face as a white person's face, how it took years to convince myself that I was not the aberration other people wanted me to be, but was instead practically the same as the Americans I watched on TV. I also recalled how this was not the first time I'd seen a reflection and imagined myself as a white woman with golden hair.

PART ONE

SUN CHILD

1980–1990

1.

mong my people, it is a widely held belief that an infant would become whatever its mother had craved—sugar and a child would turn out sweet, for instance, or plantains and the baby would grow sturdy. Pregnant women were therefore advised not to spend too much time in the sun and certainly not to stare at it directly, for fear that their baby would be born anak araw, a sun child, the strangest creature whose skin was so pale it glowed, and who couldn't open its eyes except to squint, destined to be nearly blind, an affront against nature.

Yet on the long bus ride from my parents' house in Manila to my hometown of Talacsan in the province of Bulacan, my grandmother Nanay Coro told me that as soon as she held me in her arms, she was sure I was a blessing. She refused to allow anyone to talk about me any other way, especially because I was destined to live in America, the richest of countries, where Mama's father, Lolo Bert, had settled, full of people who looked like me. And anyway, I wasn't like other anak araw. My mother stayed away from the sun when she was pregnant but craved sweet corn, and so that was how I must have ended up with corn silk hair and fair skin.

Though I did burn in the sun, I wasn't near blind like I was supposed to be, only nearsighted, which was lucky since I wouldn't have known what to do with myself if I couldn't read. As our bus sped across the highway through an endless series of rice paddies, which I perceived as patches of yellowish brown since it was April and the fields had been harvested, my grandmother assured me that I was meant for a better future than her and our ancestors, farmers who had tilled soil in the fields surrounding our village for generations.

"This is because you are fair and beautiful," she said, "not dark and ugly like me."

I learned not to protest because I'd heard similar words many times before, not just from her but from other relatives and neighbors in Talacsan, where I lived until I was three. I'd spent the last two years going to school in Manila and only making weekend visits back to the place I still considered home, but after my grandmother discovered that Mama had been locking me in my bedroom to go out after I fell asleep, and having learned that a distant cousin had died in a fire in the middle of the night, she insisted that I return to Talacsan and wait another year to start first grade with other kids my age.

"There are people in Manila who think I look abnormal," I said.

"They're just jealous they don't have a child like you."

I looked forward to living in Talacsan again, where no one found me strange. We eventually got to the bus station in Baliwag, the closest city to our municipality, where Nanay and I walked to the jeepney stand for our town. There were no jeepneys when we got there, which meant that it would be at least a thirty-minute wait, so Nanay Coro decided to stop by the dry market to get some supplies. On our way, we passed by a store that sold cassettes, and I asked my grandmother if she would buy me one. Papa owned cassettes back in Manila, but I'd never had one of my own.

We came in from the afternoon light, and I blinked as my eyes adjusted to the darkness of that tiny stall, where a woman sat over a glass cabinet filled with cassettes. We were in a hurry, so Nanay Coro asked the store owner to suggest a tape for me to buy. The woman contemplated for a moment, then opened the cabinet to pull out a cassette titled "Small Voice," with a picture of a girl in pigtails named Lea Salonga.

"She's not as white as you but her voice is beautiful," the woman said.

The vehicle was nearly full when we returned to the stand, but people made room. The jeepney had padded seats and open windows on two sides. In the middle were various goods obtained from Baliwag—fruits and vegetables, sacks of rice, even an actual chicken in a wire cage. There were murmurs once we got on, and I sat on Nanay Coro's lap.

"Your skin is so white!" the woman next to me exclaimed as she touched my arm. The jeepney rumbled then began to move, and I looked out the window to observe the path to my village.

We turned onto a dirt road that led to our municipality, San Rafael, Bulacan, and drove through a succession of villages— Caingin, Pantubig, Poblacion—groups of mostly wooden houses with thatch roofs, the larger ones raised one story high to protect them from floods, with a few newer ones made of concrete blocks piled on top of one another, filled with cement, then painted in bright, pastel colors. Our route took us by the vast Angat River, visible down a slope, past trees and rows of raised wooden houses near its bank. I craned my neck to see the other side of the river as the jeepney passed, just a flurry of green and brown patches, and I asked Nanay Coro whether there were boats that traveled across the water.

"Sometimes," she replied. "But most people just go by land."

"They could build a bridge."

"The river is too wide here," she replied. "They can only do that in America."

Everything seemed easier in America—easier to live, easier to travel. As I gazed across the river, I recognized that even though I loved it here, there was another part of me that was so curious about elsewhere, and I would always have to pick between my riverbank or the other, home or away from home, the Philippines or America. The thought of it left me with a sadness I'd never felt before.

Though I grew happy again when I registered the long stretch of fields that led to our village, as the jeepney's motor emitted a soft roar on its way up the long hill, our family house near the top, a wooden structure raised on a foundation of stones. I was home.

I ran up the stairs and told my younger aunt Tita Nanette, a plump girl only three years older than me, that Nanay Coro got me Lea Salonga's cassette. My grandmother took out a portable tape player from inside a dresser, as the three of us sat on the wooden bench in our common room and listened to the tape for the first time. I was unprepared for the beauty of Lea Salonga's voice—clear and resonant as a church bell—so it took me some moments to notice that she sang in English, and I didn't fully understand her. But once I did recognize the language her songs were in, I sensed that Lea didn't sing in English like other Filipino singers I'd heard on the radio, because she sounded actually American, in a way I couldn't describe.

My grandmother and aunt left me to prepare dinner, but I stayed on that bench and listened to the entire album, then listened to it again, and so many more times over the following days and weeks that my family teased me about having a crush on Lea. I'd been exposed to English through TV shows and American pop music on the radio, but when I listened to that girl, I felt an urge to learn the language like her, so I could sing her songs as well as she did. I tried to copy her pronunciation, and over time, I too became aware of v's and th's that didn't exist in Tagalog, and that my tongue needed to relax so I could pronounce English's softer sounds. If a Filipino girl like Lea could develop the ability to perfect her English and sound American, then I became hopeful I could someday learn English so well that everyone would just think of me as an American boy, that no one would ever know where I actually came from.

One night, I figured out that I could listen to Lea Salonga in the dark before bed, even when my grandparents and aunts slept with me on the seagrass mat in our common room, under a giant mosquito net. If I pressed my ear against the tape recorder's speaker, I could play "Small Voice" low enough that I wouldn't disturb them but loud enough that I could hear. I mouthed Lea's words when she sang and found to my wonder that the direct contact between the speaker and my ear formed a connection between Lea's voice, my mind, and my mouth, so I felt the eerie sensation that Lea was singing through me, as those wondrous sounds vibrated inside my body. For a moment, it felt as if I was Lea Salonga herself, and that feeling made me want to be her, so much that I wouldn't mind being a girl if only I were blessed with her voice.

The next afternoon, after she had finished her chores and the sun was no longer too punishing, Nanay Coro took me to see relatives on the other side of our village. My grandmother used an umbrella to protect me from the sun, as we left our house and walked down the dirt road that ran through our hamlet of a few hundred people. We passed the town chapel, a couple of sundry stores, and porches where mostly men and a few women whiled the day away playing billiards or cards. Nanay Coro greeted everyone and encouraged me to do the same, though I tried not to be overly enthusiastic so we wouldn't end up lingering too long.

Our neighbors were used to me by then, not like in other towns, where children and their mothers often ran after me to touch my hair and skin. Still, several women we passed exclaimed, "He's so white!" when they saw me. I'd learned to take my special place in our village for granted, how I could command attention just by showing up, make people squeal or clap with a cute expression.

One of the houses on our path belonged to Nanang Lita, a distant cousin of my grandmother's, who had a twelve-year-old son named Jembong. We found him sitting on top of his mother's cement porch balustrade, in bright blue shorts and a thin, sleeveless shirt, one leg on the railing and another swinging down to the ground, supporting himself with one hand behind him like one of those pinup girls I'd seen in Papa's magazines.

"Have you found a boyfriend yet?" Nanay Coro teased as we passed.

Even at his age, Jembong was already well-known in our village as bakla, a boy who acted like a girl and liked other boys. I'd seen plenty of bakla on TV, though that boy was the first I'd met in person, as he covered his mouth with one hand in an expression of playful shock.

"Ay, I'm too young," Jembong replied. "I want to remain a virgin until marriage."

The neighbors behind him laughed. "You know you can have a boyfriend and still be a virgin," my grandmother joked.

"I know, but we must remember the words of Our Father," he said, as he put his palms together, closed his eyes, and feigned prayer. "'Lead us not into temptation,' and by temptation He means boys." This produced a fresh peal of laughter from our neighbors, and I found myself laughing too even though I didn't know exactly what "virgin" meant, just that it was good to be one like the Virgin Mary. I was also perplexed over how Jembong allowed himself to be made fun of so openly, even if it was just my grandmother's good-natured ribbing. It was clear enough that Jembong provoked so much laughter because everyone assumed he could never get a boyfriend, that no one ever wanted to love a bakla, which was also the constant theme of those comedies on TV, the desperation of these creatures who were tolerated but never wanted.

We continued our walk and passed by my great-grandmother Inang's house, where she had planted a fruit orchard in the back. She gave us some guavas she picked herself, before sending us off to Nanay Coro's younger sisters, Mommy Seleng and Ine, who lived next to each other just a few houses down. Once we got there, we sat on Mommy Seleng's porch with her four children, who were a few years older than me, and Ine came over with her two sons.

As the adults were catching up, I decided to go inside the house to get myself a glass of water. I walked around the porch to the front door of the low structure with unpainted cement walls and a metal roof that clanged when it rained, unlike our own traditional wood-and-thatch dwelling. I took off my slippers as I went inside, and the cement floors felt cool under my feet. I walked to the kitchen in the back, pulled up a chair in front of the sink, reached for a glass on a metal rack, and opened the faucet to get my water.

After I filled my glass, I sat next to Mommy Seleng's bright blue plastic-covered kitchen table to drink; I could hear voices from the porch but couldn't understand what they were saying. I liked being alone with my thoughts, a quality that felt different from other children in my village, who often spent all their waking hours with people, playing among other kids or helping family with chores, then sleeping with their entire household in the same room. I realized how much I enjoyed getting relief from too much attention and promised myself that I'd spend more time alone inside in future visits to my great-aunt.

Amid the faint human voices, I suddenly heard a low moan from another direction, which sounded like a wounded animal. I thought I imagined it until I heard the sound again and stood up to find where it came from, somewhere near the back of the house. I got to a door to another room I hadn't realized was there, with windows that looked onto the kitchen, covered by green curtains from inside so I couldn't peek through them. I reached out my hand to open the door, but the metal knob resisted me. It was locked. I took a step back, then another, and was ready to turn away when I noticed a shadow from inside the room, humanlike but swaying in an odd way as it moved closer, got bigger. It wasn't long before I spied fingertips on one of the curtain edges, and I wanted to run, but curiosity and fear tied up my feet. An older boy's face emerged behind those fingertips, a face I recognized because it was mine but dark, mine but with drool coming out of its open mouth, mine but without comprehension in its glazed eyes. The boy I thought was an animal moaned again, louder, and then again, and again. I resisted the urge to scream, ran back to the entrance, and encountered Mommy Seleng in the living room, who rushed to the moaning boy, then my grandmother, who took me in her arms.

"That's your uncle Amang," Nanay Coro whispered.

She did not say anything else as she walked me back to the porch, nor did Mommy Seleng when she returned to join us. Our family went about that visit without mentioning my uncle again as I pretended to read a book and controlled the urge to ask about him, even though I was afraid of the answers I would get, since I knew that Amang, like Jembong, was related to me in a way I couldn't entirely name. I was also different from everyone else, and even though people thought I was beautiful most of the time, there were those who thought I was cursed, and no one knew my secret that I might be like Jembong, even though I had not quite figured out if I truly was. As I stared inside my book, I remembered suddenly how I'd cried for so long the first time I woke up in the middle of the night, only to find the door to my bedroom locked. I had to imagine that I was actually the ghost people sometimes told me I resembled, that my body didn't feel fear because it wasn't really there. It was the only way I could get back to sleep. Seeing Amang, I wondered if my parents would have stayed with me had I just been a normal child, if they would have loved me and not sent me to my grandmother to be raised. Seeing Amang, I realized how being different could get you locked up in a room all your life.

Since my family decided to wait a year to put me in first grade, I didn't have school in Talacsan, so I spent my days finding ways to entertain myself. I often lay on our common room floor, made of bamboo slats that were cut by hand, and ran a finger down the surface of the wood, searching for knots my eye might have missed, then used my thumb and forefinger to measure minute differences in the thickness of the bamboo. I looked up to the top of our ceiling, trying to pick out details from that distance, the variations of brown in the bundles of thatch that formed our roof, the long strands of leaves that held those bundles together, and the bamboo poles that met at the top, which gave that part of our house its triangular shape. I was just any other kid in our village whiling away the time, until I sat up and noticed the color of my legs, remembered that no, I would always be different, and tried as best I could to talk myself out of my sadness, with reassuring words about my beauty and intelligence.

I also loved insects—spiders I fought on bamboo sticks with other kids, beetles whose legs I attached to a string and flew like a kite—though ants were by far my favorite. I set aside small pieces of dried fish on the windowsill by our kitchen and watched them carry the food inch by arduous inch, until the ants took the fish down the wide bamboo pole that ran from our window casing to the ground. I loved the way those ants worked together, each a seamless part of their collective, no single one distinguishable from another.

My grandmother wanted me to play with other children and often went with me down the hill to the neighbors next door, who had a covered porch where kids played games like jacks and pickup sticks. I was lousy at first, but I spent hours playing those games on my own, until I could catch the ball without even looking and pick up all the sticks in a single turn. But there were games I could never be good at, like jump rope or kick the can, and especially hide-and-seek, where the other children let me be a hider but never a seeker because the game took much too long. Invariably, these children would get bored and run into the field to play tag, or go to the woods to climb trees, and I wasn't allowed to join in because I was accident-prone, and my skin burned in the sun.

"It's all right," my grandmother said. "Those other kids aren't white like you." And when she said white, "puti," I could tell she also meant beautiful, intelligent, better, more special. If I couldn't have that sense of being like everyone else, that feeling of shared destiny like those ants or those kids, then I could at least find a way to feel good about standing apart from them.

I was proud to have gone to school for two years in Manila, when the kids my age in our town hadn't even started yet, and many of the older ones didn't know things I'd already learned, like the English alphabet or the nine planets of the solar system. Many of them couldn't even read properly, while I always had a stack of books ready for when I was left alone, my favorite ones the picture books with nursery rhymes, which Mama's father, Lolo Bert, had sent from America, with their sturdy cardboard pages and vibrant drawings. Mama didn't have the patience to read to me, and Nanay Coro had never learned English properly—she only finished sixth grade before she worked on the farm all year—so I mostly read to myself and tried to learn words I didn't know from television or asked one of my aunts when I couldn't figure something out.

The other problem though was that everyone else had parents and relatives who looked more or less like them, other children they could bond with and emulate. I had no one. From my earliest memories, Nanay Coro told me I wouldn't grow up like her or any member of our family or community, because I was white and would someday live in America. But without anyone to model after, I often asked myself what my future would be like, how I would live as an adult.

I'd never met any other anak araw, nor did I come into contact with any actual Americans. The only anak araw I was even aware of was Redford White, a comedian who was often a guest on variety shows and always seemed clueless about what was going on, because people said he came from a backward part of the country and being anak araw made him defective, almost retarded. I cringed when I watched Redford on TV and wondered whether this was what people thought about me behind my back, resolved to study as hard as I could so that no one would ever think I was retarded just because I was anak araw.

My grandmother sensed my loneliness, and we grew inseparable. The two of us took the jeepney to Baliwag once a week, where she went shopping for food and supplies and I got sweet treats like yema or polvoron. She taught me to ride a water buffalo during her trips to supervise the fields that she began to hire other people from our village to farm. She brought me to the mango orchard behind our house where we picked fruit together, as she climbed the trees and dropped the fruit on the soft ground for me to pick up. But the times I enjoyed most were when she attended to my daily needs, because that was when I felt the deepest connection between us, like I was any other grandchild instead of being who I was, someone who could never feel truly one with her, because I was born fair and she dark, in a world where that difference seemed to matter so much. But when Nanay Coro cleaned my ears with a cotton bud or pulled my fingers and toes one by one until the knuckles cracked, that was when I felt most like the child I would have been had I not been born anak araw, something I found so hard to admit to myself I wanted, because my mind refused to dwell in the impossible and preferred instead to be so good at being the person I was fated to be that no one could ever guess I was unhappy with myself. I was so convincing that even I often forgot I wanted to be brown like everyone else, an admission I only re-called as bursts of feeling, instantly dismissed.

My despair over being different took on tangible form whenever I observed the women and children of our village spend lazy af-ternoons probing one another's scalps for lice, settling on sets of stairs in groups of three or four, including my cousins and aunts. I was excluded from this activity because my eyes were too poor to pick out those tiny brown creatures in people's heads, so I never got the pleasure of crushing a louse against one thumbnail using the edge of another, the satisfying crack of its tiny body. It was such a simple wish to be part of this ritual, yet its simplicity made it all the more heartbreaking, even when I convinced myself it was fine, that I could just watch TV or read a book instead.

Even worse, it took so little time for me to get deloused compared to other kids, because the dark lice were so easy to spot against my hair. Nanay Coro must have noticed my annoyance when my Tita Nanette—who often felt more like a sibling to me than an aunt—took more than twice as much time to get cleaned of lice, and my grandmother started checking me for those insects more often, directing me to sit below her on the wooden steps outside our house door.

She seemed to take a really long time one afternoon when I was six, the summer before first grade, which I looked forward to because I loved the prospect of learning English better, but also felt sad because it would mean not being able to spend nearly as much time with Nanay Coro. My grandmother took out a fine comb and worked it through my hair a half dozen times, to rid it of louse eggs. Then she began to examine my scalp, inch by inch from top to bottom in rows, like a farmer pulling out weeds in a field.

"There's something I need to tell you," she said as she worked. "We want you to start elementary school in Manila."

"But I like it better here."

"Your mama misses you."

Though I felt sad when Mama sent me away, the fact that she never visited made me question how much she wanted me back. I also knew she couldn't take care of me the way Nanay Coro did. But I did long to have a mother who was devoted to me the way other mothers in our village were, who nursed their babies until they were toddlers and seemed to keep an invisible cord between them and their children at all times, a second sense about their well-being because they thought about their children more than they did themselves.

I wanted to face Nanay, but her hand was on my head, and I could tell from the tone of her voice that she was sad in a way she didn't want me to see.

"You need to learn how to live with your mama and papa," she continued. "You won't have me when you go to America."

It was only then that I absorbed how my grandmother would not be coming with us, to that wondrous life I'd been promised half a world away, a place full of people like me. It confused me to know that I would someday belong with strangers just because we had the same skin, when I felt so close to my grandmother, and couldn't imagine being closer to anyone else. But my family's insistence convinced me there was something better than my grandmother's love out in the world, and it was a future I had no choice but to accept.

My grandfather Tatay Gaudencio came home one afternoon carrying a large cardboard box from Lolo Bert, my other grandfather in America. He took a small knife and leaned over to slash against the many layers of packing tape, then stood up when he was done.

"It's for you," he said as he stepped out of the way.

My entire family surrounded me while I opened the box, which reached above my waist. A wondrous smell wafted out even before

I looked inside. The scent was clean and fragrant, free from the odor of animals and sweat I'd grown used to in our village. I forgot where I was, lost in the smell of America, dreaming of giant houses and endless toys. When I came back to myself and realized I was still in a small village in the Philippines, my first thought was that I wanted to be wherever that smell came from.

My family helped me take out what was inside. There were several bottles of shampoo, which up to then I'd only seen in plastic sachets. There was soap in bright boxes, and many pieces of colorful clothes—shorts and collared shirts with an animal on the front that Tita Jackie, the elder of my two aunts, told me was a crocodile, which meant that the shirt was expensive. But I was less interested in those clothes than the heavy presents at the bottom, which I took out one by one.

The first was a giant book with a shiny black cover, so heavy that I needed to set it down. I mouthed the title in big letters on the front, ASTRONOMY, and marveled at a picture I recognized as the Earth from outer space. The other book was a collection of fairy tales, made of thick shiny paper and full of color images. The third item was not a book but another box, and inside was a plastic contraption with a keyboard called a Speak & Spell, which began to talk when I turned it on. I squeezed into the empty cardboard box and rested my back against one of the walls to play for hours that afternoon, and for several days after, with the talking machine that predicted the wonder of America, while that box's fragrance became embedded in my mind even after I couldn't smell it anymore, and Nanay Coro finally convinced me to throw the container away.

My English learning sped up after I got that box of presents. I discovered the UHF channel that only showed American programs from the Angeles U.S. Army Base in Pampanga, the province next to us, and watched it all day even though I had to constantly adjust our metal TV antenna just to catch the grainy signal. I found a show called *Jeopardy!*, where contestants answered all sorts of questions I didn't understand at first, but was able to piece together over time when I started watching it every day, facts about the U.S. Constitution, the capitals of the world, and great books I hoped to someday read.

Though even as my knowledge of English broadened, I still listened to Lea Salonga several times a week, as though her album bridged the world I came from and the one I looked forward to. I'd learned the whole tape by heart and sang songs from it throughout the day, including "When You Wish Upon a Star" and "Rainbow Connection," whose melody I loved and which seemed more tangible to me because I saw rainbows often enough. I loved all the songs on the cassette, though I wasn't as fond of "Thank You for the Music" as the others, its rhythms more complicated and confusing. I listened to it often enough, but because it was near the end, I was just as likely to skip it and fast-forward so I could turn the tape over and start from the beginning.

But one day, I lay in our common room as I often did on idle afternoons, the breeze from under the spaces between the floor's bamboo slats my relief from the summer heat. I looked up at our high ceiling and observed the holes in the thatch, from maya birds who took the pieces of dry grass to build their own nests. My grandmother would bring workers over to patch up the holes before the rainy season began, but I would be in Manila by then and wouldn't experience that feeling of new protection from the coming monsoons. The TV was on in the background, a show that played songs from America.

I vaguely registered that a new song began, its first chords somehow familiar, though not familiar enough to stir me from my rest. But when the first lyrics came on—"I'm nothing special. In fact I'm a bit of a bore"—I sat up because I recognized that this must be the original singer of "Thank You for the Music."

I was halfway across the room, so the images were just blurs to me, until I crawled closer and got to my usual spot a couple of feet away from the screen. The singer was part of a band that performed in front of a crowd of young people. Her hair was the same color as mine, her skin light and cheeks rosy like other Americans I'd seen on TV. The way the crowd adored that singer, reaching out their hands to touch her, they must have found her beautiful too, the way people around me thought I was beautiful.

"I've been so lucky," she sang. "I am the girl with golden hair." I suddenly realized what she meant, that the hair I'd compared to corn was actually much more valuable, like the gold chain and cross pendant that hung from my grandmother's neck, her most valued possession. I imagined myself as that performer, a golden-haired American woman singing in front of thousands of other Americans, who lived in a mansion like in *Dallas* or *Knots Landing*. But by the time she sang, "What a joy! What a life! What a chance!" a few moments later, I had already returned to my own body, the body of a boy in the Philippines who just happened to have her hair. My future may hold riches, but I would not live it as a beautiful woman.

Still, I felt more special after that, more able to withstand the loneliness of being the only one of my kind. Even if I didn't belong with my family, my village, or my country, at least I was lucky to have a future in America where I would lead a wonderful life, because my hair was gold, my skin fair. I never skipped "Thank You for the Music" after that, except I sang "boy with golden hair" instead of "girl," because I was a boy.

2.

The day I left Bulacan for Manila to live with my parents, Nanay Coro and I flagged down a jeepney that took us back to Baliwag, then a bus that deposited us at a crowded station where my grandmother held my hand tight, in an area called Balintawak. From there, we took a tricycle to the squat, two-story concrete building that housed Mama and Papa's cramped apartment in Caloocan, on the outskirts of the city.

Neither of my parents were there when I arrived, just a young woman named Charito who Nanay had hired to take care of me. I didn't see Mama and Papa until they came for dinner that evening, and I noticed that my mother's arm was around my father's, which I didn't remember ever seeing before.

"I'm so happy you're here," Mama said as she hugged me, though the way she said it made me feel as if she was acting in a soap opera. Papa said hello and nodded in my direction, cool even though he hadn't seen me in months, so I copied him and tried not to get excited.

I hadn't been close enough to my parents to see their faces too well, though I was aware that Mama was fat-cheeked and plump with wavy hair she cut short, which was unusual for women, and it looked a little like a dark helmet on her head. Papa's frame was thin but sturdy, his manner swaggering, which I also found unusual, since the man of our household in Talacsan, Tatay Gaudencio, moved with gentleness and deferred to my grandmother.

A few days later, I went downstairs and was surprised to find Mama awake earlier than me, and even more surprised when she told me she was taking me to Fiesta Carnival. We dressed and then boarded a bus to that giant indoor fun fair with a large sign in front, the letters filled in with different-colored lightbulbs.

"Your Lolo Bert took me here before he went to America," she said. "The horses were my favorite."

She motioned to a ride where painted wooden horses went around in a circle, but it didn't look as much fun as the one next to it, where mothers rode little cars with their kids in a large paved area, and bumped against other cars. But Mama wanted to go to the horses so that was where we ended up, and I tolerated the repetitive music so I could get to the ride I wanted. Once we were at the cars, though, I sat in Mama's lap and she seemed to enjoy ramming other cars and making the mothers scream. Afterward, she walked me over to the sorbetero with his wagonful of ice cream, where she got herself a chocolate and me a cone of coconut.

"Isn't life beautiful?" she remarked as we sat on a bench.

"Yes, if I can go to the carnival every day."

Mama chuckled as she took a lick of her cone, and she seemed impossibly young to me. She had me when she was seventeen, and though she was a few years older than Papa's younger sister Tita Jackie, my dutiful aunt who had just started college seemed more adult.

"I have something to tell you," she said as she turned and smiled. "You're going to have a sibling."

I looked down at her stomach and saw the beginnings of a bump.

"Aren't you happy?" she asked when I didn't respond. "We'll be a bigger family."

"I like my family in Talacsan."

A flash of movement as if the world sped by; a sting of pain. Mama had slapped me across the face. I started to cry.

"Be quiet or I will leave you here and never come back."

As I rubbed my cheek, I wondered if I could find the way to Talacsan on my own. It didn't seem so hard, though Nanay Coro had warned me many times that someone would kidnap a white boy like me if I wandered off alone. I needed Mama. I stifled my tears.

"Your grandmother poisoned you against me."

I didn't want to get slapped again, so I said nothing. I stifled more tears and imagined I was so white I was invisible. Somehow, I managed to hold on to my cone, as the ice cream melted and began to coat my fingers. Mama told me it was time to go, and I followed her back to the bus. I pretended not to notice when she held out her hand.

I saw little of Mama and Papa in Caloocan. I was alone indoors most days, leery of the unfamiliar kids in my neighborhood who gawked at me. Also, the only open space to play outside was the street, and I was afraid of getting run over.

Mama left for work early and often came home when I was already asleep, bringing people who woke me up with their chatter, though she warned me not to come downstairs while she was with friends. My only companion was our maid Charito, who kept me fed and shared a bed with me.

Papa ran a car repair business, but as far as I could tell, this just meant he was out all night and slept through the morning most days, our only contact during the couple of hours it took him to get ready to go out again. He was friendly sometimes and even invited me to hang around with his drinking buddies, but I never took him up on it and he didn't insist. "You are your grandmother's true child," he said, and I heard resentment in his voice I couldn't decipher. I might have gone with him had I known I would grow up to be the kind of man he was, but I felt different even then, and not just because I was white. I was afraid Papa would realize this the more time we spent together.

I did look forward to school, at a Catholic academy called Notre Dame that was run by nuns, not like the Montessori school I went to for kindergarten. I found it amusing that students called one another by their last names, less amusing that we had to form strict lines to go anywhere—from morning prayer to class, at recess and at lunch. Though I did enjoy being just one of the kids, not singled out at first, and when teachers did notice me, it was because they noted how quickly I understood lessons, how often I got perfect scores on assignments. The homework was tedious, since those nuns emphasized rote repetition, so I waded through many pages of pointless drills on subjects I'd already memorized in class, like the different farm animals in science or the concept of the Holy Trinity in religion. Thankfully, it was work that was easy enough to get through in front of the TV.

Inside that electric box, I finally found an American boy to be like, shortly after I started first grade. A program called *Silver*

Spoons started to come on a few times a week, and I tried to catch as many repeat airings as I could even though I didn't totally understand what was going on. Thankfully, I was with Tita Jackie one of the first times I saw the show, and she filled in the gaps as we sat in front of the TV in Talacsan, where I continued to spend weekends even while I was living in Manila. The show was about a boy named Ricky, who showed up one day at the grand home of his rich father, Edward, to introduce himself as Edward's son. Tita Jackie also taught me the meaning of the show's title, that to be born with a "silver spoon" in your mouth meant you were really rich.

"Silver is quite expensive," she explained, "so only rich people could afford it."

"We don't even use spoons," I replied. "If there was a show about us, it would be called *Hand Spoons*."

Tita Jackie laughed. As we watched the program together, she explained that Ricky behaved better than his own father because Edward had been spoiled all his life and acted like a child.

"You must learn good habits now so that you grow up responsible and mature," she said.

I completed her sentence in my head: *not like your papa.* The parallels were obvious, and I sensed for the first time how my aunt resented the liberties my father took because my grandmother indulged him, while everyone expected Tita Jackie to fulfill a dutiful daughter's role. I also wondered, when I learned that Ricky's mom did not tell Edward he had a son, whether Papa might not be my real father, if that was the reason I was so white and Papa didn't care much about me. Maybe Mama had an affair with an American, and I would someday find him in a giant house in the

United States, where I could have as many books and games as I wanted. Another part of me knew this couldn't be true, but I enjoyed the fantasy anyway.

That show also gave me a template of what life was like in America. Instead of our wooden chairs and benches, families there sat on padded sofas. When I pointed to what looked like a giant hole in the wall, Tita Jackie explained to me that this was a fireplace, which Americans needed because it got cold there when it snowed, a concept I still couldn't quite grasp, something like ice that fell from the sky, except soft.

Though as the show went on, my focus became solely on Ricky and how I could imagine him as an older, American version of myself. I got really close to the TV and scrutinized the boy's mannerisms, any hints that would give me a better sense of what I could be like once I moved to the U.S. *Silver Spoons* came on Saturday evenings right before bedtime, and my family prepared our common room as soon as the show was over, laid out our sleeping mat and pillows, put up the mosquito net. I went to bed with dreams of being Ricky, living a blessed boy's life in America.

One early Sunday morning, while Nanay Coro was in the kitchen preparing breakfast and the rest of our family was still asleep, I sneaked out of bed to the far side of the house, through a curtain, to the only private room that had a mirror, which was attached to a carved wooden dresser. In that mirror, I practiced the gestures I'd observed from Ricky the night before, the way he put his hands in his pockets and shrugged, how he made an angelic expression with a slight smile that emphasized his ruddy cheeks, then blinked several times. Once I was done, I stood at the back of the room, so that I couldn't see the details of my face, only saw a boy with blond hair and fair skin, which made it so much easier to imagine myself as an American boy who shrugged and cocked my head exactly like Ricky. I continued to do this over the following months, and then years, until I'd absorbed many of that blond American boy's mannerisms unconsciously.

America began to form itself on the other side of my mirror with a version of me inside it. I began to see a white American boy in my reflection, even as I was a Filipino anak araw in my daily life. Seeing that American boy, I also began to see my future in America so much more vividly: adventures in the snow, Santa Claus at Christmas, arcade games, a giant bedroom of my own, a mansion made of stone. The mirror became a bridge toward the wondrous place I was destined to inhabit, a fantasy that my white skin made real.

I returned to Harvard to speak at a panel in March 2018. Though I'd spoken at a number of universities, it did feel significant, but also amusing, that my alma mater had finally invited me back. I was such a troublemaker in college, a self-branded queer radical who got removed from protests and threatened with arrest for public indecency.

I decided to come to Harvard Yard a few hours before my talk, not quite spring, too cold to walk around without a coat, the trees still barren. I came through the side entrance facing Massachusetts Hall, on a Friday afternoon in the middle of the semester, and encountered the usual sprinkling of human figures, a couple of students with expressions of grave attention, tourists taking pictures in front of the bronze John Harvard statue. I had the overwhelming feeling of being out of place as I passed that monument and came to the other side of the Yard, the part I had traversed hundreds, maybe even thousands of times before, from my dorm at Wigglesworth in the very corner of that vast lawn, toward my various classes where I also felt out of place.

Back then, it was the typical alienation of being a poor college student in the world's richest school, but over time, it turned into feeling alienated from the person Harvard wanted to make of me, someone who was supposed to think freely so that I could be groundbreaking and innovative, yet also conform to whatever arbitrary standard the university decided I should meet. Harvard reminded me of a fickle father who encouraged you to break the rules, except you were never allowed to undermine his authority. From the distance of a quarter century, I now had enough perspective to acknowledge how my experiences at that school had shaped me, and that many of my conflicts with administrators were a form of acting out desires I couldn't reasonably expect them to understand, let alone fulfill. Yet speaking at Harvard was a final, grudging admission that the institution I fought with for so long was also one that gave me the tools to be the person I ultimately wanted to be, someone who made an impact in the world while remaining true to the parts of myself I cherished, which I managed not to give up even though Harvard tried to discipline them away. But now, accepting how I'd grown into a person that both I and Harvard approved of also made it harder to grapple with the struggle it took to get to that place, as if feeling even a modicum of satisfaction betrayed the part of me that suffered for so long. I wondered about other people I could have become had I made different decisions—a professor in the Philippines or the dutiful grandson who took over the family business once my grandfather died. Or I could still be a gay man in a twenty-year relationship with the love of my life, no doubt married, maybe even with adopted children.

In that agitated state, there was only one place that could ease my mind. I felt pathetic as I scaled those three dozen concrete steps up to the entrance of Widener Library, but it really was the building on campus where I felt most safe. When I entered through the gilt-and-glass doors to that building's lobby, encased in marble with a row of pillars on each side, the opulence no longer intimidated me, knowing how this part of the building was for donors and tourists, while the best part was what the public didn't see.

The guard at the entrance directed me to the privileges office, through a door near the back corner of that vast room. A gray-haired, pink-skinned man with metal-rimmed glasses, light blue shirt, brown tie, sage green cable sweater, and a dour expression—the very image of a stodgy librarian—met me when I got to the wood-paneled counter, and I told him I was an alum who wanted to visit the stacks. He asked for identification, and I handed him my passport: blue, American.

"Year?" he asked.

"Nineteen ninety-seven."

"Ah," he said as he raised an eyebrow, "that was before the database." The man set down my passport and shifted to a row of brown hardbound books on a shelf beside him, pulled one out, and shifted back toward me as he glanced down at my passport and thumbed through the pages.

"You'll find me under 'Marc,'" I said. "I was a boy in college, but I became a girl."

"Fair enough," he replied without taking his eye off the book.

He found my name, wrote down my information on a bright yellow card, and then handed it to me. "Show this to the guard."

I proceeded to the circulation desk, pleased with myself that I still knew where it was. I showed the monitor my pass and saw the gray door before me like it was a portal. I turned the spherical metal knob and went in.

Sudden silence, the smell of old paper, the same low ceiling I could reach with a decent jump, the same feeling of comfort, of something like home. Even the mute echo of footsteps felt the same as I wandered down the gray marble floors, one remnant of opulence from the other side of the door, the other that this building housed the largest university collection in the world. I spied a set of narrow stairs that led down and took those all the way to the Dante section on level D, which the university kept, maybe because it was such a good joke, even after it switched from its in-house system to the Library of Congress classifications. From there I found the tunnel to the library annex and section HQ, where all the LGBT books were—it figured the university would consign them to another building—and laughed to myself over the under-grad joke that HQ meant Harvard Queer.

Eventually, I found myself back on the first floor, whose stacks were most familiar because they housed the English literature section. Like I often did when I felt agitated in college, I picked a row randomly from among the few hundred on that floor, turned on the light switch, and meandered among the shelves to find a book I might like. On this particular afternoon, I found myself in the R section and turned my head sideways to peruse the titles, brushing the books I scanned with a finger. When I reached Salman Rushdie, I was surprised to find *Joseph Anton: A Memoir* among the books there. I had no idea he'd written a memoir. And not just any memoir, but one about being exiled from his own country. I sat on the cold marble, my back against the gray metal shelf, and started to read. That too was like college, and even before that; no matter how upset I was, or how scared, I somehow always managed to find the right book.

My brother, Ramon Antonio Talusan Jr., was born on September 21, 1982, three months after I started first grade, brown and dark-haired like a Filipino child was supposed to be. My father gave him his own name, and I disliked my brother immediately, jealous of the attention he received from my parents, especially Papa, so I mostly ignored him and kept to TV and books, while Mama played the role of doting mother. I looked forward to being back in Talacsan and away from my brother for the summer, in Nanay Coro's arms and her undiluted love.

But Mama decided that I would spend the summer in Manila instead, and when I protested that she wouldn't have enough time for me, she said that I could come with her to her clerk job at a printing press called Philippine Graphic Arts. Her office—a room with about a half dozen other clerks—was too crowded and noisy for me to read in, so I explored various parts of that complex where thousands of books got made every day. I watched production artists cut large sheets of film and assemble them into templates for book pages and learned to love the sweet and rusty smell of ink when I walked through the printing facility, with gargantuan presses in a vast room that ran through rolls and rolls of paper to make books. The room's high ceilings reminded me of a sparse church, where the miracle of bookmaking was performed every day.

I eventually settled in the press sample room with its raw wood floors, gray walls, and fluorescent lights. It was an unremarkable place except for its numerous stacks of books on metal shelves that surrounded the room, which was usually quiet since hardly anyone went inside. The press mostly produced English-language books, many of them for children, but I found myself drawn to the books for adults. One afternoon, I found a book on a low shelf called *The United States and the Philippines: A Study of Neocolonialism*, its cover red, white, and blue, though the American flag was made to look like a building with smoke coming out of it, and the smoke was in the familiar shape of our country, groups of islands that reminded me of a kneeling woman. I opened it to find dense masses of words I couldn't parse into sentences, along with graphs I didn't understand, something about the U.S. having so much more money than the Philippines. I kept the book to read when I got older, curious about the relationship between my current and future homes.

I also brought my own books into that room and sat on the floor with my back against one of the shelves. I pored through the book of children's stories Lolo Bert had sent from America, hardbound in a mottled sea green. It contained all sorts of tales, though I found myself less drawn to stories of princesses in castles, which felt alien to anything resembling my life or the future I envisioned for myself. I liked the stories involving animals better, like the Aesop fable about the dog who got too greedy and mistook his own reflection in a pond for another dog, so ended up dropping his own bone into its depths. It reminded me of our own folktales, like the one about the girl who turned into a pineapple—a fruit with many eyes—because she refused to obey her mother who told her not to sew at night.

Though among all the stories in that book, the one I kept going back to was "The Velveteen Rabbit." It was about a stuffed animal who wanted to be real, and other rabbits made fun of him because he was just made of cloth and sawdust, not fur and flesh. And even though my brother was only crawling then, I knew that he was real in a way I could never be, that he belonged with everyone else around him in a way I didn't. It struck me how there were plenty of real rabbits in the story but only one velveteen rabbit, so maybe that was why he was lonely, not because he wasn't real but because there was only one of him.

I got used to getting out of Mama's way, though I still held out hope that our relationship would improve. So it made me happy when she came home one day with a bright expression on her face and called me over to tell me that a friend of hers had heard about a TV show starring Redford White, and that they were looking for a kid to play his son. She wanted to take me to audition.

Maybe I should have been more excited over the prospect of playing Redford's child, but the idea seemed far-fetched, and I wasn't even sure Mama would follow up on it. But when Saturday morning came, Mama and I boarded a jeepney to a complex called Broadcast City in the Diliman area of Metro Manila, a set of modern, rectangular buildings painted white on the outside. We entered a waiting room crowded with a few dozen light-skinned children, and I realized I'd be meeting other anak araw for the first time. Though as the mothers began talking, and as I observed that most of the kids were darker than me, I discovered that most of them were not really anak araw, but either kids who had American fathers or mestizos with Spanish blood.

But I did observe a boy across from me in the waiting room, standing between his mother's legs, who I recognized as anak araw from the way he squinted his eyes. He seemed really shy though, and I wondered how he would do performing in front of a camera if he couldn't even pry himself away from his mother's arms.

I went over and introduced myself to the boy, whose name was George. He told me that his mother heard about the audition on TV and that they came from Bataan, a province near my grandmother's. I couldn't help but judge him as we spoke, how he seemed so unsure of himself and kept blinking too much, so it really looked like there was something wrong with him. Having learned from Ricky on TV, I controlled physical tendencies that made me look weird, like squinting too much and looking down to see where I was going. George, on the other hand, seemed not to know or care that he came off as odd, though Redford White was like this too, funny-looking, so maybe the two of them would be good at playing father and son.

When my turn came, I walked into an office with Mama and sat on a chair in front of a confident man with an unusually square jaw for a Filipino, and I wondered if he was half-American; he introduced himself as the director, Steve. He asked me normal questions about where I was from and my favorite subject in school. I told him science, specifically astronomy, which we hadn't studied yet, but I'd read about it from the books my grandfather had sent from America. He handed me a script and asked me to read several lines.

"You're a good reader," he said, then told me to keep the script to study, and he would have me read it with Redford after lunch.

"He's not only so intelligent but very hardworking," Mama said as she came over to kneel next to my chair. "He spends his days staring at books."

I didn't know Mama had noticed, and I turned to face her as

she effused about me, realizing that I'd never been this close to her for this long, that there were details of her face I hadn't discovered. I knew her cheeks were chubby, her hair wavy and cut short, but I hadn't noted that the skin on her face was rough and marred with tiny pimples, many more than I could perceive from far away.

She wasn't as beautiful as Papa was handsome, I realized, and that was why he looked at her with such indifference, the reason she constantly grasped for his attention. I rarely saw the two of them in the same room together, but when I did, during those rare times when Papa was home for dinner or when the three of us watched TV, she glanced at him lovingly while he remained indifferent, which seemed to make her crave his attention even more.

I wondered what it would be like not to be beautiful or smart, not to be white like I was, not to learn things fast. This must be the way to Mama's affection, to show off qualities she didn't have, because I was an extension of her, and she thought of my achievements as her own. I resolved to be as smart as I could to please her, so I could see her smile at me that way again, and hug me so close.

There were only four other boys in the waiting room when Mama and I returned, and I was sad not to see George there; I was the only anak araw. I did not expect to enter an actual studio with a set when my turn came. That was when I met Redford White, and maybe it was an advantage that I wasn't a fan, because I wasn't nervous; he seemed pleasant as we ran our scene several times just sitting on the set's living room sofa, with Steve instructing us through a loudspeaker while he sat on a high chair. It was a scene where my dad tries to convince me to put on pajamas and go to bed so he and my mom could have time alone, but I trick him into putting on pajamas instead and run out of the bedroom to my mother.

Eventually, Steve asked us to stand up and go to the bedroom set to do the scene there.

"You left your script," the director said over the loudspeaker.

"I don't need it," I replied.

An assistant handed me the script anyway, as Steve gave me instructions about when to enter the room, when to sit on the bed, and when to run away while Redford tried to catch me. I kept the script in my hand but didn't look at it, having committed the words to heart after I read them so many times, because I didn't want to have to put it close to my eyes while I did the scene. The whole thing still seemed like a game, though I did register that Steve was pleased with me, when he said he couldn't believe I memorized my lines so fast. Two weeks later, Mama came home with the news that I'd gotten the part.

3.

My brother had been sent to live with Nanay Coro by the time my show first aired, as Mama decided she couldn't take care of him and also manage a son who was starring in a sitcom. So Mama didn't send me away as a baby because I was anak araw after all; she just didn't like raising children. The night my show first aired, my mother invited a group of her friends to watch on our TV. I was expecting Papa to be there, but he wasn't.

I'd spent the past month working on the show, being introduced to the cast, following directions, and doing scenes. It seemed like everyone in the crew made the show a big deal and told me how my life was going to change. But I was used to getting attention all the time for being me, so the thought of being on TV didn't feel that different. I found the challenges of being on set more exciting, memorizing lines and blocking, playing my character for laughs, a part that suited me because I was the smart one while my father was dumb, and that was funny because I was so young.

So I was surprised to feel my heartbeat in my ears, when we finally sat down to watch the first episode of my show, me in my usual spot on the floor close to the TV while Mama and her friends were on the rattan couch behind me. As the episode began, there was a laugh track when I first ran into the scene while my TV parents were talking.

"You're such a big boy," my TV dad observed, a nod to the incongruity of the show ending its previous season with my mom pregnant and starting the new one with me fully grown. "How did you grow up so fast?"

"That's because I don't eat vegetables," I replied, then smiled and blinked like I'd seen Ricky do on *Silver Spoons*, as the laugh track came on again and there were chuckles from Mama's friends. Though their reactions fell away as I continued to watch, and I found myself mesmerized by the odd sensation of being someone else. For a moment, it was as if dreaming of being Ricky had transported me inside that television and I had become him, a real American boy who lived in a giant house and got everything he wanted. Then I started speaking in Tagalog and I was myself again.

The show ended, and Mama's friends clapped, then gushed about how smart and talented I was. I got more and more used to that praise over the following weeks, as my addition to *Bisoy* gave the show a ratings boost, and I began to get recognized on the street. A magazine even wrote a story about my relationship with Mama, which ran with a picture of her holding my hand as though she were taking me to school, the two of us an ideal image, her the envy of the country for having a child who was not only smart and white but also the star of a TV show, as I grew to understand that I was expected to play the same happy, clever boy not just on set but whenever I was in public. I sat with that magazine alone in our apartment and wondered whether her beaming face meant that Mama would never threaten to abandon me again.

<hr />

I did a good enough job those first few months, as I got my script on the weekend and prepared my lines for two, sometimes three evenings of taping each week. Everyone was kind on set, Redford and other supporting characters like my TV grandfather and the maid, but I was especially drawn to my TV mom, Isabel Rivas, a dark actress with short wavy hair, whose modern, forward manner reminded me of Mama, not like the shy women in our province. But while my mother was chubby and eager to please, Isabel was slim and impossibly cool in her tube tops and tight jeans, and she often stroked my hair or kissed my cheek; she really was a more ideal version of Mama. Her life was also the subject of gossip magazines, always rumored to be with one debonair actor or another, which excited me in a way I couldn't define.

I noticed that Isabel often disappeared whenever we were on break, so I once decided to follow her into a hallway to see what she was up to. She opened a back door, and by the time I caught up with her outside as a streetlamp lit her face, she already had a cigarette in her mouth, her back against our studio building, one of her sandaled feet resting on the wall.

"So why are you here?" she asked.

"I just wanted to say hello."

She let me lean next to her as she finished her cigarette. I looked up, and her mysterious beauty moved me then, the way light reflected off her large, dark eyes, how the end of her cigarette burned right before she exhaled a puff of smoke through her nose. I felt the power she held to entice whatever man she wanted through my nerves as my body tingled. It was a power Mama didn't have, nor anyone else in my vicinity, and looking at her, realizing it was a power I myself would never possess, I felt a sadness I couldn't explain.

"Promise me you'll never smoke," she said as she flicked the cigarette butt away. "It's very bad for you."

I nodded. She rested her hand on my shoulder, and we went back to set.

One Sunday afternoon when I was eight, early in *Bisoy*'s run, I kneeled on a chair over our glass-topped rattan table to work on an assignment. I loved the permanent scrawl of pens and the narrow lines of my elementary school paper unlike the wide spaces in kindergarten. I was writing a letter to President Ferdinand Marcos for school, on the occasion of his upcoming birthday, September 11, 1983. The TV was on like it usually was during the day, though I was focused on making the letter great, so the president would read it and invite me to his palace. I loved President Marcos with all my heart because he was the man who restored order to our country, the man who saved the Philippines from the NPA, according to my social studies teacher. I had no idea who the NPA were, but I knew to fear them because they were evil; they lived in the mountains and killed people. My eyes were inches away from the page as I wrote, "Thank you for everything you've done for our country" in English, then "Salamat po. Salamat. Salamat." I was so engrossed that it took a few seconds before I registered the shift on the TV, the stern voice of an announcer, and the jarring images on the screen.

I walked to the television and sat when I couldn't understand what I saw. Mostly gray pavement, a wall of white with windows in the background, metal stairs leading to the ground, a bloom of darkness next to a body clothed in white. Then the announcer's solemn words: Ninoy Aquino had been shot.

The man explained that Ninoy was a senator, but the president had imprisoned him for being a dissident before allowing him to go to the United States for medical treatment because of a heart condition. Ninoy lived there for many years but had decided to return even though there was fear for his safety. The announcer said all this in vague, careful language, but I began to feel uneasy at the thought that Marcos put Ninoy in jail just because he disagreed with the president.

As I watched this lifeless man on the ground and what I now recognized was a widening pool of blood around him, a sudden memory seized me. I had traveled with my grandfather when he campaigned for a municipal council seat; it must have been when I was four. Tatay Gaudencio liked bringing me to campaign stops because children from remote villages were curious about me and came out of their houses along with their mothers, who my grandfather made speeches to on a megaphone.

We were coming back from one of those stops in our family jeep, military green with a dark khaki cover. I rode in the back and looked outside through a clear plastic porthole as the headlights occasionally revealed a tree or the bottom of a house. Suddenly, a body-shaped, too-bright figure appeared in my line of sight, then another. I crouched between the driver and passenger seats to look ahead and saw another body, indistinct but unmistakable, lying by the road among dirt and stone. With a calm voice, my grandfather said the people in this town were peculiar because whenever they had the urge to sleep, they simply lay down wherever they were and stayed there until they weren't tired anymore. He suggested I sleep too since it was getting late, so I leaned against the cloth cover and closed my eyes. But seeing Ninoy lifeless on the ground, I grasped that what I had seen were dead bodies, and Marcos had something to do with their murders.

Over the following weeks, the TV news became preoccupied with Ninoy Aquino, though I could tell those announcers weren't telling the whole truth. Thankfully, the American UHF channel from the Angeles Army Base aired a documentary on Ninoy, which talked about how he was Marcos's major opponent before the president declared martial law in 1968 and ended up ruling the country for more than a decade, even though he was only supposed to serve a four-year term. There had been no elections in our country since Marcos came into power, which Ninoy loudly criticized before the president put him in jail.

But after Ninoy suffered his heart condition, Marcos allowed him to go to the United States to get treatment in a city called Boston, where he settled in exile. I was not familiar with this word, "exile," and had to look it up with a magnifying glass in my Webster's dictionary. It meant being forced to live outside your own country against your will, a thought that saddened me. Ninoy was able to stay in the United States instead of in a Philippine jail under one condition, which was that he could not criticize the president or his administration. So to still speak his mind, Ninoy came up with a series of jokes that could be interpreted various ways.

In an interview for the documentary, Ninoy, wearing a crisp

white shirt and glasses with wire frames, smiled wide as he told one of his jokes. "The ambassador of Japan once visited the Philippines and made a speech. Keep in mind that in Japan, there is no distinction between 'l' and 'r,' so Japanese people often pronounced the two letters as if they were the same, so the ambassador said, 'You know, you Piripino pipor, you are very rocky. You have a president who robs you, and a First Lady who robs you more.'"

I was struck by how clever and brave Ninoy was to come up with something so witty, though Marcos could have put him back in jail. But Ninoy knew that it would have been a risky move for the president; it was much easier to imprison someone for yelling and inciting violence than for making a funny joke. So Ninoy managed to avoid prison, until he decided he could no longer remain in the United States, and ultimately died for his country.

I had read about heroes in our history books, the ones who fought for Philippine independence against the Spaniards, men like José Rizal and Andres Bonifacio. But here was a man who was immensely brave and had also mastered the intricacies of English so well that he was able to make sophisticated jokes in that language, yet remained unquestionably proud to be Filipino. I began to wonder why I was so quick to want to be American.

That idea was in the air as I began hearing the phrase "colonial mentality" on TV, along with "neocolonialism." I remembered the book I'd taken from the shelf at Mama's printing press, *The United States and the Philippines: A Study of Neocolonialism*, and began to read it, surprised at how much more I understood in less than a year. The book argued that even though the Philippines was supposed to be independent after World War II, America still controlled the country economically. Not only that, but Filipinos were brainwashed to believe that Americans were superior, which meant that we still behaved as though we were colonized rather than as fully independent people. I recognized myself in those words and felt shame.

Though watching myself on TV was still exciting, working while going to school got really hard. In the beginning, I fought with Mama to be in class at seven in the morning even when my tapings went past midnight, only for me to get yelled at when I fell asleep on my desk. So I started to skip, though I cried when I got my report card and realized I was no longer the top student in my class; I wasn't even on the honor roll. I also grew more bored at work, as I got used to the routine of learning lines and blocking, looking cute, doing the same joke over and over again, me being clever and Redford dumb.

I tried to stay focused to please Mama and the director, but the boredom wore on me and, combined with my exhaustion, made me less and less enthusiastic about working on the show, which led to more takes and our tapings getting longer.

One night, as I tried to wrap up a scene with Redford at one in the morning, I couldn't get my blocking right and kept running into the living room too soon.

"Marc, you're not concentrating," Steve said over the studio speakers.

"I'm tired. I want to go home," I replied.

"You can't go home until this scene is done."

I rubbed my eyes and tried not to cry. "Let him take a nap," Redford said as he hugged me from the back and patted my head. "We can wait."

Steve nodded and let me lie down on a couch while the cast and crew waited. I somehow willed myself to finish the scene after I woke up and was ready to sleep in the cab on our way back home. But I knew by the way Mama pulled my arm when the car arrived that she wouldn't leave me alone when we got in.

"I can't believe you embarrassed me like that!" she yelled. Mama spent the next few minutes enumerating my faults, how I'd been unfocused and unenthusiastic, how I was an ungrateful child. "You're so lucky to be on TV, and you're throwing the chance away."

"I don't even know where my money goes," I replied. "You're just spending it when you go out."

Mama held my shoulders and shook me. "You can't speak to me like that!" she yelled, and as my teeth clattered, I knew my whiteness could save me from many things, but not this. When we got home, my mother pulled my arm so hard I felt like a puppet, except I owned bones that flinched at her tug. She did not turn on the light when she dragged me up the stairs. In the dark, Mama shoved me facedown on her bed and I wanted to disappear. I knew how. I couldn't just be white; I needed to be transparent, a figment without feeling or shape. *I am a ghost. I am a ghost,* I chanted inside, to every whack of her broom, as she made my white flesh red. But soon my incantation worked and I hung in the air, that ghost of myself. I became that ghost whenever Mama hit me if I misbehaved, if I talked back, if I smiled too wide or too little, if I said too much or not enough. I accepted the pain because parents beat their kids where I was from, but I couldn't accept the injustice of Mama hurting me whenever I wasn't perfect, while she allowed herself to make every mistake. I didn't grow to hate Mama because she beat me; I hated her because she was unfair.

4.

I was on one of my visits to Bulacan, which had grown more rare since I became an actor, when my Tita Jackie came from college in Manila one Saturday morning as I read on the floor of our common room.

"I have some bad news from your mama," she said. "Your show has been canceled."

"But why? The ratings are so good."

Tita Jackie explained that the network decided to replace us with a news program. She conjectured that since the government owned the TV station, maybe the administration wanted a show about the real lives of Filipino people.

"Will you be okay?" she asked.

"I think so."

I lay on our floor and looked up at the ceiling to think. *Bisoy* was canceled. I could lead a normal life again. I could go to school every day and not have to endure late-night tapings. I could go back to Talacsan every weekend. Maybe Mama wouldn't beat me as much. But then I remembered how exhilarating it was to see myself on TV and felt a twinge I didn't expect.

When I went in the following Monday to do our last taping, Steve and other crew members reassured me I wouldn't have trouble finding work. Because the cancellation was so sudden, the scriptwriters didn't have time to write a proper ending, so the last episode gave no indication that there wasn't going to be another one, as I pretended to run away even though I was just hiding in the bushes of our backyard and Redford couldn't find me. When Isabel finally looked around and noticed where I was hiding, she started talking about how it was too bad she didn't know where I was because she brought me cake, and I sprang out of the bushes to hug my TV mom for the last time, the kind and beautiful mother I didn't have in real life.

I wasn't done with show business though; I was actually booked on a talk show called *Seeing Stars with Joe Quirino*, so I returned to Broadcast City the following Friday. Another guest that night was Lea Salonga, the singer I'd admired for so long but had never actually met in person.

I went on first, and the cancellation hadn't been announced yet, so I had to pretend there was nothing wrong as the host asked me mundane questions about being a sitcom kid. When I got off the soundstage, my eyes adjusting to the darkness, I spied a figure in a baby doll dress and pigtails with ribbons standing at a distance from me. It was Lea Salonga. A crew member was leading me toward the exit to the dressing rooms, and I would pass her on my way there. I prepared to pause and say hello.

But as I got closer, I noticed that Lea's gaze was pitched upward and her eyes were glassy. She was focused on her performance, maybe going through her song in her head. I didn't want to affect her concentration, so I only gazed at her in wonder as I passed. Instead of returning to my dressing room, I stood in the back of the studio as she sang "Top of the World" by the Carpenters.

"I'm on top of the world, looking down on creation," she sang during the chorus, and how could she not be? She looked too big for her dress, on the cusp of puberty at twelve years old, with that voice and that beauty. I couldn't help but compare us to each other, how I had no real talent besides looking cute and memorizing lines like a trained monkey. In her presence, I understood what real, transcendent talent was like, and how it didn't just come naturally but must have been nurtured over many years. This was what I sought rather than fame, something I was both good at and passionate about, instead of a job I didn't like even though it brought me attention.

Life felt normal for a while after my show ended, as I focused on school and returned to the top of my class. Though soon enough, Mama took me to auditions again, and I got small parts in movies. This seemed fun at first because I only needed to act on weekends, and only for a couple of days at a time. I played the young Redford White in a parody Western, and I was part of a gang of waifs in an action movie called *Idol*. These jobs also didn't seem particularly interesting, but they at least kept Mama happy, as she and Papa decided to separate and the two of us moved in with her new boyfriend, so I started third grade in a different school.

Though over time, as Mama focused on her new relationship, she also began to lose interest in my career. She got pregnant again with my half sister, who was born when I was ten and she had to raise herself since she wasn't Nanay Coro's grandchild. Pretty soon the money from my acting dried up and we had to move to a dilapidated house in Cavite province south of Manila, which extended my bus trips back to my grandmother by two hours. The house flooded every monsoon season, so its wooden frame smelled of rot, and seawater bleached the legs of our furniture. I also had to switch to another school in the middle of the semester, my third in less than three years.

So much was happening in our country in the meantime, as more and more people gave themselves permission to criticize the administration after Ninoy Aquino's assassination. Because of the complaints, Marcos decided to hold special elections in February 1986, and Cory Aquino, Ninoy's widow, was put forward as his opponent. I watched on TV as ballot officials staged a walkout two nights after the election, when they saw hundreds of thousands of votes for Marcos appear out of nowhere on their computers.

On February 25, 1986, millions of Filipino people took to the streets to overthrow Marcos, when he declared himself president even after the walkout. I was proud to be Filipino then, awakened to the unique qualities of our people, our selflessness and desire to cooperate with one another, to band together as one to expel an unjust leader.

My mother had just given birth to her fourth child, even though she had left the third to the care of a maid she could barely afford. I wasn't sure when she began to gamble, but it was hardly a secret by that time when I was eleven, as she and her boyfriend disappeared for days, leaving me with the maid to fend for myself, since I was self-sufficient and would do my homework on my own. I resented being punished because I was conscientious, unable to fail, unable to prove to others that Mama neglected me, because I had no sense of self if I wasn't perfect, and I was too ashamed to be known as a child worth abandoning.

The spirit of change that swept through our country after the revolution compelled me to evaluate my life. I had lived with the promise of going to America for as long as I could remember, had molded my entire self for that future. But the last few years taught me the vast gap between perception and reality, how a leader I'd grown up believing to be good turned out to be the embodiment of corruption, and learning that the United States kept Marcos in power to serve its own interests made me suspicious of my loyalties. If the American government were to approve our petition to immigrate, which my parents filed even before I was born, they would have done it already. I became convinced that this dream of America was destined to stay just that, so I began to envision a future without the promise of moving there. America must have been just another fantasy Mama had concocted, like so many of the promises she had broken, to spend more time with me, to take me places I'd never been, to love me like a mother should.

It didn't even make sense that Mama would want me around, except she was set against me going to Talacsan because she must have wanted to own my accomplishments and prospects for herself. Since I'd proven such a useful cash cow while I was acting, she figured that having me stay with her, a son who was sure to grow up successful, would mean that I would someday provide for her like dutiful children did in the Philippines. Except she didn't want to do any of the work of raising a child. While Nanay Coro provided for me without expecting anything in return, Mama gave me nothing but expected everything.

Mama's one concession was that I could still visit Talacsan on weekends. But once school was done the summer before I started sixth grade, I decided that I wouldn't return to her house and would continue my studies with my grandmother indefinitely. Because Mama had threatened to go to court when I'd brought up my wish to live in Talacsan in the past, and Nanay Coro did not want to keep me with her against my mother's wishes, I knew that I needed to talk to Mama before I left her for good.

It was past noon on a hot day when my mother came downstairs, bleary from one of her gambling binges the night before, as I watched TV in the living room. I caught sight of her plump face in a bright blue, flower-print house dress before she sat on a rattan chair behind me. A variety show called *Eat Bulaga* was on, hosted by a trio named Tito, Vic, and Joey who had starred with Redford White in a number of movies. The thought of this made our change in circumstances even more stark, how I was the star of my own sitcom less than three years before, until Mama got too addicted to even take me to auditions.

Still sitting on our concrete floor painted an ugly earthen red, I turned my body to face Mama. I'd planned what I was going to say for days, but her weary face gave me pause because she was sure to be in a bad mood, her hair unkempt and head bent as though she could fall asleep again. But she could leave for weeks at any moment, so I had to take this chance and speak to her.

"I'm going to school in Talacsan next year."

Mama said nothing and I wasn't sure if she registered my words, so I stood up and was about to repeat myself when she said, "Are we talking about this again? You're staying here."

"I'm old enough to decide for myself."

Mama stood up, and though her movements were slow, I still took a step back. But I noticed that since I'd grown over the past year, the two of us were now nearly the same height.

"I am your mother," she said through bared teeth as she took a step toward me. "I decide where you should go."

"You're not a real mother," I replied. She ran to the corner to pick up a broom and held it up by the bottom of the wooden handle wrapped in red plastic, near the sweeping bristles made of thousands of yellow reeds. I walked toward her, and she raised the handle to threaten me, as my focus turned to the innocent household item that had been the tool of my pain over many years. She'd never beaten me in daylight before, and seeing that instrument, associating it with Nanay Coro's tireless efforts to keep her home clean, I forgot my fear.

"Your grandmother didn't hit you enough!" she shouted. "That's why you turned out so ungrateful."

"I have nothing to be grateful for," I replied, and watched my fingers splay to grab the handle, felt the alienness of plastic as my palm wrapped around it. We struggled for a few seconds, but Mama's widened, fearful eyes invigorated me, and I finally wrested the broom from her hand. I raised that broom high like a trophy and smiled when my mother flinched. I wanted to hit her, so I could prove myself the terrible son she failed to raise, but the last person I wanted to resemble was my mother. I threw the broom aside and ignored Mama's sobs as I walked back to my room.

My bags were ready when Nanay Coro arrived to pick me up the next day. I told her the news, that Mama had allowed me to continue school in Talacsan for good. My mother wasn't there to speak for herself; she had left to gamble the previous afternoon.

In Talacsan, I woke to the echo of roosters in my dreams and the brightening dots of sky through the gauze of our mosquito net and the thatch roof that covered us. Those maya birds had once again poked holes in that roof, but village men would no longer cover them with new thatch, because we were about to move to another house my grandparents had built, a dizzying two-story concrete-and-marble edifice that announced their success.

As I turned my body to get up, I was surprised to find my brown brother, who slept on his side as he faced me, mouth open, no longer the toddler in my memory but a five-year-old boy. The two of us rarely saw each other since he got sent to live with Nanay Coro. A clutch of scabs littered the side of his face, no doubt from scratching after insect bites. He revolted me, how dark and unkempt he looked, the child I would have been had I come out of the womb like everyone expected, a dark boy like my father.

"Pangit," I said when he opened his eyes. Ugly.

I watched the indecision in his almost-black pupils, over whether he could keep the hurt inside himself. But as his light and smart brother, in a culture that taught siblings to follow a strict hierarchy, neither of us had doubt that if I called him ugly, he was ugly.

The tears I expected flowed out of those eyes, though I was

surprised at the loudness of Tonton's cries when he opened his mouth, and the pleasure I felt in hearing them.

"Stop bothering your brother!" Nanay yelled from the kitchen, halfhearted and indulgent.

"One little two little three little Indians," I chanted as I tapped my palm against my brother's mouth, transforming his cry into an Indian call. This made him wail even more, as only shallow, halting breaths interrupted his cries. A tiny part of me wanted to stop, but a bigger part wanted to cause him the worst pain, arbitrary and unfair, even when the many beatings of my own childhood made me wince at any sign of violence, unable to even watch mundane action movies. No, words and smarts were my weapons, taunts and clever forms of torture. I kept calling Tonton ugly, kept chanting and tapping his mouth, until Nanay Coro ran into the room to take my brother away.

Soon enough it was the first day of school, and as I buttoned up my uniform in the mirror shortly after sunrise, a short-sleeved white cotton shirt with the school insignia embroidered on the pocket, it felt comforting to be dressed like everyone else, as if I was just an ordinary schoolkid. There were no fantasies behind the glass, no dreams of a fabled life in America, just the reality of a Filipino student about to start sixth grade in a place he loved. Going to school also made my life in Talacsan feel defined and permanent, clear evidence that I'd taken control of my future.

A white van stopped outside our house and took me, my brother, and my youngest aunt to an L-shaped, four-story concrete building, which faced a paved courtyard and our municipal church on the other side. This was St. Paul's, the private Catholic school well-known for sending its graduates to prestigious colleges in Manila like UP Diliman and Ateneo, the Jesuit school Papa attended before he dropped out.

Our van arrived right before morning exercises, so I didn't get the chance to talk to any of my new classmates, as we stood in a neat line to sing the national anthem and say our morning prayers. I followed the other students to our classroom on the second floor, a perfectly ordered rectangle with a blackboard on one short end, windows along one wall, and five long rows of dark wooden desks, alphabetically assigned except for mine, since I had to sit in the front row because of my eyes. My first-period English teacher simply noted that I was the only new student in my section, before she assigned a composition on our summer vacation, and I wrote about returning to my beloved Talacsan but left out the part about fleeing my own mother.

The lessons seemed similar enough to my old school as several periods went by, until midmorning when we came downstairs for PE, and the boys were separated from the girls as we merged with another section. The teacher told us we would start with a game of basketball, our class against the boys in the other group.

The dozen of us gathered around to form a huddle, and a boy named Samuel Dominguez asked us who would like to start. Several hands went up, and he picked four other students to join him, as our tallest player got to the middle of the court and the teacher threw the ball in the air to start the game, while the rest of us sat on benches under an awning.

I usually couldn't tell people apart from a distance, but I found myself tracking Samuel's lanky frame from the speed with which he weaved through other players and the way he ran down the court with the ball after the other team scored, but invariably passed it to someone else on our team to make a shot. Because basketball was such a national obsession in the Philippines, I'd watched games on TV with my grandfather and knew that Samuel played a position called point guard, which Tatay Gaudencio told me was the most important player, because he determined what everyone else was going to do. Our team jumped into a several-point lead in the first few minutes, before Samuel took himself out of the game to give someone else a chance to play.

"You're new, right?" Samuel asked as he sat next to me on the bench. His face was flush with exertion, and I could smell his fresh sweat. "What position do you play?"

I turned my head to look directly at him, his smile open and lopsided, a dot of a mole above the left side of his lip, the part of his mouth that was more upturned.

"I don't play basketball."

I grinned when his forehead crinkled and his thick eyebrows disappeared under his bangs, as his eyes bulged out in shock.

"What do you mean?"

"I can't even dribble. My eyes are too weak."

"You don't need your eyes to dribble. I'll show you after class."

Once the bell rang and our teacher declared the game over, with our team the winner by a dozen points, Samuel stayed behind with a basketball under his arm, which he passed to me and I thankfully caught. He told me to close my eyes.

"Just feel the ball when it comes off your hand, and then listen to when it bounces on the ground."

I did as I was told as he put his hand on top of mine and we bounced the ball together. After a while, he took his hand off and I felt the sensation of that object's textured surface against my palm and heard the pleasant squeal of the ball, almost like a breath, right after the thud when it bounced on the ground. Samuel was right. I didn't need to look at the ball to dribble, and I even managed to walk and bounce the ball at the same time before we headed off to the canteen for a snack.

My lessons with Samuel continued over the next few weeks, even though it soon became clear that while I could manage to dribble and even pass all right, the basket was just a blur so I couldn't shoot the ball. Still, Samuel's lessons allowed me to do a credible enough job whenever I had to do my few minutes of required playing time. Through Samuel, I started hanging out with a loose gang of boys from our class, kids like Dek Igaya, Don Flores, and Ramil Cruz.

It felt different to be friends with a group who regularly got together, not like my previous schools where I just made friends with a couple of kids who did well in class like me. I also liked that the group didn't have a specific leader, or it would be Samuel and not me if it did, except he was too easygoing to care.

Samuel and I were equivalents in that we were both talented— him at sports and me at academics—and through him, I learned how to stand out while remaining humble. Samuel was always happy to help, quick to share credit when our team won, and didn't act superior even though he was better than everyone else. I had a habit of showing off whenever I could, how I got perfect scores on tests without studying too hard or grasped material faster than the other kids. Over time, I learned to control my need to always be better, to help Samuel and our other friends do their schoolwork.

Though what cemented my bond with Samuel was an incident that happened midway through sixth grade. Our school day went from seven to five with an hour break for lunch, when the school van drove me home to eat. But I hadn't finished my homework one day and so decided to have lunch at school with Samuel—who lived far away in Baliwag and usually stayed—at the canteen as we ate our pork adobo and rice on green trays. It was a pleasant change getting to spend more time with my best friend, so I figured I'd have lunch at school from then on.

But two periods later in religion class, I felt an uncomfortable rumbling in my stomach and excused myself to go to the bathroom. I tried to hold it in, but by the time I got to the boys' lavatory at the end of the hallway, I had already soiled myself. Thankfully, no one was there to witness my embarrassment, as I went into one of the stalls to figure out what to do. I couldn't go back to class and tell my teacher in front of the other kids, but going to the principal's office seemed even worse. I wouldn't be able to face anyone at school again if they knew what had happened.

So I decided to wrap my underwear in toilet paper and throw it into the trash, then wiped off what had gotten into my pants, which were thankfully dark brown. I took a deep breath in the mirror as I washed my hands and set my face so that no one would suspect anything. I returned to my desk and continued the rest of class with Sister Antonia, the kindest of the nuns at school, and I almost decided to go to her after the bell rang to say something because my stomach still felt unsettled, but I couldn't.

During the minutes between classes while the teachers switched rooms, our assigned monitor, Grace, stood up and walked around while the rest of us stayed in our seats. She came from a rich family and was known for being fussy and neat, which was probably why she got chosen to be monitor in the first place.

"Does anyone else smell something?" Grace asked as she wandered near the front of the class where I was sitting.

"I know what you mean," another girl said as she sniffed. "It smells like poop."

Other people started sniffing too, and I joined them, pretending I had no idea where the smell was coming from. But soon enough, Grace came back close to my seat.

"Is it coming from you?" she asked as she looked down at me, her eyes wide and incredulous.

It felt for a moment like I was falling off a cliff, as if the perfect image I'd cultivated for years would collapse in a single moment, how this incident would follow me grade after grade, and I would be forever known not as the smart and white one but as the kid who pooped himself and was stupid enough to think he could get away with it.

"Someone stepped on dog poop and tracked it inside," I heard Samuel say behind me.

"Yeah, that's why it smells bad," Don Flores said, and a couple of other boys followed. We all checked our shoes, and even though no one found anything, our social studies teacher came in, so we settled down to our lesson again. I could still smell myself, so I was sure anyone near my seat with a sensitive nose could too. But thankfully, no one brought it up again, and Grace sat a safe distance away.

As our teacher began writing on the board, I stole a glance at Samuel two seats behind me. I couldn't see his expression, but I could tell he was looking at me too. I was sure he knew, and I wanted to mouth "thank you" but couldn't, so I let the matter remain an unspoken secret between us. As my gaze lingered on Samuel, I became aware of something even more shameful: I was hopelessly smitten with my friend.

5.

For weeks, I refused to move into our new house. Nanay tolerated my whims, set out the seagrass mat, and stayed with me even though everyone else had started sleeping in that opulent building with its two terraces, multiple bathrooms, and beds just like the Americans. It felt cruel that I had just learned to appreciate my own upbringing when my family decided to adopt Western ways, and I was sentimental about my childhood in our wood-and-thatch home, the breeze from the gaps between the bamboo slats on the floor, the open wood flame we cooked over instead of the stove Nanay had installed, and the washer she bought for clothes.

But over time, Nanay coaxed me into spending more of my days in the home that represented the pinnacle of her dreams, her final ascension from peasant farmer to prosperous businesswoman. She pointed out the built-in bathtub next to my own room and reminded me that I liked the idea of having a door to close when I read or studied, even though I was afraid to find it locked from the outside in the middle of the night. I relented one day and agreed to sleep in my bedroom in the corner of that house, on the second floor where I could survey the fields we owned beyond the paved yard and the mango orchard at the edge of our property, one of several parcels of land my grandparents had amassed. I slept in my bed made of dark wood and carved with curlicue patterns, hoping not to dream of Mama's old apartment, where I first slept on a bed and was beaten. After a peaceful sleep, I went downstairs the next morning and rested my head against the cool marble floor, then spent most of the day reading there, occasionally taking breaks to cool my head again. I looked up not at the bundles of thatch I was used to but at a series of concentric wooden rectangles that started from the edge of our ground-floor living room, polished and varied in shades of brown, which converged onto a crystal chandelier in the middle. The wood was attractive enough, though the chandelier struck me as a cheap try at those fancy flourishes in American TV shows. I avoided looking at it but decided it was comfortable on the floor and I could get used to the house after all.

As our jeepney passed the lone movie theater in Baliwag on the way to the market one afternoon, I noticed a poster for an American movie—I could tell just from the muted colors and the orderliness of the design, in contrast to the more chaotic posters that accompanied Filipino films. I told Nanay Coro that I wanted to stop, so she rapped on the roof of the jeepney as the vehicle ground to a halt and we got out.

I'd never seen our local theater show an American movie, so I was determined to see this one no matter what it was. When I got to the modest lobby, I saw that the poster was for *Dead Poets Society* and showed a group of young men in red sweaters carrying an older man who wore a long-sleeved shirt and tie. Nanay Coro wasn't interested in seeing a movie in a language she barely knew, so she agreed to let me see *Dead Poets Society* on my own while she went to the market.

I took my seat in the second row of the near-empty cinema, which didn't bode well for American films playing regularly in Baliwag. I gathered after the first couple of scenes that the boys in the poster were students in high school who wore uniforms like me, though mine was a short-sleeved button-down, while theirs was a jacket and tie, which made them look like they would become businessmen someday. They also lived in their school instead of going home, a concept that was alien to me though not entirely unpleasant.

The older man in the poster turned out to be Mr. Keating, the boys' English teacher, a charming figure who taught his students that poetry was the source for humankind's deepest feelings and insights. There was a scene where he read a line from a poem by Robert Frost that we had gone through in my English class, "Two roads diverged in a wood, and I— / I took the one less traveled by, / And that has made all the difference." Watching Mr. Keating explain how the poet encourages the reader not to follow everyone else's path, it occurred to me that my classes only focused on making sure we understood the literal meaning of what we read. I had never been asked to interpret a poem, much less expand on what it meant for me personally.

As I sat alone in the dark, I watched as Neil, Mr. Keating's most promising student, wrestled with his desire to act in a Shakespeare play called *A Midsummer Night's Dream*, while his father wanted him to focus on getting accepted to Harvard and becoming a doctor. I'd heard passing references to Harvard as the best school in

America—it had been a clue on *Jeopardy!*, and UP Diliman, the most prestigious state school in our country, called itself "The Harvard of the Philippines." Though that movie was the first time Harvard took concrete shape in my mind, as a university that countless students over many generations had aspired to attend. But Neil wanted to make decisions for himself, so he defied his father and did the play anyway.

I gasped when Neil's father unexpectedly entered the theater just as Puck began his first speech. But Neil turned out to be masterful in his role, so much so that I understood him. I understood Shakespeare! I understood that Puck was a fairy in the woods who delighted in bringing lovers together, and that he traveled with a gang of other fairies.

When Puck delivered his last monologue at the end of the play, it was also Neil speaking directly to his father: "Gentles, do not reprehend / If you pardon we will mend." I found myself so moved not just by Neil's sincerity but by the layers of nuance in those lines, of a fairy begging an audience's pardon if they weren't entertained, and also of a son for acting against his father's wishes, while the actor who played Neil was also a son, and I wondered whether the actor's own father disapproved of his profession, the choices he made in life.

I marveled over these complex ideas and realized, really for the first time, that I had a passion for literature, which I had nourished over many years without much of a thought. I started out reading books from America just to learn English, but in the limited scope of my life, literature evolved into the prime way for my imagination to transport itself to other worlds. Movies and television supplied me with an influx of images, but it was really books that stretched my capacity to come up with ideas, a quality I'd had for as long as I could remember but wasn't aware could be put to any use. I couldn't exercise my talents in the Philippines, where the smartest students routinely turned into doctors, which I, like Neil, was expected to become. The Philippines could not give me adequate training to be a great poet in English anyway, and I lived in a country where actors didn't typically mine the depths of Shakespeare but rather appeared in cheesy comedies or telenovelas. *Dead Poets Society* unearthed my regret that the dream of America I'd nurtured as a child didn't turn out to be true.

I was sure Neil's father would forgive him after seeing how great he was, but the man took his son directly home and ordered Neil to enroll in a military academy the following day. While the rest of his family went to bed, Neil returned to his room, took off his shirt, and opened his window in the middle of a snowy winter. The next set of images would play in my mind repeatedly over many years, of Neil shirtless and shivering, staring longingly out the window, the white landscape around him an eerie blue in the middle of the night, the trees ugly and black like witches with gnarled arms. I knew something bad was going to happen but did not expect Neil to find his father's gun and shoot himself, which I'd never seen a Filipino movie depict, in our Catholic country where suicide was the gravest of sins.

I left the movie thankful that I didn't have a figure in my life as controlling as Neil's father. Even if my choices were limited at home, it was better to have a small set of options than to have a future I wanted and other people got to have, but that I somehow couldn't pursue. I would make an excellent doctor, and my family would be proud of my success. In my country, that felt enough.

———

Maybe this was just how the mind worked, that as soon as you decide something is out of reach, then you notice everything that brings it tantalizingly within sight. That year I turned fourteen was also the year when Lea Salonga was cast to play the lead role of Kim in the London production of *Miss Saigon*, which would eventually go to Broadway. This was a route to the West I hadn't envisioned; Lea was so talented that powerful men searched the whole world to find her, then brought her to their land as a star.

I bought the recording when it was released in early 1990, which was when I learned the full scope of the plot, how *Miss Saigon* was not just about a talented singer from my country fulfilling her dream of becoming a star on Broadway; the musical itself was about a similar dream, of women from our neighboring country of Vietnam hoping to come to America through the power of love.

The show begins when Kim enters a Saigon bar for the first time, forced to sell her body after her village is burned and her parents killed. A shy American soldier named Chris becomes enamored of her, and one of Chris's marine buddies purchases Kim for his friend. When Kim realizes that she will join a man for the first time, she sings of her inner dreams, the fragments of fantasies she's created from her limited knowledge of America. She believes it's a land of wealth and that not all soldiers are evil, as she longs for "a man who will not kill / who'll fight for me instead."

Chris is the perfect representation of Kim's dreams, a rugged and kind man who falls in love with her innocence and pledges to protect her at all costs as she sings of him being the sunlight to her moon, the force of blazing energy in contrast to her mystery. Even as the war ultimately wrenches the two lovers apart, there is never any doubt that the American soldier only has the best intentions and that their fate is the fault of circumstance rather than his character.

I listened to that tape over and over again and found myself dreaming Kim's dreams despite myself, even when I knew that Americans were never as kind as they were made out to be. But in my budding adolescence, I couldn't help but be swept up in this union between an Asian woman and an American man, and not just any Asian woman but someone from my country I had followed since I was a child. I sang Kim's parts along with Lea, so that her voice became my voice, and in the darkness of my room, her spirit also became mine. I too dreamed of being a woman capable of getting a rugged and kind man to fall in love with her.

When I woke up after those nights listening to that album, there was no one else I could think of but Samuel, who embodied all the qualities Kim fell in love with when she found Chris, someone unfailingly masculine who was also gentle and loyal. Samuel was the one with whom I imagined a future together, even though this too was impossible, because no one would ever love a bakla.

Though there was an afternoon that gave me hope. A pool resort called Eight Waves opened close to our town, a short drive from Samuel's house, and the gang agreed to meet there so his father could drive us to the resort to spend the day. There were too many of us in the car, so I sat on Samuel's lap in the front seat.

It wasn't unusual for Samuel and me to touch; we often walked with our arms around each other's shoulders or rested our heads together when we were tired. We were rambunctious out of our school uniforms that day, headed for an adventure all to ourselves, without parents or teachers looking after us. We were still boys who acted like boys in many ways, but that start of our independence marked the dawn of our time as men.

"Stop wiggling around!" Samuel yelled, and slapped me on the thigh.

"They keep hitting me on the head," I replied as I tried to swat at the boys behind me.

"Can't we just talk? I'm sure they'll stop if you ignore them."

"The game last night was brutal," I said, aware of what would rile Samuel up. "Jaworski's getting too old."

Samuel blew air out of his mouth after I took a dig at his favorite basketball player, Robert Jaworski, who was both the point guard and coach for Añejo Rum but was slowing down as his team kept losing to their rival, San Miguel, that season. I grinned as Samuel defended Jaworski and assured me Añejo was going to come back, and I pretended to be interested. I just enjoyed being inches away from him, feeling his breath in my face as we continued along the newly paved road to the resort.

The wind from the open window drowned our voices when the car sped up, so I looked out onto brightness and the green rice paddies, freshly planted, until we reached a section full of potholes that the floods had eroded. As we negotiated this path, I felt Samuel harden underneath me, and I tried to keep my body from tensing up. Samuel was aroused in a way I'd never dared to expect, and even though I knew it wasn't exactly me that triggered this physical reaction, that it was the car's motion and the newness of his adolescence, I still hoped it was a little bit me, that part of him didn't consider it so monstrous, the thought of being with a boy who was also his best friend.

I glimpsed the outline of his naked form for the first time as we changed together to swim, when he stripped down to his white briefs, though he wrapped a towel around himself to change into his trunks. It was also the first time I saw him shirtless as we swam in the pool, noticed the beginnings of hair under his arms like the hair under mine, except mine was barely visible, while his was a pattern of swirls I would muse over day and night, like knots I needed to untangle.

I returned to Talacsan for my grandmother's funeral in October 2015. I'd only been back one other time since transition, and only for a couple of hours, to convince Papa to let his mother see the house she so lovingly built, after he claimed it for himself as head of the family when my grandfather died. By then, I understood that Papa hated Nanay Coro for forcing him to marry Mama, that she ruined his life for doing so, and his cruelty in her old age was revenge. If my grandmother was at fault, it was only in favoring my father and raising him to believe that he didn't need to follow the same rules as everyone else. It was an upbringing I knew well, having spent plenty of energy countering its negative effects as an adult, even as I was grateful to Nanay Coro for giving me a sturdy sense of self through her unconditional love.

I had last seen my grandmother alive ten months earlier, when I visited her during a reporting trip to Manila. I picked her up from my cousin's house in an out-of-the-way section of that sprawling metropolis called Cainta, a place she had no connection to, and so her only wish was to go back to Talacsan, not to live in her house but just to see it. As my grandmother held my hand and marveled at how white I still was, I realized how much of me was a product of her own fantasies as a dark peasant farmer born into poverty, who may have loved me regardless but favored me over everyone else because she connected my color to the wealthy, powerful Americans who had conquered our land. That I'd gone to better schools, gotten more degrees, made more money than the rest of my family was proof that I'd become a manifestation of her fantasies, even as I bristled at the thought that my consciousness was built around a fundamentally mistaken belief, that there was something about my color that made me better, apart from the belief itself.

I also realized how much Nanay Coro valued money because it was where she rested her dignity, having come from nothing and become something through her wealth. So she asked for money the entire trip, a simple refrain, almost a chant, "Wala akong pera, wala akong pera," even as the cousin who accompanied us pointed out that she had nothing to spend her money on. But because Papa had commandeered her property and her dear husband had died, money was the only measure by which she could regard herself. On our way back to Manila after Papa refused to let Nanay Coro come inside her own house, I went to an ATM and gave her forty thousand pesos, about a thousand dollars, the maximum I was allowed to take out, even when I knew that the money would either idle under a mattress or be given to cousins I barely knew.

My grandmother died in her sleep, stripped of her dignity, on a single bed in a tiny back room at my cousin's house in that obscure corner of Manila. After Papa bullied her out of her own property, the only person who could have stood up to him no longer existed, because that person was me, but me as a man, and me as someone who hadn't left.

This was how I found myself back inside a house that was once my grandparents' pride, which Nanay Coro was only able to inhabit again as a lifeless body during the three-day wake before her funeral. That once-grand home was in a sorry state, much of its expensive furniture gone, roof and ironwork rusty, ceilings and walls stained brown from water that had seeped in during monsoons. The only opulent feature that remained untouched was the marble floors, which I only realized then were nearly identical to the Widener Library stacks at Harvard, the same square tiles and shade of gray.

I spent the first night of my grandmother's vigil sleeping on an old upholstered chair near her casket, while Papa showed up to gamble in the wee hours and I pretended not to see him, then woke up and bathed in rusty water the next morning. The entire day, neighbors from our village and nearby towns visited Nanay Coro, almost none of whom had met me as a woman, nearly all of whom I didn't remember because I left too young and too long ago. There was an old woman who asked about my brother, meaning me, and another who asked if I'd given birth to children, thinking that my surgery involved making a womb. But just like it was during my childhood, many of those villagers marveled over how beautiful I was, and with my light blond hair down to my shoulders, wearing mascara and lipstick, how I was even more beautiful as a woman than the man they'd never met, their extrapolation of the boy they remembered.

A friend from school named Dek Igaya visited on the second day, the one member of my old gang who also lived in my village. He and I sat on a long bench with an ornate, carved back, one of the few pieces of presentable furniture left in the house. Dek was a predictable outcome of the dark, baby-faced kid I once knew, especially when he still sported his bowl cut and straight bangs.

"I'm sorry it took this long to visit Ninang," he said.

It was only when Dek used the word "ninang" that I remembered Nanay Coro was his godmother, which reminded me of the revered role she once played in Talacsan, a legacy that my father had obliterated, having sold nearly all of my grandmother's property to fund his wayward life. Though maybe the loss was just as well since I, his only surviving legitimate child in the eyes of Philippine law, would not have been in a position to carry that legacy on. Maybe my brother Tony could have taken over, but he had died nearly a decade before. I wondered if I would have given him my share and position as male head of the family—Philippine law did not recognize transgender women—or, flush with the prospect of wealth, I would have become a different version of my father.

"Hershey Rodriguez died of a heart attack," Dek said out of the blue. "It's too bad she won't make it to our twenty-fifth reunion."

He told me about the last time our class reunited, at a restaurant in Baliwag the previous summer. Dek regaled me with a long list of updates about various friends like Richard Paguia and Mirabella Desiderio, the top students in our class who had become doctors. Many of the old gang like Ramil Cruz and Don Flores had gone to work abroad.

"Samuel Dominguez stayed here though," Dek said. "He's a manager for a corporation in Manila."

I expected to hear Samuel's name and was glad I didn't have to ask. I was also proud of myself that I didn't follow up with more questions, allowed what existed between me and Samuel to lie firmly in the past.

"We talked about you at reunion," he admitted. "It's amazing you've become a woman. We didn't even know you were gay."

I was tempted to explain that gay and transgender were distinct identities in America but decided to set it aside, knowing they overlapped in our country.

"You really had no idea?"

"No," he said as he shook his head. "We were really surprised."

I felt disappointed over how I hid so well that even my most intimate friends didn't know me. I was still sure Samuel did though, regardless of what he said.

Dek was there for my grandmother's funeral mass two days later. Papa refused to represent our family like he was supposed to, so I was called upon to speak without any notice, before the hundred or so neighbors, friends, and extended family members who sat in our vast municipal church that morning.

"Salamat po sa inyong pagdalo," I began, thanking everyone who came, and for those few minutes, I felt as if I had never left and had been living with my grandmother the last twenty-five years. I spoke in the innocent Tagalog of my youth, as the deferent, dutiful grandchild of a singular woman, who emerged out of her humble upbringing to become one of the most respected members of our village. I spoke of how much our family loved her, how much she persevered through many obstacles, and how much she loved the people of Talacsan even when she didn't live there in the last years of her life. By the time I finished, I'd not only forgotten I had left for America but that I was a different gender than the boy those people knew, a change that felt trivial in the face of my grief.

We buried my grandmother beside her husband at the municipal cemetery. I cried as pallbearers pushed her casket inside the raised mass of concrete that would be Nanay Coro's permanent resting place. Though I wasn't just mourning her, I realized, but the two of us together. I once told her I wanted to stay in the Philippines, and she convinced me I would always wonder who I could have become if I didn't go to America. But seeing my grandmother for the last time, and knowing how heartbroken she was when I left, how unhappy during the last decade of her life, it didn't feel like the regret I would have felt if I stayed could be any worse than the regret I felt at that moment. She would have been so much happier with me there, and I would have made her happy, which could only mean that I would have been happy myself. Maybe I would have needed to sacrifice my ambitions, been less likely to live my life openly, but as a man used a trowel to cover the side of Nanay Coro's tomb with fresh cement, so that soon my grandmother was encased in concrete, I also mourned that dutiful Filipino grandson who appeared during that mass like a ghost, someone I hadn't noticed I'd buried.

6.

We'd been in line for nearly half a day, or really, over fifteen years, before our number got called one April afternoon in 1990, and we walked through a maze of hallways to an ordinary fluorescent-lit room at the U.S. embassy in Manila, except that behind a sturdy wooden desk sat a brown-haired man with a narrow face and lips nearly the same shade as his skin. He introduced himself as Mr. Webber and motioned for my family to sit on thinly padded chairs in front of him, my younger brother on Mama's lap.

It was strange to see Mama and Papa smile at each other as though they were an actual couple. Divorce was illegal in the Philippines, and when my mother got the letter about our immigration interview, she decided it was too risky to present herself as a single mother, rather than a happily married woman with a husband who supported his wife and kids, never mind that husband and wife both lived with other people and that neither of those kids lived with them. We were a happy family for the sake of this interview, even when Mama had become a stranger to me, and I never really knew Papa to begin with.

Yet the oddness of seeing us together couldn't compare to the bizarre possibility that we could be living in America in a matter of months. After years of preparing through books and television, it felt as if I knew everything there was to know about that country, yet also nothing about actually living there.

"How do you think you'll adjust to school?"

"I have read about America since I was small," I replied. But even as I tried to impress this man who controlled my fate, what I really wanted to do was ask him how *he* thought I would adjust, since he was in a much better position to know.

"He is in the top of his classes," Mama said.

I was surprised she didn't bring up my whiteness, though I didn't either. That Mr. Webber himself didn't mention it made me suddenly aware that I really had no idea whether I would just blend in with other Americans the way my family described. They had no way of knowing, since none of them had been to America themselves.

As the attention shifted away from me and toward my parents, it struck me how cruel it felt to be wrested from the life I'd known, just as I was on the verge of discovering the adult I would become. Mama and Papa knew they wanted to be somewhere else, after life in our country didn't make them happy. At fourteen, I couldn't know what kind of grown-up I would be in the Philippines, but I desperately wanted to, just as much as I wanted to find out what my future would be like in America. I wished that all this was happening a decade earlier, when I was too young to know the difference and could have gone on to be just American, only vaguely aware of the country I came from. Yet I also ached at this thought, that I would have never known my grandmother, my friends, an upbringing and a country I'd grown to love more than the fantasy America represented.

I continued to search that white man's face for answers, as he spoke to my parents about their finances. With a mixture of puzzlement and relief, I realized I no longer worshipped Americans like him, or the promise of living in such a rich country and becoming white myself, indistinguishable from those creatures with so much power who ruled the rest of the world, who every day decided on the fates of us brown people pleading to be let into their country, a situation they themselves created when they conquered us against our will, used our land and our hands for free to enrich themselves. No, I didn't want to go, and no one could force me to leave.

It was easy enough to say this to myself, harder to figure out how to tell my family, after Mama sent news from Manila to Talacsan two weeks later that our petition had been approved, and we could move to America whenever we wanted. I joined the celebration on our front porch, where relatives and neighbors congregated when they heard the news, even as I plotted to stay home.

I sat in a rocking chair on the second-floor terrace of our new house, shortly after sunrise a few days later. I could see the brown mass of our old home in the middle distance, and the gray sloping line of the road beyond, which had finally been paved a couple of years before. A bamboo fence stood diagonal to me, beyond which was a network of low wooden huts with corrugated metal roofs, nearly all of them rusty. I'd never been able to tell the dozens of neighbors who lived in those shanties apart from one another, but my grandmother could, because she grew up among them, which was maybe why they didn't resent the change in her circumstances. This generosity of spirit allowed our village to live in harmony, and I wondered if I really needed more out of life than that happiness.

"Do you want to have breakfast soon?" my grandmother asked as she opened the sliding glass door behind me.

"Why don't you sit with me first."

Nanay Coro sat in the rocking chair next to mine, made of hardwood with caned backs, not like the rickety bamboo chair at the old house that she and I used to rock in together, me on her lap. Now, though the two of us rocked apart, the wood made coordinated creaking sounds beneath us, so it felt for a moment like we were traveling together, before I remembered that I was supposed to leave and she was supposed to stay in this village all her life.

"I don't want to go," I said.

I'd uttered those words many times before. Maybe those dozens of goodbyes were supposed to prepare us for the one where I wouldn't see her for years, to become a person she might not understand.

"Your life will be better in America."

"You don't know that," I insisted, old enough to understand that Nanay Coro had no idea what America was really like, except for blind faith and colonial brainwashing. "I can become a doctor here. And when you get old, I can help you manage your business."

Nanay Coro shook her head. "You won't be happy if you stay. You'll always wonder how vast your life could have become."

My grandmother used a word, "malawak," that I'd never known someone apply to a life. I'd heard it used to describe endless fields of land, the vast river that bounded our village on one side, the ocean that lay between me and America. I had never crossed that river, never even been beyond the main island of Luzon where we lived. I knew what she meant, that as much as I loved home, I'd also spent an entire childhood wondering about the possibility of America, the new ways of life I would find there, the person I could become. My grandmother forced me to admit that the right direction, no matter how painful, was toward that infinite horizon.

"I can always come back," I said, though even then I suspected that once I left, I could never return for good.

When June and the start of school came around, I couldn't bear to be without my friends, so I decided to continue at St. Paul's even though we were leaving for America in August. I wanted to pretend a while longer that my life wouldn't change. The work also distracted me from the wait, and sooner than I expected, it was time for us to go.

The weekend before my flight, Samuel and my gang of friends drove to Eight Waves for the last time, in two cars so I didn't get to sit on Samuel's lap. As we stripped down to our briefs in a dressing room that smelled of mildew, I marveled at how good of an actor I'd been, for no one to suspect my secret all those years. I looked in Samuel's direction, and he smiled at me like it was just another day.

We played in sky blue water, wrestling one another without care, traces of our boyhoods still in our touch. They were the last boys with whom I could be so intimate without the guilt of my desire. Except for Samuel, who I didn't touch because it felt perverted, though I allowed him to put his arm around me, reciprocated his pat on my back. I sat on his shoulders to play a game of topple and willed myself not to show any signs of want, even if he accepted my obvious love for him, the love of a friend. Or maybe he knew that my love was more but tolerated it because I was about to leave his life.

We changed back into our clothes after we swam, and I caught a glimpse of Samuel's legs in his basketball shorts as we sat together on the car ride back. There was a hint of his adult shape in the girth of his thigh, thicker than the gangly lines I'd observed in previous years. I would leave for Manila early in the morning and then get on a plane to California. So I allowed my fantasies about Samuel to wander underneath those shorts, to parts of him I would never reach.

The entire gang decided to return to Samuel's house to play basketball, but I told them I was tired and wanted to rest. Samuel offered to let me take a nap in his bed and led me through the back of his house and into his room, a part of the world I'd never been, with a low bed, plain navy blue sheets, and basketball posters on the walls.

I lay down and watched as Samuel took off his white shirt and threw it on the bed beside me, then pulled out a basketball jersey from his closet and put it on.

"I'll come back when we're done," he said as he closed the door.

I stared at that pile of white cloth at my arm's length, the nearest I could ever be to my friend, yet also the furthest, because that shirt represented the very intimacy the two of us could never have, and reaching for it would betray a person who had only been kind to me. But knowing I wouldn't see him again for many years, I grasped that shirt and held it to my face, took a deep breath as I stored his scent inside me, knowing I would never be that close to him again. It was just as well, since I couldn't imagine that he would want us together the way I did.

"You're awake," Samuel said when he came back to check on me, sooner than I expected. The shirt lay safely at my side, but he glanced at it and looked me in the eye.

"I couldn't sleep," I replied.

"So what were you doing?"

The suspicion in his voice was so gentle that I didn't notice it until his gaze cast down to the shirt. He knew me too well, and no matter how much I tried to hide, he could see the truth on my face when he looked up, as much as I could see the truth in his, as the well of our unspoken understandings—the day I soiled my pants, the time he got aroused beneath me—deepened at that moment. I wondered if he could tolerate my last wish to be with him, not even sex, not even naked in bed, but just a kiss, or even to hold his hand in the way he would someday hold the hand of a woman he loved.

"We should go back," Samuel said, and I lost my chance. Nothing seemed amiss the rest of that day, as we joined our friends for dinner and last goodbyes, the promise to see each other again, along with a hug. It was the last time I touched his flesh, smelled his skin, and I wondered if I would ever feel this kind of love, with someone who loved me the same way.

Nanay Coro knocked on my door in the middle of the night; it was time. Our bags were already packed and in the van, so the only thing left was goodbye.

"Remember that I love you always," my grandmother said as she hugged me, but the way she said it—"Tandaan mo lagi na mahal kita"—I couldn't tell if she meant that I should always remember she loves me or if I should remember that she will always love me. I chose the second meaning, the love between us permanent even when our time together was not.

My grandmother decided not to come to the airport, and I heard her wail as soon as the engine turned on. I waved back as the van sped away, grateful that I couldn't see the details of her face.

My family boarded a Korean Air flight to Los Angeles a few hours later. It was August 21, 1990, the anniversary of Ninoy Aquino's assassination, though no one else seemed to notice the auspicious date. I would leave my beloved country on the day Ninoy returned to sacrifice his life, and I felt like a traitor. I told myself a new story, that I could come back and settle in the Philippines, once I had the chance to learn what America was like.

I affected the air of a seasoned traveler even when Mama and my younger brother gaped in wonder around me. I didn't find the drab beige interior of the plane all that attractive anyway, and the uniformity of everything was off-putting, the identical seats and plastic trays, as if nothing in that aircraft had been made with human hands. The takeoff was wondrous though, even when we sat in the section of four seats in the middle of the giant plane. Mama let me take the aisle, so I at least peeked out the window, as the mottled landscape got blurrier the farther we got from the ground.

I wore a jacket my grandfather in America, Lolo Bert, had sent me, sand-colored with "Members Only" emblazoned on the breast pocket. But coming out of the arrivals terminal, it felt just as hot as it had been when we took off. Lolo Bert had visited once when I was little, though I didn't remember his face even after he hugged me; my grandfather led us to a gigantic blue car called a Cadillac to take us to my uncle's house, where we would live while we got settled.

"There is a change of plans," he said. "You will be at your uncle's nursing home."

My uncle Tito Romeo had worked as a nurse for many years, at a hospital in Chino, California. But I learned on that car ride that he'd recently bought a house that he converted into a facility to take care of old people.

"Why aren't their relatives taking care of them?" I asked.

"It's different in America," Lolo Bert explained as he drove. "Here, old people don't live with their children."

The alien concept merged with the strangeness of our surroundings when we left the airport. Instead of the lush, green fields of home, we drove on the widest road I'd ever seen, between buildings like giant boxes, the land barren except for identical trees on the edge of some roads. Giant signs for SEARS, TOYS 'R' US, and PACE were the only shifts in color amid the blue sky, the dusty earth, the gray roads that formed mazes as they intersected. Everything, everything was improbably big and wide and far, as our own giant car hurtled for miles.

My grandfather told me we were getting close. We found ourselves in a barren-looking town of squat buildings instead of skyscrapers, with no people on the sidewalks. As we passed row upon row of nearly identical single-story houses painted in shades of dust, their roofs reddish-brown, it felt as if the America I knew was just a trick of my imagination, even as I would later learn how the Hollywood that built my fantasies was only an hour away.

My grandfather turned in to the driveway of one of these houses, which I couldn't distinguish from any of the others. It had a beige exterior like the rest and a sloping brown roof, pale and discolored from the blinding sun. As I took in air, I smelled the distant odor of manure, as Lolo Bert explained there were cattle ranches on the outskirts of town.

Tito Romeo welcomed us into the house, where we found an aged man in the living room watching a talk show on TV, his socked feet flat against the carpet, also beige. I followed Tito Romeo's lead and ignored the old man while my uncle led us to our room, past two other rooms that were half-open, where I spied beds and tall contraptions, which my uncle explained were monitors for the patients at the home. As I lay in bed that night, unable to sleep, I took stock of what I'd left behind. I came from a place with varied shapes, patterns, and colors wherever I looked, a culture and history I knew. But this place seemed devoid of distinctiveness; everything looked so similar, a variation of the same mold, be it the roads or houses, even the cloudless sky. How was I supposed to find my way if everything around me looked exactly the same? I tried to quiet these fears, and didn't notice I'd fallen asleep, until the beeps of inhuman machines jostled me awake.

PART TWO

HARVARD MAN

1993–1997

7.

Harvard Square," I replied, as casually as I could, when the taxi driver at Logan Airport asked where I was going. I used my bags as an excuse to splurge on a cab, but what I really wanted was to meet my future above ground, feel the curving road that followed the bank of the Charles, the chill of early autumn when I opened the car window.

"Where do you come from?" the driver asked, as I noticed the dark skin on his nape from the back seat, the close-shaved hair below his newsboy cap. He spoke in an accent I couldn't exactly place, though I could tell it was from somewhere France had colonized.

"California," I replied, rounding out the vowel in "Cal" to imply that I'd lived there all along and didn't come from a place where vowel sounds were simple and abrupt.

"Ah, Beverly Hills?" he asked.

"Santa Monica." A friend took me to that city once, and when we got to the wooden pier that embraced the water, it made me wish I could live there.

"I'm from Haiti."

"Vous parlez français?"

"Ah oui. Comment vous pouvez parler ma langue?"

"J'étudie le français à l'école."

"Votre accent est excellent."

It was true I had a good ear and didn't need much practice to make sounds like those around me, whether in English or French. My family's premonition did come true, that once I copied their accent, white people thought I was white, or "American," as Filipinos put it, at least until those white people talked about something obvious I didn't understand, like homecoming or Jimi Hendrix.

Before I came to the U.S., it did not occur to me to question why people from home said "American" when they meant "white." I didn't ask why they called black people Negroes even when they were also American. I wasn't even aware of other races, that Americans would call my family Asian, or that there were Latinos who came from Mexico and made up the majority of kids in my high school, even though most of the students in my honors classes were white. I quickly confirmed that it was to my benefit to seem white too.

"You go to Harvard?" the driver asked.

"I'm starting this year."

"You are lucky."

I wondered whether it was the college I glimpsed in the distance, even though to me those far-off buildings were just indistinct patches of red. As I fantasized about what it would be like to walk through those grand halls every day, I also dreamed up private school friends I'd be seeing soon, a spacious house close to the beach, and a white mom and dad who bid me goodbye.

"Where are your parents?" the driver asked.

"I told them I'd rather go alone." This was literally true even though my attitude of carefree independence was not.

Because Mama did want to come, but I refused because I didn't want her to feel any part of my success. With my grandfather's help, we eventually moved out of the creepy nursing home and into a dinky apartment close to my high school, but it was also around then that Mama discovered the casinos in California. She left me, my younger brother, and our two half siblings from another man she was no longer with, to go on gambling binges that went on for weeks. This forced my other grandmother, Nanay Minyang, to come live with us, a woman whose every word was either a whine or a shout, though at least she kept us fed. I maintained my grades through this turmoil, because I knew a college scholarship was my only chance to escape.

"Why did you choose to come to Boston?" I asked.

"I did not choose," he replied. "My parents are here and their relatives before. My father drives a taxi so I drive a taxi."

I wished I could have told him how alike we were, that I ended up in California not because of rich white parents but because my relatives were there when we immigrated, in smoggy Chino and not Santa Monica. But I was already too deep inside the fantasy I'd built, for his benefit and mine.

I held my breath as the cab turned to cross the short bridge from Storrow to Memorial Drive. We passed buildings I knew were collectively known as the River Houses, dorms for upperclassmen, and as the cab wound through Cambridge streets to deposit me next to the passageway that led to my dorm in Harvard Yard, and my roller luggage rattled through the uneven brick sidewalk, I fancied that if I could dream my future into existence, maybe I could dream away my past too. Maybe I didn't have to be the child of poor immigrant parents who neglected him, who left everything he cared about to be in this country, literally half a world away. If I could turn the dream of becoming a Harvard student into reality, maybe I could just forget that I was anything other than American, live and study among my rich white friends, never have to deal with my life being cleaved. Maybe this was the place where I could erase everything about me that didn't add up or make sense, the place where I could finally belong.

I sat cross-legged on a wooden bench in Emerson Hall, my back against the wall, thirty minutes early for a class I wasn't sure I had the courage to take: Topics in Gay Male Representation. I had promised myself I would come out of the closet as soon as I got to college, but there was still a gigantic part of me that was invested in being seen as someone whose life was unassailable, who did nothing—at least in public—that anyone would be ashamed of. I was afraid to break this pact with myself, the possibilities for my future such a move would foreclose.

I considered returning to my dorm to lie in bed and think, search for answers on the blank ceiling. But I knew I'd be too scared to go back if I left, so I looked down at the floor to find some mind's rest, made of blond wood in narrow stripes of slightly different shades. I thought of our old bamboo floor back home, the same rows of wood that joined at random places. In Chino, all the houses

I'd been in wcrc built in the last twenty years, with drab carpet floors and dull-colored walls. The layers of history and handmade details at Harvard comforted me, because they felt truer to the place I grew up in.

But as I continued to stare, those narrow rows of wood unfurled a cascade of jarring images—shiny balls, a black grip on someone's hand, a puff of smoke when Mama stepped her bowling shoe in a box of rosin. It must have been around the time my show went off the air, for three years starting when I was nine, that Mama got bitten by the bowling bug and started taking me to practices and tournaments. It was strange to think of my mother as ambitious, but I suddenly remembered that bowling was an exhibition sport for the Seoul Olympics in 1988 and Mama dreamed of competing there. I even recalled that Arianne Cerdeña, one of the women Mama bowled with, won the Philippines' first Olympic gold medal, even though it didn't count in the official standings.

I remembered Mama teaching me how to bowl, how I had to stretch my fingers to fit into the holes of the mottled-red, eight-pound ball. She taught me the mechanics of the approach, the swing, and the follow-through.

"But how do I know what to hit?" I asked. "I can't tell the pins apart."

"Do you see those arrows?" she asked as she pointed to some marks down the lanes.

I nodded. The arrows were a lot closer to me, and easy to distinguish because they were black against the light wood.

"You just need to guide the ball to the proper arrow, then it will take a good path to the pins."

She taught me how to aim for the arrow to the right of center to get a strike. Over the following months, before she gave up bowling shortly after she failed to qualify for the Olympics, Mama taught me to use those arrows to hit whatever pins I wanted, when I needed to pick up spares or splits. It was only in that hallway at Harvard that I realized these lessons had applied to other parts of my life, how I'd searched for closer cues whenever I couldn't see something from afar, and how I learned to move boldly toward a direction even if I couldn't see where I would end up. These lessons became so woven into my consciousness that they helped my very decision to come to America, even when my impulse was to stay home.

Mama reminded me that going into this class was the right choice. Whatever future was in store, I couldn't bear the idea of hiding who I was, and I didn't need specifics to understand that being an out gay man was better than staying in the closet. If this was true, then Topics in Gay Male Representation was the arrow that could guide me toward my path. One of my legs was numb when I stood up, but I managed to shuffle through the tall wooden door and into the classroom.

I sat near one end of a long oval seminar table with a wooden base and a smooth black top. The room was painted an unusual shade of blue, like the sky right before dusk, which added to the sense that wherever I'd been, I was about to go someplace else.

I watched as student after student walked in, so there was a line of them standing against one wall by the time a man in a black leather jacket, white T-shirt, and tight jeans walked in, with the air if not the clothes of a professor. He introduced himself as D. A. Miller, but asked the class to call him David.

"This is an advanced seminar so I'm giving priority to upper-classmen," he said. "I can only take twelve students."

There were at least twenty-five of us in that room. I was sad to learn that the decision to take the class was not in my hands, though also a little relieved. But I figured I'd stay for the first class anyway, even if I didn't have a shot at getting in. As I looked around, I was surprised there were several women there, but not surprised that everyone else sported a knowing expression, like they had been in these seminars before.

After everyone said their names, Professor Miller distributed the class syllabus, two pages of books by authors I'd never heard of—Baldwin, Genet, Proust—along with critical essays with titles like "The Epistemology of the Closet" and "Is the Rectum a Grave?" I promised myself I'd read these books anyway, and take the class the next time the professor offered it.

"E. M. Forster's *Maurice* isn't a great book, but it's the only one of his novels that explicitly discusses homosexuality," the professor said as he walked us through the syllabus. "And please remember the correct pronunciation. It's *Mau*-rice and not Mau-*rice*. This is why your parents pay thirty thousand dollars a year for you to go to Harvard, so you won't embarrass yourselves at cocktail parties."

As the other students chuckled, I peered at their faces and imagined what it would be like to have parents who could afford full price for Harvard, to not be on full financial aid and need a work-study job to pay for living expenses.

After the syllabus, Professor Miller took what looked like a stack of brochures from his black leather satchel and passed them around. When I got my copy, I saw that it was for a beach area on the Massachusetts coast called Provincetown. The paper was glossy and thick, with photographs of wide beaches, which I could have mistaken for home except the color of the water was cooler somehow, less inviting, the green masses that assembled between patches of sand too dark and clumped.

"Do you notice anything unusual?" he asked, and I had no idea what he meant. "Pay attention to the language."

"The line about the dunes offering privacy seems suspicious," a slim Asian guy named Royce replied. "That's where men in P-town usually have sex."

"Exactly," the professor replied. "The tourist board couldn't put 'This is where gay men fuck' on the brochure, so they wrote, 'The dunes offer privacy' instead."

I tried to contain my shock, first at a professor saying the word "fuck," and second that we were talking about sex outdoors like it was no big deal. I did my best to absorb D. A. Miller's point, that texts weren't just what something explicitly said, but there were many layers underneath, which were important to tease out of gay-related material because queer people often used coded language to express themselves in a society that rejected them. He called this method of analysis "deconstruction." I wrote down the word in my five-subject notebook, which I already planned to replace when I noticed that most of the class used slim journals with ribbon bookmarks.

Still, it was hard to distill the professor's points not just because he used such unfamiliar terms but also because the discussion moved on to places in Provincetown where gay men met to "cruise," as we talked about a line in the brochure about "convenient public restrooms."

"That's a reference to glory holes," a student named Gavin said, whose confident voice I recognized even though he sat on my side of the table so I didn't get a good look at him. The class began to talk about the glory hole as a site of rebellion during the AIDS crisis, and I was once again completely lost, overwhelmed by phrases like "police state" and "the Marxist commons," as I raised my hand without thinking.

"I'm sorry but what's a glory hole?" I asked.

The chuckles in the room aimed themselves at me. Gavin leaned forward so I could see him. In the half-second before he spoke, I noticed that he was beautiful.

"A glory hole is an opening drilled into the side of a restroom stall," he said like he was reading out of a dictionary. "You slide your cock through and someone on the other side gives you head." My eyes cast themselves down, yet I felt the thrill of discovery along with my embarrassment, and that flutter in my chest because of how attractive Gavin was with his dark curly hair, thick lashes that framed seductive eyes, and full lips set against a square jaw.

Professor Miller asked us to write an essay summarizing our goals for the class, due in his department mailbox by six, so he could decide who to let in. I figured I might as well try.

I didn't own a computer, so I walked to the lab in the basement of the Science Center to work on my essay the rest of the afternoon. I wrote that I was a freshman who had just come out, that I grew up in a Catholic household in the Philippines, then moved to California at fifteen. I wanted to take the course because I'd never been exposed to gay culture before, and the class felt important for my intellectual growth. I learned "intellectual growth" from a teacher who helped me write my college essays and used it because it sounded impressive. I wanted to leave out the part about the Philippines but wasn't confident enough to pretend like I was native-born. After I turned in my essay that afternoon, I came back the next morning to find my name on the class list taped to Professor Miller's office door.

I was studying in my common room that night when the phone rang. It was Mama.

"Kumusta na, anak?"

"I'm fine," I replied in English.

"How is your classes?"

I was tempted to tell her how her bowling lessons helped me figure out my life. Maybe we could be like other families, where parents supported children and took simple pleasure in their accomplishments. After a childhood full of resentment against her, I had come to understand more of why Mama was the way she was. I had known as a child that she got left behind when her parents and three brothers moved to the U.S., because she was married, and the waiting period for married people was a decade longer than for single people who didn't have families of their own. What I didn't piece together until I got to America was that Mama was forced to marry Papa because she got pregnant with me, in a culture where unmarried mothers were the very symbol of moral failure. So my existence was the source of Mama's ruined life, and this insight allowed me to better understand why she found it so hard to raise me.

Yet that conscious knowledge couldn't undo the way Mama

ignored me all of high school and was staunchly against me leaving home, because she wanted me to make money and take care of my siblings while she gambled. Yet she also had no compunctions about taking as much credit as possible as soon as I got into Harvard, finding ways to bring up my college acceptance to strangers at the supermarket or our apartment complex.

"I learned about deconstruction," I replied. "It's a method of analyzing texts that a French theorist named Jacques Derrida proposed, which reveals the underlying signification of meanings." I continued in this vein, regurgitating the most abstruse parts of Professor Miller's lecture.

"I do not understand," she finally said.

"Then stop asking me questions."

I felt a surge of power over her, aware that for the first time, she needed me in her life more than the other way around.

"I am your mother," she said in Tagalog. "I worry about you."

"You need to worry about yourself before you worry about me," I replied in her own language, to make sure she understood. "I'm a student at the best university in the world. You're so addicted to gambling you can't even hold down a job."

"So what? You don't want me to take care of you anymore?"

"You've never taken care of me."

This brought on a litany of complaints, how she took me to tapings while I was acting, how she got me to America. I had easy rejoinders prepared, but I didn't need to argue with her version of the world at all. I could just refuse to be part of it.

"You can send me money if it will make you feel better," I said. "I don't need anything else from you. Goodbye."

I was determined to go to the first queer dance of the year, even though I was scared of many things—being out, being unattractive, being a virgin. But I really didn't have much choice if a gay man was who I planned to be, and besides, it was practically across the street from my freshman dorm, over at Adams House, where I'd gone to the first meeting of the BGLSA—the Bisexual, Gay, and Lesbian Students Association. Having procured a white T-shirt and fitted jeans from the Gap, and thankful it wasn't too cold since I couldn't afford a nice jacket yet, I left my freshman dorm and eventually found myself in the Adams House dining hall, where I encountered a hundred kids or so dancing while portraits of dead white men surrounded them.

As for the alive white men, they dominated the floor like they did at the BGLSA meeting, resplendent in their own tight shirts and jeans, dancing in the rotating glow of disco lights set up on a black metal frame around the DJ booth, incongruous amid the tall windows and dark-paneled walls. They were young men with names like Brian, and John, and Greg. I appreciated that my parents named me Marc instead of Ramon Jr. after my father, but I already knew I would never be one of those chosen ones, because even though I passed as white, I could never be the kind of white who was firm-jawed, tall, and muscular.

At least I'm not Asian. The unconscious thought became words inside my brain before I had the chance to replace "I'm not" with "I don't look," as I watched the Asian men in that room hover at the periphery of desire, those planets revolving around their white suns. We'd read an essay in Professor Miller's class called "Looking for My Penis" the week before, which talked about how Asian gay men were automatically seen as subservient and emasculated, so they metaphorically did not have penises. Gavin intoned in class that it was important to let go of these ingrained stereotypes and for Asian gay men to consider themselves powerful and desirable, even as he seemed oblivious to the way his white good looks made him the star of the class, the room's attention constantly pulled toward him. That essay was meant to unpack stereotypes about Asian gay men, to allow us to come to our desirability on our own terms, but the lesson I got was that it was a lot easier for white men to get laid, and in matters of sex, there was no real difference between looking and being white, since that was the only criterion gay men used to judge you anyway.

I spied Gavin himself on the dance floor and watched his perfect face flashing different colors with the light. He swayed from side to side with the smallest of effort, and it didn't even matter if he barely danced because he was so attractive. I'd long given up on the idea of being with him and instead settled on thinking about what it was like to have his life, to be able to attract practically whoever I wanted. Comparing myself to Gavin left me anguished, so I walked away from the dance floor and sat on a chair at the far end of the cavernous dining hall, where the happy music wasn't so loud. A tall figure emerged from the shadows toward me, and I recognized him from his long curly hair as Kit Clark, a black alum who was now working at Harvard and had introduced himself to me at the BGLSA meeting.

"Wanna be my granddaughter?" he asked as he sat down, and when I stared at him blankly: "You know, in the House of Ho."

He explained that a queen who graduated years ago started the

House of Ho, the Harvard version of the fabulous houses for black and brown gay men in the New York ball scene. I was only aware of it because Professor Miller had described the movie *Paris Is Burning* to our class, though we hadn't watched it yet.

"But I'm not—"

"What? Femme? Brown? You think I can't tell you're not a white boy? I'm very aware you're albino. Mulattos like me know these things. And girl, you gotta flaunt your femme because it's seeping out of you."

It was strange to be thought of as feminine, when I grew up around flamboyant bakla and told myself I wasn't like them. But in America, the fact that I didn't puff up my chest or speak in the lowest voice possible, that my gait wasn't halting and my hips swayed a little when I walked, this all meant I was femme, or a femmy twink, as one of the students in Professor Miller's class called me when we were discussing different labels for queer people.

I learned that a twink was a slim young man, typically hairless and blond, who attracted older men and were usually bottoms, men who preferred to be penetrated, which I figured I was too. There were also gay men who liked Asian guys, called rice queens, though many more men were into twinks, as long as they—we—were masculine enough.

Even though I'd been happy to learn an American accent from TV, I somehow couldn't bring myself to speak with my low register or make myself as broad as possible when I walked, though I did try to check the expressiveness of my hands and the sway of my hips, like Tom Lee from *Tea and Sympathy*, a play we read in class where a guy suspected of being queer had to be taught to walk like a man. I also started going to the gym several times a week, hoping that with the combination of a good body and a Harvard education, somebody nice would want me someday, and I wouldn't have to feel so alone.

"Ready to dance?" Kit asked, when "Express Yourself" came on.

I followed him to the dance floor, where a dormant part of my brain activated and I began to just move, momentarily forgetting the people around me, purely focused on the music and the beat. I started taking dance lessons while I was a child star in the Philippines so I could perform in variety shows, a hobby I kept up over the years, even though I wasn't used to dancing outside of class.

"If people still think you're white after they've seen you dance then they're just dumb," Kit shouted in my ear.

In that moment, I didn't care if my moves exposed me as a minority. I danced through a couple more songs, focused only on the music and the lights, while people poured in and the floor got crowded. I was aware that men were bumping into my body, but it took me a while to register that someone was intentionally sliding his back up and down against mine.

I turned to see the broad face of another guy from the queer student meeting named Matt. I tried to relax and pretend I was just with a friend, instead of a man who seemed to like me, even if he wasn't exactly my type, stout and barrel-chested rather than the tall, slim, but toned men I was becoming aware I preferred.

"You know this song is about blow jobs, right?" he shouted in my ear when "Like a Prayer" came on, lyrics about going down on knees and feeling a man's power in the midnight hour. The religious images I grew up with, the God I was told to hold sacred, were being replaced with this new world where it was fabulous divas who were the icons, and sex itself was a form of worship.

An hour and a few more dances later, Matt complained that it was getting too hot and asked if I wanted to go outside. I looked around for Kit but couldn't find him in the dark, so I followed Matt toward the back of the dining hall, to a door I didn't even know was there, which opened out to the street. He asked me if I wanted any food, and when I shook my head no, he wondered if I'd been to Dunster House, where he lived.

"I can give you a tour," he said when I shook my head again.

"Sure," I replied, though I wasn't sure at all.

There was a quiet that followed as we walked down brick side-walks in that early autumn night, and I didn't know whether the goosebumps I felt as I crossed my arms were because of the cold or something else. We reached that set of buildings that bordered the river, and Matt led me through a dining hall that looked eerily like the one at Adams House.

"We're sister houses," Matt explained. As if he forgot he was supposed to show me around, we walked up a flight of stairs directly to his suite and sat alone in the common room because his roommates were out.

"Do you want a beer?" he asked.

"No thanks."

I wanted to say yes because I knew that was what he wanted, but my distaste for alcohol trumped my desire to please him, because men in the Philippines like my father sat around getting drunk all the time and I refused to be like them. I wanted to explain why I didn't like beer, but this would have meant telling him

I wasn't white, so I didn't. Instead I settled into a cobalt blue bean-bag chair as he opened his mini-fridge and took out a Budweiser. When I heard him pop the can open, my senses felt suddenly alert, as I noticed the swishing sounds his jeans made while he walked back and sat on a chair. We talked about mundane things like the political philosophy class I was taking, how he was a senior government major but planned to go to med school. I decided I would sleep with him if he asked me to, that I didn't really have enough experience to know what my type was. Maybe I would actually enjoy being with a large hairy guy, and D. A. Miller kept telling us we needed to figure out how to dissociate romance from sex, to fuck and have fun, rebel against prudes and people who wanted to make villains out of promiscuous men because of AIDS.

"Do you wanna see my room?" he asked. After I walked through the door and saw the part of his single bed that the light from the common room could catch, I wasn't prepared for the moment when his hand reached from behind to touch me on the opposite shoulder, then turned me around to kiss me. Or maybe there would never be a moment when I would be adequately prepared to kiss a man for the first time. Or for him to push me just enough that it was easier for me to lie in his bed than to stand up. Or for him to follow and lie on top of me, our lips still fastened together.

My eyes adjusted to the new darkness as he stood up to wiggle out of his sneakers, then take off his clothes. He pulled my legs so they dangled down the side of the bed, then undid my jeans and pulled them down along with my underwear. I heard two soft thuds, the sound of my sneakers falling to the floor.

I let him take off my shirt, and he lay his weight against me again, as the hair all over his body pierced my skin when we kissed. I felt that strum of desire like my desire for all men, but not the desire for only him, and I thought maybe we should stop, but I didn't know how to say that, didn't want him to be disappointed in me so I focused on that desire, the desire I felt for all men. I thought he would like it if I touched his penis, so I did, and he moaned. I felt both desire and nothing when he touched mine. I knew enough to know that he wanted me to do more, so I slid down the bed and took him inside my mouth, but I didn't know I would smell his sweat, didn't know his hair would tickle my nose while I tried to hold on and he told me it felt so good as I bobbed faster up and down.

"Don't go too fast," he said. "I don't wanna come."

That was when he slid me back up the bed and lay on top of me again, rubbing up and down against me, and I thought maybe this wasn't too bad.

"I wanna fuck you."

Matt tried to flip me over with one hand, but my body wouldn't let him.

"I don't think I'm ready," I said.

So he let me suck on him until he came, and when he asked me how I wanted to come, I told him to lie on top while I jerked myself off, as I closed my eyes and dreamed of Gavin's body when I expelled the desire inside me.

"Do you want me to walk back with you?" he asked when we were done.

"I'll be fine," I replied, though I wished he invited me to stay, wished I would have wanted to say yes. On the walk back in the even cooler air, I wondered if I would ever be ready, before I entered the Yard and spent a sleepless night thinking not just about what I had done but what my body didn't want to do.

Matt and I slept together two more times, once after a BGLSA meeting and another time late at night when he knocked on my ground-floor window. Each time he wanted to fuck me, and each time I wasn't ready. Each time I asked if we could hang out, and each time he said yes but didn't call. So the fourth time, after he knocked on my door again late at night, once again tried to guide the back of me against him then reached for my head when I resisted, I realized I would never let him fuck me and turned on the halogen lamp beside my bed.

"What are we doing, exactly?" I asked, his nudity suddenly absurd to me, his large hairy body and his erection. He put on his white briefs, but this didn't lessen the absurdity of him, his penis still erect, the briefs too tight so his hairy belly flowed over them as he leaned on my dresser.

"Well this is over," he said, then began to put on his shirt and jeans. "You know what we call you? Fresh meat." He told me he only came to the first couple of BGLSA meetings every year to check out the new boys, and how much of a waste of time I turned out to be, as the cruelty I realized I'd always known he was capable of oozed out of him. He didn't come back for another meeting, nor did I encounter him again.

Matt was the first of several men I slept with my first year at Harvard, none of whom wanted to stick around for long. At first I expected to go out on dates with those men, who I met at queer events around town or in chat rooms on the internet, and followed up our trysts with enthusiastic invitations to hang out. But over time, I learned that this wasn't what those men were looking for, at least not from me, and I thought to myself that a guy like Gavin probably didn't have this problem, that there was a line of men who wanted to be his boyfriend all the time while he remained aloof and unattainable. But because I was new to America, new to Harvard and this sophisticated world, no one wanted me to stay with them beyond one or a few lays, because I was a novelty and not much else.

8.

Amid my sexual turmoil and failed attempts at social adjustment were my classes, which I tackled with the same gusto I'd always had, though my efforts didn't yield the same positive results. The administration liked to promote the idea that each of its students was more or less equally capable, so the college didn't acknowledge the gap between those who'd gone to private schools versus someone like me, who was the first kid from my working-class public school to go to Harvard, and was one of the least-prepared students there. Most of my peers also had people around who'd finished college to advise them that it probably wasn't a good idea to take an upper-level English seminar my first semester, one that assigned hundreds of pages of reading every week, many of which were abstract theoretical texts that other students in the class had already been exposed to. When I got my first paper back, on a Roland Barthes theory of photography book called *Camera Lucida*, I was horrified to discover that my last-minute spellcheck had replaced "Lucida" with "Lucinda" throughout the whole paper.

"We were not amused," Professor Miller wrote, and refused to grade the essay until I gave him a copy with the correct title. His pronoun use confused me until someone in class explained that he preferred to give his paper comments in the "royal we" like the Queen of England, an affectation I found delightful as I too tried to develop that ironic air gay men were known for.

It was just as well that I had no family to go to by the time Thanksgiving came along, since I had my final paper for Topics due the following week and looked forward to working on it without any distraction. Though Papa had settled in New York with his new family, and his second wife, Clara, had invited me to Thanksgiving dinner, I chose to avoid my father and recede into my schoolwork, which through the years had been a more reliable companion than he ever was.

Not having any friends in town, or really any friends at all, I decided to splurge on dinner at a Chinese restaurant in Harvard Square, instead of eating alone at the Union with other freshmen who had friends to eat with, or even worse, who might pity-invite me to be part of their group. After my meal, I crossed Mass Ave and entered the Yard, then walked around the back of Widener Library to get to the Science Center, the one facility on campus that never closed. I was determined to at least outline my paper that night on masculinity and femininity in Tony Kushner's *Angels in America*.

I'd first heard about the play while I was a junior in high school, when it ran at the Mark Taper Forum in Los Angeles. I'd taken a beginning composition class at the local community college over the summer to help my English, and the professor recommended me for a job at the tutoring center afterward, because many of the students who asked for help were also recent immigrants, and she thought I'd be a good example for them. One of the supervisors was a stout, bearded guy named Michael, who despite being quiet was always ready to help whenever I didn't understand a pop culture reference, or take over when a student preferred to work with an older tutor.

We occasionally made small talk, and I happened to ask him what he was up to one weekend. He said he was going to see an amazing play called *Angels in America* for the second time.

"It's about gay men in New York coping with AIDS," he said. "It's the best play I've ever seen."

I sensed him gauging my reaction. We lived in a conservative part of California, and it felt like he was coming out to me just by talking about the play. No one had ever come out to me before.

"That sounds interesting," I replied.

"You can come with me if you want."

"Maybe," I said, in a way that meant no, and neither of us brought it up again.

Our relationship was never the same after that, and we lost touch when we didn't work the same shift the following semester. Walking to the Science Center, I realized with a start that Michael might have been hitting on me. I wondered what it would have been like to have sex for the first time with someone thoughtful and kind like Michael, instead of a person who merely thought of me as a fresh trophy to be won.

I was so lost in thought that it took me too long to register the particles floating under one of the Yard's tungsten lamps. I looked up to find what must have been hundreds of solid droplets that formed soft shadows against the light—so this was snow. I put out my hand and allowed a solid droplet to land on my palm. I'd read that each snowflake had a crystalline pattern all its own, but to me it just looked like a delicate white circle tinted blue, in contrast to the pinkish hue of my skin. I allowed another flake to fall against the sleeve of my dark jacket to see if I could pick out more detail, but I couldn't. I felt a tinge of self-pity for being blind to the uniqueness of snowflakes but consoled myself with my singular perspective, how snow to me could only mean a gathering of entities that were all alike, a comforting thought on Thanksgiving night.

I went on my way to the fluorescent-lit, unromantic Science Center, a building that looked like blocks stacked together to resemble a Polaroid camera. By then I'd been set up with a computer at the disability lab, which had a giant monitor so I could enlarge my text.

As I began to draft my paper, I found myself focused on *Angels in America*'s two extremes—the hypermasculine closeted lawyer Roy Cohn, who distances himself from his AIDS diagnosis, and the ultrafemme Prior Walter, a nonprofit worker who moonlights as a drag queen and tries to cope with the prospect of his longtime lover leaving him when he finds out Prior has the virus. Over a couple of hours as I refined my argument, I reread my favorite scene in the play, which starts with Prior looking in the mirror as he tries to make himself feel better by putting on makeup. A woman named Harper appears out of his reflection, a Valium-addicted Mormon whose husband works for Roy Cohn and is secretly gay. She tells Prior that she's aware of his illness but that the deepest part of him is free of disease. When Prior asks her how she knows this, she says, "This is the very threshold of revelation sometimes," and that phrase, "threshold of revelation," became an immediate part of my internal lexicon, because it felt so inventive yet utterly familiar.

I ended up making the argument that the mirror, a site of feminine vanity, becomes the font of Prior's self-awareness, the bridge through which he is able to access his fortitude in the face of AIDS. I compared the Angel breaking through his ceiling to a figure from his fantastic reflection breaking through a mirror into reality, to serve as his guide as Prior begins to recognize himself as a visionary, someone who fully accepts himself, including the femininity that Roy Cohn takes such great pains to hide. Roy, in contrast, never looks at himself in the mirror—literally and figuratively— and therefore does not possess the power of self-reflection as he denies his homosexuality throughout the play and eventually dies alone, with neither a chosen family nor a community to comfort him.

I wrote the whole draft in a fugue, and when I finally thought to look at the clock on the wall behind me, it was four in the morning. I read through what I had written and, for the first time, felt worthy of being at Harvard. I wasn't sure whether I would feel this way the next day or even the next hour, but I tried to hold on to that feeling as I put the pages in a folder and left the computer lab to go back to my dorm.

It was eerie to come out of that room and find the facility half-lit with absolutely no one outside, not a single student or even a guard, as if there had been some cataclysmic event while I was working on my paper and I was now the only person in the world. I approached the building exit, a wall of glass with a revolving door in the middle, and sensed even from afar that there was something different about the landscape beyond, brighter, until I remembered as I got closer that the snow must have now settled on the ground.

Though I was unprepared in my fall jacket, it still felt warmer outside than I'd anticipated, maybe because of the excitement of seeing snow for the first time, which was still falling at a languid pace. I walked through the giant arched gate into the Yard and traversed the long diagonal from one side of that field to the other, Widener Library in front of me, Emerson Hall to my left, on my way to Wigglesworth, my dorm at the southeast corner. I got to the end of the path but didn't feel like going inside, so I turned around.

There was only a single set of tracks in the snow, and those tracks were mine.

That image from *Dead Poets Society* flashed through my head, when Neil looks out his bedroom window in the middle of a snowstorm and sees only white, but could not see himself in that world because his father was forcing him to study medicine instead of following his own dreams. But here I was, alone at the center of the most famous school in the world, and I was only responsible for myself, free to find my own way. I was poor but independent, with no obligation to my parents or even to my grandmother, the person I loved most in the world, because I already far exceeded her expectations. In that white, unpeopled landscape, I felt the overwhelming freedom of being able to study whatever I chose, become whoever I wanted.

I experienced that sense of freedom again, on New Year's Eve a month later, when I finally watched *Angels in America* on Broadway. It didn't matter how conflicted I was about accepting Papa's invitation to come to New York for winter break; I had little choice since the idea of going back to Mama was even less appealing, and Harvard shut down the dorms. But going to New York at least allowed me to finally see that play, which I loved so much that I decided to explore theatre as a career. The production started at eight and went for three and a half hours, so when I got out of the show, I discovered that the street had been blocked off in preparation for the ball drop, and I decided to stay while the rest of the audience rushed to their New Year's plans. I leaned against a wall next to a giant picture of Prior as he watches the Angel descend over his bed. I could see the bright, pink-hued sky from the part of Times Square where many thousands of people were and heard the unearthly roar of that crowd counting down to midnight, their even louder cheers once the new year, 1994, began. Somehow, it didn't matter that I was alone in the world, not just because I had no real friends or family but because I'd never met anyone who came even close to sharing the collision of circumstances that formed my very being. I was an outcast among outcasts, but I didn't feel despair because I'd come to accept the blessing of my unique experience.

I knew you were albino, but I didn't know you were from the Philippines," a woman named Camilla told me as we waited in the buffet line at reunion dinner, May 2017. She still had traces of her girlishness from twenty years earlier, though the lines around her eyes had also given her the appearance of a benevolent mother.

"I didn't come to the States until I was fifteen."

"That's incredible," she said, and I wondered how her image of me had changed because of this new information. I didn't witness the moment when Camilla found out I was Filipino, at a career panel earlier that day where I talked about how the expectation of a linear job progression was not part of my upbringing in the Philippines. I wondered how many other people in that room revised their image of me when they realized I was a different race than they imagined. Over the years, I'd witnessed many averted glances, abrupt halts, mumbled excuses, when I revealed information about me that contradicted people's assumptions. But unlike in college, I'd learned not to care nearly as much.

"What have you been up to?" I asked her.

"Well, I left the church for one thing," she said. "My husband and I were both members."

I wondered if Camilla sensed my own view of her shift then, from reserved politeness to empathy. I remembered her going from table to table at the Freshman Union, introducing herself the first week of school. But unlike so many people I met that year, who felt as though they were nice to me as a form of charity, Camilla really did seem interested in my life, my intention to major in English, my interest in theatre, the parts of me I was willing to disclose. Though that changed after our first few encounters, when she kept asking me if I wanted to come to Bible study because she had become a member of Boston Church of Christ, a controversial group that targeted college students, who in turn tried to convert other students with single-minded focus. I noticed other people avoid Camilla, so I did too, though it felt like such a shame because it seemed as though it was the company of others she most reveled in, which was maybe part of why she became so attracted to that church, not knowing she would end up more isolated.

"It was very difficult to leave, but the church tried to control too much of our lives," Camilla continued. We went on to sit at different tables for dinner, but we found each other several times over the next three hours, drawn together by what I came to recognize as the incongruous, shared experience of having to clarify who we were now to people we knew but hadn't seen in a long time. My equivalent of her "I'm not with the church anymore" was "I'm a woman now," a request to interact with us on different terms than our past selves. I also wondered how much she regretted her college life, how she had been so drawn to that church that she wasn't able to focus on much else. Thinking of her made me think about what it would have been like if I had been a woman in college, to have skipped my days as a gay man. But while I wished I'd been more open about being Filipino at Harvard, that I'd had the self-assurance then to tell anyone who judged me to go fuck themselves, I couldn't bring myself to wish I had never been a man, because my life as a man was part of the complexity of my being, this unusual person I had become, someone whose insights I cherished. In the superficial climate of a reunion reception, where we mainly talked about facts and only grazed over feelings, I wished the same for Camilla, an acknowledgment of what her past provided her, even when she found herself turning away from it.

I also couldn't help but feel that Camilla and I were alike in another way, because the experience of being gay felt in some ways like belonging to a strict church. Feminine men in the gay community were relegated to such inferiority that I eventually couldn't stay, even though I belonged there in principle. It wasn't that I didn't resonate with being a gay man—in similar ways to Camilla joining BCC because she was a Christian—but it was the specific, masculinity-obsessed form gay male culture took in America that I eventually couldn't tolerate. Gender transition provided me with much greater freedom of expression, the ability to determine the forms of femininity I wanted to embody, instead of feeling like I had to negotiate every feminine accessory or mannerism with a strict gay church that constantly threatened to reject me. I would have probably been bakla had I stayed in the Philippines, remained in that more indeterminate space in a culture where that was possible.

Though I knew how easy it was to imagine a different future because you're unaware of the challenges that came with it. I had to remind myself of my aversion to feeling inferior and how bakla, while tolerated, were still seen as second class. I'd learned over time that the imagination simplifies the complexities of real life, so that the life other than the one you're living tends to seem better no matter what. Chances were that there would also be unforeseen obstacles in my other imagined future.

"I hope we keep in touch," I told Camilla as our evening wound down, and I meant it, even though our ideological differences felt more stark as I anticipated the outside world, the bridging of our emotional lives so much easier to hold within the confines of a Harvard dining hall, the span of a dinner.

"I hope so too."

I spent the rest of freshman year in that same state of vacillation, between long spaces of loneliness and slivers of belonging. The adjustment from my life in Chino, California, to Harvard often felt like a bigger transition than the move from the Philippines to the U.S., especially when I was doing it alone, without family to guide me, without friends who in some way approximated my experience, not just of being poor or new to America, but of being gay and looking white even though I wasn't. I submitted myself so completely to Harvard's norms, ones that were defined by centuries of white elitism, that over time, the distinction between who I was—a Filipino person who looked, sounded, and acted white— and a person who was actually white became more and more uncertain, even to myself. Yet my difference continued to burn inside me, as I wondered constantly whether people could tell I wasn't white and whether they'd judge me inferior if they found out I was Filipino.

Theatre ended up becoming my refuge, my tool, and my distraction, a space of make-believe where I didn't have to confront my life's paradoxes so directly. I auditioned for a dozen shows but didn't get cast, so I ended up doing backstage work, helping out with lights and stage management. In the spring of freshman year, I got a grant to direct Martin Sherman's *Bent*, a drama about gay men in the Holocaust, because the head of the selection committee was queer himself and loved the play. The climactic scene featured two men making love with words as they stood at attention and apart, under the watchful eye of SS guards. The production got good reviews from the *Crimson* and a local gay paper, which led to a summer internship at the Nora Theatre Company, a troupe that was affiliated with Harvard. Maybe I directed that particular scene well because its yearning for connection in a seemingly impossible situation was something I felt, hooking up with plenty of men but unable to find someone who wanted to spend the night.

The internship thankfully meant that I didn't need to leave Cambridge that summer, so I didn't return to either California or New York, determined to see my family as little as possible. I moved from one Harvard dorm to another, then to Adams House the fall of my sophomore year, the queerest of the dorms that also happened to be closest to Harvard Yard and the rest of campus.

The day I moved into Adams, I called Papa's house to give him my new number. Clara picked up the phone and told me that Tatay Gaudencio, my grandfather in the Philippines, had died in early July, but no one knew how to reach me.

"Didn't you feel a sign the day he died?" my stepmother asked. "It was July 2."

I stayed quiet rather than admit that no, I had felt no such sign, nor did I believe that I could have. I ran far away from religion when I came out, especially the Catholic Church, which still deemed homosexuality a grave sin. But I did feel a moment of sorrow over the person I was, someone who had a stable set of values, who would have gone to my grandfather's funeral and comforted Nanay Coro in her time of grief. But there were no phones in Talacsan, so it was a challenge to console my grandmother from America. I had to call an aunt in Manila, who would pass the message along to her, and hope my grandmother would be there when I called again. I had intended to do this as soon as I settled in but ended up not getting to it in the rush of starting classes and meeting people at my new house. Nanay Coro traveled for hours every week to see me when I was young, but she was so focused on turning me into someone who would succeed beyond expectation that I never fully learned how to put the needs of others before my own. A suspicion grew in me that I was more like my father than I was willing to admit, but I escaped into work instead of confronting my deepest faults, which led me to abandon my beloved grandmother at the hardest point in her life, a failure so complete that I didn't even recognize it as failure at the time.

Instead, I focused on moving into Adams and the second chance it gave me, to be around a new set of people and present a better version of myself than the one who first came to school. I had in my first year dutifully gone to the gym multiple times a week and had grown to adopt that knowing, ironic manner cool gay men were known for. I also saved my work-study money to get my hair cut at a proper salon and found more colorful, stylish clothes.

So maybe that was why, after a year of stilted adjustment, I found an auburn-haired girl walking toward me while I was having breakfast alone in the dining hall before the semester started.

"What are you doing up so early? Classes haven't even started yet."

"I grew up on a farm, so I wake up with the sun," I replied, not quite awake enough to remember my story, that I'd lived in California all my life.

"Lucky," she said. "I have to go to work."

She asked if she could join me at the square table and left her tan leather backpack on a chair when I nodded. This gave me time to ponder how pleasant and beautiful she was, in a flower-print dress cinched at the waist, then billowing out and down to her shin. Her attention puzzled me, but I figured she preferred to have company, any company, rather than sit and eat alone in a dining hall that was practically deserted. She introduced herself as Lucy when she came back.

"Do you know what your schedule is at the museum yet?" she asked. "You're in the Development Office, right?"

It turned out that Lucy was an art history major who worked at the Conservation department and had seen me at my work-study job.

I apologized for not recognizing her, made an excuse about being too absorbed in my thoughts when I was walking around. We started discussing our favorite pieces at the museum, and I told her about encountering a map of the London Tube as part of a show called "What, If Anything, Is an Object?" and how it shifted my perspective on art's function, how works that we officially designate as art are more like models for a larger world that was full of art, rather than rarefied and separate from that world. I noticed how I sounded like I knew what I was talking about, how I'd absorbed lessons from my classes and my museum job, ideas I would not have been exposed to back home, as I spoke in a borrowed language that once again felt incongruous and new. Lucy's attentiveness confirmed my inkling that I, offhand, had said something smart and that she looked forward to more conversations with me.

After a few minutes, an ebullient friend of Lucy's named Omiyinka came by, standing next to our table while she sipped a mug of coffee. She seemed so relaxed in our world even though she was black, and I wondered whether she hid her alienation like me. But unlike me, Omiyinka was beautiful, waifish with a long neck and delicate features that pleasantly contrasted with her boisterous personality, her voice echoing against the walls in that cavernous space. Lucy and Omiyinka left together to go about their day, but over time, they became regular meal companions, along with other beautiful women like Dana Gotlieb, Asia Goodwyn, Danielle Sherrod, as if a single year of college made me eligible enough as a fabulous gay man to have them as friends.

It was fitting that the year I figured out how to be friends with women at Harvard was also the year when I first dressed up as one for Drag Night, an experience that left me intrigued despite its scary conclusion, those men trying to get me in their car and my fear of getting beaten up. Still, I found myself tantalized by the pleasant surprise that I looked better as a woman than I expected. Between study sessions at cafés or on my way to rehearsal, I browsed through the goth nail polish colors at Newbury Comics and came out with a shade called Gangrene, which I wore clubbing at Liquid on weekends and took off when I got home. I also discovered the basement at Urban Outfitters, where I obtained cheap women's clothes that I was thankfully small enough to fit in.

But even through these mild gender experiments, I continued to maintain as masculine an image as I could muster, aware that my attractiveness depended on it. I was happy to decry the gay community's overemphasis on desirability in discussions with other queer people, the problem with personal ads where men used "straight-acting" as a point of attractiveness, how terrible it was that "No fats, no femmes, no Asians" often appeared in those ads. But I also made the utmost effort to be as un-fat, un-femme, and un-Asian as possible. Un-fat was easy enough, and over time, un-Asian became habitual too. Un-femme was harder, but I found that my weekly outings at Liquid released my feminine energy and allowed me to be masculine enough the rest of the week without feeling unduly burdened.

These patterns exerted themselves during those weeks after Halloween, in that year when my relationship with Papa continued to mend, maybe out of necessity for both of us since he loved bragging about his son who was at Harvard, and I needed somewhere to go for winter break. Still, I tried to see my family as little as possible while I stayed in Queens, either holed up in the room one of my sisters gave up when I visited or out into the city for as long as possible. I would have skipped the traditional holiday dinner, where Filipinos feasted on Christmas Eve and stayed up until midnight, if I had friends in the city to go out with. Instead, I accepted my presents without much enthusiasm, reminding myself whenever I felt guilty that this was what Papa had been like my entire childhood, barely there even on those rare occasions when he was physically in the house. It felt good to implicitly deny his existence at school, to allow people to think that my father was white, allow them to imagine him as a supportive part of my childhood.

"You still have work? What are you writing?" Papa asked when I came downstairs to get a snack one night. I explained to him that at Harvard, final papers and exams were due after the holidays.

"I'm doing this paper that applies social contract theory to the status of women in Shakespeare's tragedies."

"I read many Shakespeare plays so I can help you."

"I don't need your help. I've read everything Shakespeare has written." This was not an exaggeration—I spent a good part of the previous summer going through my giant edition of *Riverside Shakespeare* from cover to cover.

"You think you're better than me? If I was white like you I could also go to Harvard."

"Lazy people don't get into Harvard."

It hurt that he wielded my whiteness, as though I didn't have the ability to get to where I was without it. It hurt even more that he wasn't entirely wrong, even though I would never admit this to him. In Filipino families, confronting fathers like this often led to children getting kicked out of the house, but I was fully aware that Papa, for the sake of his pride, needed a son who went to Harvard more than a son who obeyed him without question.

Papa and I avoided each other after that encounter. It was convenient that he and Clara worked long hours, him as a limo driver and her as a home-care worker, so I didn't have to see them much anyway. That immigrant house became a mere way station between my trips into Manhattan by subway, as I breathed in the culture that cosmopolitan city had to offer—the MoMA, Central Park, the Rose Reading Room at the New York Public Library—and in the process shifted further and further away from the values and priorities of my own family. Poor Asian immigrants didn't normally go to Harvard, and even when they did, they were often in premed or engineering, fields that came with some guarantee of financial stability, so their diligence could help lead their families out of poverty. But not me. I preferred to behave like the white kids at school who were too rich to care about money and had the freedom to major in the humanities, expend their energy on activities like theatre and dance, which had no tangible practical value.

In that week between Christmas and New Year's, I spent nearly every morning taking the E train to Times Square to go to the TKTS booth for discounted Broadway tickets, then proceeded to whatever other excursion I'd planned, passing a stretch of porn theaters on Eighth Avenue. I didn't have the gumption to enter, even though I'd hooked up with a number of men from online. My devout Catholic upbringing still made it hard for me to accept that I could be the "type" of person who would frequent a porn establishment. It had also become ingrained in me to avoid any risk of doing something illegal, because I only had a green card and could feasibly be deported if I committed a crime. On top of that, seedy cruising spots reminded me of AIDS, which in 1995 still felt like an automatic death sentence, even when there were significant advances in controlling the disease.

Yet as winter break drew to a close, I found myself determined to get over my fears and be the renegade queer that D. A. Miller presented in class as a figure to idolize, a white gay man who used sex as a form of political rebellion in the time of plague. I probably would not have been able to swallow my shame were it not for this impetus, which reminded me of the People Power Revolution in the Philippines, except the rebellion happened in bed instead of in the streets. This fervor boosted my lust, so I was able to gaze into the eyes of an old man behind a booth painted red, who asked me for ID before selling me a ticket for eight dollars and told me with a smirk that I looked about fifteen. The Latino man sitting on a stool by the door also grinned as he tore my ticket in half, which made me aware that my youth might be a prize. I walked fast through the tiny lobby to find the darkness of the theater, determined not to chicken out, so determined that I found myself disoriented when I got to my seat near the front row, because I had not thought this part of the plan through. In a video playing on the screen, all pink skin and no body hair, I watched two men fucking like automated dolls that a precocious, naughty child had set in motion. It was oddly meditative, watching these men, as my mind filtered out sound and only focused on their bodies, so the movie became just a moving abstract painting of flesh, except I got aroused after a while and came out of my trance.

In the meantime, a number of men had gotten closer to me. They all seemed older, which I didn't mind, some of them fat, which I did. With only the reflections from the screen against their faces, their bodies shrouded in winter clothes, I distinguished race in subtle movements, the slouch and syncopated gestures of Latinos compared to the languid language of white men, their more erect posture, along with a couple of Asian guys, who I dismissed as possible hookups. Even though I told people at school I had no preference when it came to race, I had only slept with white men, because I'd been brainwashed to want them even when I resented their attractiveness. So when I ended up flanked on three sides with implied offers of sex, young Latino men in front of and to my left, a white man to my right, it was the white man whose gaze I met, who sidled from a couple of seats down to move right next to me and feel the erection under my tight black jeans. When I turned to meet his gaze up close, I noticed the gray in his temples, the lines around his eyes, as he blinked in a way I could only interpret as self-conscious.

"Wanna go to my place?" he whispered, and grinned when I nodded. I noticed the rapt eyes around us when we stood up and heard the faint hum of panic between my ears, the feeling of being nothing but meat to devour. But when the man reached the aisle and turned, I caught his face in the dim light of the screen again and saw kindness there, which pulled my feet toward him. We exited the darkness to the dim light of the lobby, then the less dim light of a late winter afternoon. We walked one, several, a dozen blocks uptown, not saying a word to each other, as if locked in a spell that speech could break. He let me inside a narrow apartment building and led me up several flights of stairs, to a door that opened to the sight of a queen bed, faint afternoon light filtering through a single window the same dimness and cool color as the movie screen, except lovelier, as I sat on the bed and he knelt on the floor to unzip my pants. He seemed surprised yet pleased when I took off all my clothes and slid up, then received his own naked body, so that what happened between us was reciprocal and un-rushed, my kisses tender, my mouth hungry.

"You haven't done this before," he said afterward, as he sat up to turn on a lamp beside him, while I lay on a pillow with my arm on his lap, feeling the softness of his flaccid penis and the prickle of his pubic hair.

"Not really," I replied.

He asked me how I got there, and I told him about being from California, being at Harvard, coming to New York for the holidays, but not the rest.

"A Harvard man," he said. "I'm even luckier than I thought. I was sure you wouldn't pick me."

"Who should I have picked?"

"One of the younger guys."

"I like older men," I replied. "We should exchange numbers. We can meet up the next time I'm in town."

"That's sweet, but you're just saying that 'cause you're new. You're hot and blond and you're even smart. There are too many guys for you to sleep with instead of little old me."

He refused to take my number, but I managed to get his and a name, Marvin, on a page in the back of my Filofax, before I put my clothes back on and returned to the street, now dark, wondering if I really could think of myself as hot. Maybe I was becoming more attractive as I acclimated to America and got buffer. But part of assuming the mantle of a smart and hot white man was the confidence that came with it, the feeling that I could conquer the world. My attitude needed to catch up.

9.

Even as the world began to affirm my body as a masculine gay man, this only made my mind flow further into the fantasy of being someone else. I found a partner in these flights of fancy, a boy named Jamie Park who was part of a musical singing group called the Noteables, which I briefly joined before I got too busy to make rehearsals. It turned out he loved *Miss Saigon* too and even owned recordings of the show in several languages, which he offered to let me listen to. He came up to my room with his CDs one Sunday afternoon in March.

Soft-spoken and pensive, Jamie confused me because he didn't strike me as a closeted gay man even with his love of musical theatre, but I felt immediately close to him in a way I couldn't account for. We sat together on my single bed with my boom box and the Laura Ashley floral sheets I'd gotten on a whim, which I deemed too feminine and replaced with a navy blue set whenever I had male company that wasn't Jamie.

"I've been obsessed with how low Lea Salonga's voice gets," he began.

Jamie played me the section of *Miss Saigon* right after Kim and Chris first sleep together, and she tells him she's never been with a man before, which Chris says must be a lie. Kim then tells the story of how everyone in her family died during an American at-tack, which was why she moved to Saigon to become a bar girl, a verse that's rendered in low, determined notes: "I have had my fill of pain / I will not look back again / I would rather die."

"A lot of women can't even sing those notes, but we can," Jamie said when the section finished, and he rewound so we could sing along with Lea Salonga and then shift to our falsettos once her voice got higher. He played me the Korean recording, where the girl who played Kim had to go up an octave because she couldn't hit those low notes. He played me recordings from Germany and Japan, but they only highlighted how rare of a singer Lea Salonga was, the coolness of her timbre and the evenness of her voice qual-ity across the span of her range, as we listened to the whole orig-inal album together.

It was the first time I'd listened to *Miss Saigon* in several years, ever since the disillusion of dreaming an America that did not materialize when I actually got here, which left me feeling de-ceived by that show. But sitting in bed with Jamie, I realized I'd found my own American dream to fulfill, one that depended not on a lover's beneficence but rather on my industry and will.

At the same time, *Miss Saigon* reminded me of a kind of love I would always be drawn to, even if I felt destined never to find it because I was the wrong gender: the ardent, protective love of a man for a woman. I had not been intimate with anyone the last time I listened to that show, and now that I had, I recognized how distant my relationship was from the love I felt vicariously, over the sacri-fices Chris and Kim were willing to make for each other, him to protect her and her to be loyal to him. It wasn't even that I couldn't find that kind of love in another man, but that the man I was couldn't open himself up to the protection of another man the way I imagined I could had I been a woman. I couldn't help but express my masculinity for others like the way I hid my flower-print sheets, the way I could only wear women's clothes when the occasion allowed, at Drag Night or going out to clubs. I'd read Montaigne's famous essay, "Of Friendship," for one of my classes, where he claims that male friendship is superior to marriage because it is a meeting of equal minds, but it seemed to me that the union between a man and a woman could be equal in the same way, while a union between men, at least one where I was involved, couldn't have that dynamic where one person heroically protects the other. So the woman who gets carried into bed or lifted to safety was destined only to exist in "The Movie in My Mind," the title of a song from *Miss Saigon* that expresses a Vietnamese bar girl's impossible fantasy of coming to America, but for me transmuted into the fantasy of being that woman who a man would move heaven and earth to protect.

At least I had tiny outlets for these fantasies, portals that allowed me temporary glimpses into a world I couldn't belong to. Apart from Drag Night, I learned that students at Adams House were welcome to dress in drag for events like dances, readings, and parties. I'd recently read *Emma* in my Major British Writers class, which was my first exposure to Jane Austen, and found the machinations of old English society immensely fascinating. One of the house traditions that seemed to match this elite, aristocratic view of the world was our monthly House Tea at the master's residence, which featured women in their Sunday best picking up round cucumber sandwiches with thumb and forefinger. It was on this occasion that I decided to wear a dress I'd picked up at a thrift store, light yellow with puffy sleeves and a built-in petticoat, as well as a periwinkle pinafore that covered the torso. I walked out in the early spring air, too chilly for my dress, to the master's house on one end of our enclosed courtyard, and I overheard youthful conversation when I got closer to the house's stone steps, animated men in suits, women draped in shawls discussing their latest ideas about art. I only encountered smiles when I went inside and poured some tea into a porcelain cup, then sipped with my pinky finger outstretched, an affectation I learned from I had no idea where. Soon enough, the master himself, Professor Robert Kiely, motioned me to come over to the main living room, ceilings low because people were smaller when the house was first built, where he stood with a distinguished-looking man in a well-worn grayish-brown tweed suit, with small eyes as if in a permanent squint and a puff of wavy hair, nearly white, surrounding his head like a bed skirt.

"I'd like to introduce you to one of our fine students, Marc Talusan," Master Kiely said, entirely unfazed by my clothes even as the other man eyed me in barely hidden confusion. "He just directed an excellent musical that you have to see."

Master Kiely described my production of *Falsettos* as the best show he'd seen at Harvard in years, how it managed to be both funny and deeply moving in its portrayal of the AIDS crisis. I forgot what I was wearing for a moment, as my mind transported itself to that time in high school when I sang a song from the show for a festival, played a gay character when I hadn't even come out of the closet. Then I looked down at my floofy yellow dress and reveled at how far I had come.

"And Marc, this is Seamus Heaney; he's a visiting professor in poetry and is living at the house while he's here."

The master left the two of us to talk, and we realized that we lived in the same entryway, his suite at the bottom and mine on the fourth floor, a cellist named Julia Tom between us who practiced in the early mornings. I admitted to him that I often sat on the stairs beside her door to listen to her play.

"Is there a composer you very much like?" he asked me.

"I don't know a lot about classical music," I replied, "or poetry either, to be honest."

"That's all right. That's what you're in school for."

I was thankful for Professor Heaney's kindness, and as I left him, I promised myself that I would devote more time to poetry, and would take a music class so I could at least learn about the composers whose pieces my cellist neighbor played. I felt inspired to return to my room and find poems to read, so I walked back to the courtyard where there were more people after the sun came out and it got warmer. I decided to trace a meandering path through the gathered guests, waving at friends I recognized, before I headed to my entryway.

"That girl looks like my girlfriend," I heard someone say just as I left the invisible loop that bound the crowd, and I didn't turn around so he would keep thinking I was a girl.

When I got to the end of the winding circular stairway that led to my room, I settled in bed with the party just a set of fuzzy figures outside my window and opened my thick *Norton Anthology* with its onionskin paper to look for the section on Christina Rossetti. I'd been thinking a lot about the last poem she wrote, called "Sleeping at Last," and realized when I opened the page that I already knew it by heart, as my eyes passed over the first stanza:

Sleeping at last the trouble & tumult over,
Sleeping at last the struggle & horror past,
Cold & white, out of sight of friend & of lover,
Sleeping at last.

As I read, I found myself focused on those ampersands as they appeared between and in the midst of the troubles of the poet's life, and somehow imagined them as figurative symbols of a woman unable to escape the expectations of society. Though I'd just started reading her, I was aware that so many of Rossetti's poems dealt with the plight of women, whether succumbing to male temptation in "Goblin Market" or the way women exist only to look beautiful in her sonnet "In an Artist's Studio." Rossetti herself never married despite having a number of suitors, which was also true of Jane Austen and Emily Brontë, whose sister Charlotte, meanwhile, didn't marry until her late thirties, a few months before her death. It was as though these women could not be both devoted to their personal passions and fulfill the expectations of their society; they had to relinquish romantic love to be fully themselves.

I was supposed to have it better because I was a man. I was supposed to make my way in the world unencumbered. Yet reading that poem, I realized how little of myself was really mine, when so much of me had been molded by my desire to be worthy of other people's approval. I keenly felt what it meant to be trapped in between with nowhere to go, to never be truly alone, to never be seen as yourself even by the people you know best. Ironically, it was wearing my dainty little dress that gave me a sense of true rebellion against the expectations of society, yet still, I could only do it on specific occasions, because I was too afraid that doing it in my daily life would lead to rejection.

Instead of dwelling on these thoughts, I turned to the index of that thick volume to look up Heaney and discovered a whole fifteen-page section devoted to his work. The next time I went downstairs and for the rest of that year, I walked gingerly when I passed his door, to make sure I didn't disrupt a bout of inspiration.

On a stone bench that was cold to the touch, a shy man named Thomas told me in a crackling tenor, overtones piercing the low rumble of cars on Memorial Drive, that he was a graduate of MIT, that he specialized in holograms, that he wanted to be with someone nice. His teeth were too big for his mouth, but he had an otherwise presentable face, a nose like half a steep mountain that I liked, since I came from a land of flat noses. It was a brisk April morning in JFK Park, one of those days when the grass glowed nearly yellow in the bright sun.

I had placed an ad in the gay newspaper: "19, blond/blue, 135 lbs, 5'6", Harvard student looking for an intelligent man, 18–35." I didn't have the money for more words. They assigned each ad a voicemail extension, and Thomas's was the first of more than a dozen voices, men in their mid-twenties to over forty. I picked him because he sounded smart if scared, and I decided to go out with the ones I liked in the order they left me messages.

So there he was, voice made flesh. It didn't take us long to kiss on that bench, hungry in public, surprised at our own audacity. As our mouths opened, tongues searching, the kiss became a danger-ous adventure when we started to grope each other. His breath was faintly acrid, his skin papery as though about to tear, but none of that mattered, or maybe it did, because with my newfound confidence, I could tell that he wanted me more than the other way around, that he was immediately sure of me, that I was someone he could love.

Thomas and I started going out every weekend and sometimes during the week, me sleeping over in his apartment across the Mass Ave bridge. When he began to call me his boyfriend, I started keeping a journal because I'd read a diary of gay life at the turn of the century and felt inspired. But almost as soon as I began to write my diary in a Keith Haring notebook, bodies outlined in red on a black background, I found myself expressing hesitation about Thomas. "My heart isn't skipping the way it's supposed to or is that just an annoying romantic notion? This is becoming really confusing," I wrote, and maybe that should have been a cue for me to slow things down. But how could I stop when I had a boyfriend, and a boyfriend had been what I'd been wanting for so long? Having someone who wasn't exactly right seemed better than having no one at all.

During my summer internship between sophomore and junior year, I learned in the mosquito-ridden lawns of the Berkshire Theatre Festival that I had no patience for the petty politics of the stage, as I observed behind-the-scene dramas that negated everything I loved about the shows I saw. The only enjoyable parts were the late-night parties with the crew and supple dances with Allen the prop master, encounters that extended to his bed. I should have called Thomas and told him it was over, but Allen lived in New Jersey during the year, so we made no sense apart from dancing close, a compatibility that reminded me of entangled, wrestling spiders in bed, the joy of one wrapping another in silk, sensual yet suffocating. Maybe this was what sex would be like until I had more experience, my spirit not quite at one with my body, the ending a relief from getting disentangled instead of the transcendent pleasure I'd been promised.

I returned to school determined to tell Thomas about the affair and break up with him, but he was so eager to see me that I couldn't, though maybe that was just cover for the ego boost he provided, the knowledge that I was the center of another person's world. He lived in a high-floor apartment on Beacon Street just after the bridge, with expansive views of the Charles from his living room window, which was probably what I liked most about him. What he liked most about me, it turned out, was that I fit into his fantasies of nabbing a twink despite being a nerd. In his apartment late one night shortly after I got back from the Berkshires, I got out of bed to use the bathroom and found him awake when I returned.

"Just stay there," he said. "I want to look at you."

Thomas turned on his bedside lamp, and I felt the light unclothe me. I stood still for a few seconds before Thomas got up himself and asked me to turn toward the full-length mirror beside his bed, oak-framed and propped up on a stand.

"I like watching myself," he said.

I always thought the mirror felt incongruous in that sparsely furnished room, and it was only then that I understood its function. Thomas stood behind me and massaged my torso, his chin propped against my shoulder; I felt like a lifeless toy. For a moment, I thought he would try to jerk me off and I wondered how far my tolerance went, but thankfully, he instead stepped from behind me to stroke himself.

"It's like we're porn stars," he said, and I reached for my own penis because I knew this was what he wanted. Looking at Thomas's scrawny body in the mirror, I began to understand that we weren't so dissimilar, that we both wanted to be desired. But somehow, being with me fueled his fantasies, and as I observed our bodies, I gained even more evidence of my high place among the rungs of attractiveness. Marvin, that guy I hooked up with from the porn theater in Times Square, told me I needed to enjoy being young and blond, and I responded to that call by getting Thomas, sleeping with Allen. But it was in that mirror, witnessing firsthand how another man projected his fantasies onto my body, that I came to a concrete understanding of my beauty's worth.

Yet I also felt a visceral repugnance, at being merely the surface of Thomas's lurid fantasies, at myself for recognizing his desire to be beautiful as my own, how I too would want to see myself in the mirror with a man who was my better physical ideal if I had the chance. But there was something else. Looking at my image, smooth skin on a naturally slim body, the toned slopes of gym-defined muscles, I realized that the only way for me to go further up those rungs of desire was to fill out my body so I could become broader and more masculine. But even though I wanted to feel my most attractive, to have hordes of men falling at my feet, I realized how the body that could achieve this outcome was not the body I wanted.

"Can we finish in bed?" I asked, and Thomas relented. I turned off the light, and darkness once again wrapped itself around me.

I wondered if Thomas saw my naked body in his mind when he brought me to climax with his mouth, while I only felt sensation.

In the morning, he asked if we could spend the day together, and I should have told him it wouldn't work out, but I'd never broken up with anyone before and didn't know how. So instead I told him I needed to study, which was always true, and I left his apartment to take the number 1 bus back to Harvard.

Because another thing I liked about Thomas was that he kept me focused on school, since having a boyfriend quieted my deep-seated fears of really just being an ugly freak despite my best efforts to cover myself up with my gym-toned body and Harvard education. I took five English seminars that spring semester junior year, which meant at least a thousand pages of reading a week, a schedule that would have been daunting to most anyone else but was one that gave me a lot of satisfaction. I usually ordered a sack lunch from the dining hall and set up by seven in the morning at the newly opened Starbucks on Dunster Street, since none of my queer artsy friends ever set foot there, and would study in the same booth for upwards of twelve hours until it was time for dinner.

My reading covered a variety of topics, from a literary criticism survey that started with Aristotle and ended with Foucault, to a tutorial on AIDS literature where I devoured practically every play, novel, and memoir related to the disease that had been written up to that point, and wrote pages upon pages of response papers every week. But the class I most obsessed over was a nineteenth-century novel course that visiting professor Isobel Armstrong taught, because it introduced me to a whole array of women authors and characters I came to intensely adore.

Though I'd been exposed to Austen, the Brontës, and Eliot in previous classes, I'd only been assigned their well-known books, such as *Emma*, *Jane Eyre*, and *Middlemarch*. Professor Armstrong introduced me to unlikely heroines like the unassuming Fanny Price from *Mansfield Park*, the type of virtuous person I aspired to be but could never manage, or Lucy Snowe from *Villette*, another governess character like Jane Eyre but one who has a much more complex inner life. Though the book I clung to despite its imperfections was George Eliot's *The Mill on the Floss*, for all sorts of reasons like its heroine Maggie Tulliver's precociousness and the variety of her romantic entanglements, how she first falls for a studious hunchback in Philip Wakem but ends up swooning over the handsome rake Stephen Guest, even though he's informally engaged to her cousin. Of all these heroines, Maggie seemed to be the only one who recognized the ardent pull of desire, as she runs off with Stephen during a boat ride on the Floss, the river that the book is named after.

And that river! It was a body of water that had played such an important role in my life, from the Angat, which defined the boundary of my childhood, to the Charles, which symbolized my induction to this new world, and my distance from the one I left behind.

At the end of the book, when Maggie decides to return to her village a dishonored woman instead of marrying Stephen, she ends up drowning in that same river with her brother, Tom, after it floods. I read the book in April, around the time I was making plans for the summer, and that ending threatened the protective fort of learning I had built around myself. On my spring break visit to New York that year, Papa told me that my younger brother Tony had been arrested, because he was driving with a friend and an illegal gun had been found in the car. Tony too was seen as a different race when he got to the States, except Latino and not white, a perception that led to him getting involved in gangs and now facing juvenile detention at thirteen.

"Maybe you can come to California and help him," Papa said.

As the most educated person in my family, I was certainly in the best position to navigate the American legal system with my brother. But going back to California also meant getting sucked into the muck not just of Tony's arrest but of Mama's addiction and the overwhelming expectation that I existed to support my family like a good Filipino child. When I finished *The Mill on the Floss*, I became convinced I couldn't drown with my brother, that I needed to reach the bank of American success before my family dragged me down.

So instead of planning to go back to California, I applied for a summer grant to do research on women's literature at the British Library. When I got my acceptance, it meant that I would once again drift further away from my family and travel to Europe for the first time, alone.

10.

May 2014, a month after I published my first article about being trans, I woke up at dawn between two naked men, on the top floor of a town house in Park Slope. I'd followed the rules of straight womanhood for over a decade, and it hadn't made me happy, so I wanted to test my boundaries, push myself to be with people in ways I hadn't before. That was when Barrett and Jason came along, a bisexual couple I met online who were interested in dating a woman.

I turned on my side to face Barrett, the one with whom I felt a stronger romantic attachment; Jason felt more like a friend I enjoyed having sex with. Bald and a decade older than me, Barrett had left his own rural upbringing in Alabama to become a modern dancer and interactive artist in New York, which led to a career as a digital consultant and allowed him to unexpectedly come into wealth. He and Jason didn't know I was trans when we first met, but I sent them one of my articles and, as I had hoped, they treated my gender as a nonissue.

Barrett opened his eyes and smiled. I could tell they were hazel but not much else, though I'd examined plenty of close-up eye pictures before, and filled in details with my mind—dark rings around his irises, dilated pupils because of the dim dawn light and, maybe a little bit, his attraction to me. He tilted his head to indicate that we should leave the room together, and I followed him down a set of wooden stairs with steel pipes for rails, part of this couple's industrial aesthetic in a house they designed and renovated themselves.

"I'll get us some coffee," he whispered as he proceeded to the kitchen on the ground floor while I stayed on the second, an open area lined with bookshelves, a peacock-green velvet couch on one side and a mid-century dining table on the other. Off that big room was a smaller room they used for guests. I noticed that the door was open, so I went inside.

Barrett and Jason also used the room as a walk-in closet; I noticed a shelf of stylish shoes on one side along with suits on wooden hangers. On another end of the room was a giant mirror, framed in ornate gold leaf, leaning against the wall. I stood in front of it and looked at myself, as morning light illuminated my body, and recalled how comfortable I'd been walking around nude in Barrett's presence. It was a relief to feel safe without clothes in front of someone else, after years of asking men to turn lights off, for fear they would find something overly masculine about my body, my too-slim hips, my muscular shoulders and back from years of lifting weights, a fear that did not go away even when men admired that body for being powerful and athletic.

"Admiring yourself again?" Barrett asked as he poked his head into the room, then went in to stand behind me. "I'm sure it feels great to be almost forty and have the breasts of a teenager."

I laughed, not just at the joke but at the openness of our relationship. The past decade when I decided to be private about my transition except to those I was closest to, the men I'd been involved with had accepted my history as fact but had also been all too willing to deny its reality, something never to be discussed again once revealed. Though really, I was more responsible for this than they were, because their reticence was an echo of my own shame, my silence like trying to suffocate my history by refusing to breathe. It was such a relief to exhale.

"It's funny," Barrett continued as he stared at my reflection. "I know you're trans, but I can't really tell. It's a lot harder to see you were an Asian man when I can't see you as Asian to begin with. To me you're just a woman with a dancer's body."

I nodded. I knew by "woman" he meant "white woman." I wanted to be pleased but was surprised at myself that I wasn't. We left the room and had coffee at the dining table, but Barrett's words kept playing in my head, "I don't see you as trans," coupled with "I can't tell you're Asian." The way he looked at me was exactly what I'd honed over many years, this trick of perception, and it puzzled me that I was dissatisfied over having accomplished it, a state of being so many trans women sacrifice so much to achieve. Maybe I didn't feel the satisfaction because I hadn't sacrificed too much, only had reassignment surgery, hadn't gotten implants or done facial feminization.

Though remaining undisclosed for a decade was burden enough, so it wasn't that. It was something about how my gender and race reflected on each other like a dizzying hall of distorted mirrors. When people looked at me and only saw a white person, I understood that being white wasn't actually better, that I only coveted whiteness because of what I associated it with—wealth, education, and beauty. But for someone like me, whose whiteness was literally skin deep, who did not have any actual European ancestry, to be perceived as white could only mean that whiteness is nothing more than illusion. In an ideal world, I wouldn't need to go through so much effort, make so many sacrifices to gain the privileges of whiteness, and other brown people who are not albino would have just as much access to those privileges if they wanted it.

I flinched when Barrett told me he only saw me as a woman, because my experience with race forced me to understand that womanhood wasn't real either. I wanted to be a woman because I wanted other people to perceive my qualities through the lens of that gender, but having molded myself to their expectations, I now understood how much of an illusion gender was too. To become a woman in the world's eyes, I made what felt like a huge sacrifice at the time, reassignment surgery, but in hindsight was really a cosmetic change not unlike a nose job, a shift in a body part's aesthetic appearance while keeping its function intact—the only difference was the meaning our society invested in one body part versus the other. Had I lived in a world where men were allowed to dress and behave like women without being scorned or punished, I wouldn't have needed to be a woman at all.

Over the following months, I grew alienated from Barrett and eventually stopped dating him, not because he did anything terrible but I just didn't want to see myself through his eyes. I came to understand that what I wanted was to be seen as my complete self—my gender, my race, my history—without being judged because of it. I wanted people close to me to see an albino person who had learned how to look and act white so the world would more readily accept her, and understand how that had been a key part of her survival. I wanted people to see how that albino person was also transgender, how she transitioned to be able to express her femininity and had surgery so she would be perceived as being like any other woman, her qualities appreciated on those terms. And if she ever hid who she actually was, it was only so that she could be granted entrance into worlds she couldn't otherwise reach, worlds that should rightfully belong to everyone, not just those who happen to uphold the prevailing standards of whiteness and womanhood.

I waded past pools of London tourists in a vast corridor that summer between junior and senior year, crowded around manuscripts encased in glass. At a reception desk, I pulled out a letter of approval from my black leather satchel, which had been mailed to me after my faculty advisor wrote on my behalf, and presented it to a librarian, who motioned for me to walk through a metal turnstile. At the end of a dim corridor, I found myself in the British Library's main reading room, a vast, circular space reserved only for scholars.

When I got to the central hub, another librarian directed me to the manuscript room, rectangular and wood-paneled, with row upon row of oversize desks to work at. I wanted to call up all my favorite women writers that first day, but I felt self-conscious and only ordered a number of Christina Rossetti's notebooks, including the one that contained "Sleeping at Last." I continued to be obsessed with the way she used ampersands, especially because different editions of her work printed the poem differently.

The librarian delivered the stack of notebooks to my desk, and

I skimmed them to find her last poem, a slim volume bound in brown cloth, which when I opened it revealed another cover in a sanguine red, Rossetti's original notebook. In contrast to some of her early manuscripts, which were carefully copied in a formal hand, "Sleeping at Last" seemed casual and dashed off, the letters less even, as if the poet didn't care as much for appearances when she got older. As I suspected, she used ampersands throughout the poem, which were converted to "and"s when her brother William Michael Rossetti published it after her death. Though when rendered in manuscript, her ampersands veered sideways and weren't those formal, erect &s they became in print. So by the time I got to the last lines, "Singing birds in their leafy cover / Cannot wake her, nor shake her the gusty blast. / Under the purple thyme & the purple clover / Sleeping at last," that last ampersand no longer conveyed the feeling of being trapped like I once argued in a paper. If anything, it just felt like she had done what she needed to do and was ready to rest. I experienced another surge of affinity with her, how tired I was of leading my life to be judged appealing to others. But the thought of letting go felt impossible, when it was that superficial image of myself as a beautiful, sophisticated white man that kept me from sinking into despair.

I ordered many other manuscripts the rest of the week, favorites like George Eliot and Charlotte Brontë, who both had exquisite handwriting, unlike Virginia Woolf, who was almost illegible, and was one of the first authors to switch to a typewriter. It felt so indulgent to have access to every manuscript in the BL's collection, and I spent many hours daydreaming about the lives of those women, their struggles and their brilliance. I'd grown into a hearty feminist by then, fed with French theorists like Cixous and Irigaray, along with Woolf's *A Room of One's Own*, which described the BL's main reading room as resembling the head of a bald British man, its perimeter lined with the names of famous thinkers throughout history, none of them women. Having grown up with no notion that women were in any way inferior—the president who took over from our dictator a woman, my grandmother fully equal to my grandfather in terms of running their business affairs, an indigenous culture that did not promote the idea of male superiority except for the colonial influence of machismo—the idea of women being kept out of intellectual pursuits simply because of their gender was infuriating, and studying their efforts to produce art under these conditions enraptured me.

But once the weekend came around, I left those manuscripts to be a young American gay man in London. I wore cutoffs, a white ribbed tank top, and steel-toe boots to the Tube, got off in Soho and the winding Old Compton Street, the queerest part of that city. I was too self-conscious to try this look back home, but no one knew me in London, so the guys there would have no idea that the blond in the construction worker costume spent his weekdays smelling musty books in the library.

It was too cold to be sleeveless in London, even during the summer, but I was determined to carry off this fantasy version of me. Though as I rounded the corner onto that street, the goosebumps on my arms forced me to ask who in their right mind would wear my shirt when the temperature was in the sixties and falling. Everyone would know how desperate I was for attention and laugh at me. I was about to do an about-face when I spied a smile, and then two, among the passersby, telling me I was all right. I walked into a café to order a cappuccino, and two guys at the next table said hello. The cute one with curly hair and ruddy cheeks asked if I was American, and I said yes, knowing that my looks and accent erased my history for this man, who told me he could tell because I had that American confidence.

After my coffee, I stopped by a pub even though I didn't drink, my surroundings suddenly moody and pinkish-orange from light that reflected onto a tin ceiling. I ordered a club soda and sipped it slowly, pretending it was a gin and tonic, when a stout man with red hair and a nose that reminded me of a tulip bulb came over and got close enough that I could smell stale beer on his breath.

"Excuse me, but are you Oriental?"

The word "Oriental" took me aback. I hadn't realized that was what Asians were still called in England. "Yes, I'm part Asian," I said.

"But you're blond."

I nodded.

"You see, I fancy blonds, and I fancy Orientals, but you're both."

I couldn't detect malice or expectation from him, just a drunken face of desire. I laughed and said thank you, finished my drink, and walked out of the pub, leaving the man with a dazed, open-mouthed expression, as though he might run after me or say something else, but he didn't. I started forming smart comebacks in my head as I ambled down the street, *It's like you won the lottery*, or, *Well isn't this your lucky day*, but these imagined retorts were flimsy covers for my feeling that wherever I was, I was only a shell of myself. I was already a shell when people thought I was white, but even if someone could tell I was Asian, they couldn't see the life I led, the struggle it took to come to America and be the person I became. What they saw was a fetish in the most basic sense—a mere trinket, a form of amusement, pure novelty. I wanted to play this game of desire, to exult in those eyes that covered the surface of my body. But I couldn't get the deeper want out of myself, the one I'd tried to keep hidden all my life, to be seen and loved for who I was.

I rounded the curve at the end of the street and saw one of those red phone booths I'd seen in pictures. I walked inside and I occupied myself with tourist tasks, called the National Theatre to find out what time their box office opened the next day, got information about trains for a day-trip to Brighton Beach. When I finished, it was just about time to grab a quick bite then see a matinee of the London production of Stephen Sondheim's *Passion*. I needed to get lost in the fantasy of someone like me, except not how I looked or seemed but who I was inside. Before I left the booth, I noticed a card for a men's bath taped next to the phone, snatched it impulsively, and put it in my pocket.

The Queen's Theatre was within walking distance of Old Compton Street along the busy, meandering, and narrow roads of Soho. I managed to get seats in the center orchestra, looking up at a raised, open stage from below, not like on Broadway when I first saw the show, where the actors were at eye-level and a gilded proscenium framed the scene. When the curtain opened and the show began with Giorgio and Clara in bed making love, I felt like a clandestine voyeur instead of an invisible observer on the other side of a screen.

I'd written a long paper on *Passion* for my junior project the previous semester, so I'd studied it intensely and knew every word, every entrance and exit. I didn't plan well, had no shirt or jacket to cover my arms in that air-conditioned theater, but the cold was comforting because it dulled the shock of seeing the person who most resembled me onstage.

I wasn't one of the beautiful lovers, not the gallant captain Giorgio or his married beloved, Clara, even though her name meant "light" and her skin was nearly as pale as mine. My twin was Fosca, a shockingly ugly woman who scares the captain when they meet for the first time, but he makes conversation with her because she is his commander's niece. They figure out that they're like-minded readers and sensitive souls in this remote Italian outpost, even though Fosca rebuffs Giorgio when he suggests that learning is the purpose of reading. To Fosca, reading is about dreaming in other people's lives, "I read about the joys the world dispenses to the fortunate, and listen for the echoes," she sings.

It was as if Fosca was singing the person I truly was. Her name means "dark" in Italian, and she is not only a gloomy presence in the play but is also sick with a mysterious illness, and so ugly that other men make fun of her because they consider her a freak. Her only solace is books, where she can project her fantasies onto fictional characters, knowing she can never have what she wants, to love and be loved. No matter how attractive I became, how much I buffed up or got the right haircut, the fact of me always remained, and that was the person who would always be unlovable. So I made sure to hide him under layers of muscle, confidence, and erudition, so that maybe no one would ever find out, so that I could maintain the illusion that I was worthy of love, even if what I ended up being loved for was not who I actually was.

But *Passion* gave me hope, however far-fetched, when Fosca in her ugliness falls in love with Giorgio, becomes obsessed with him, and he wildly rejects her after she follows him to the top of a mountain, as rain like his fury erupts from the sky. But over time and as his married lover comes up with more elaborate excuses not to leave her husband, Giorgio finds himself drawn to the uncompromising clarity of Fosca's love, the purity of her longing. They finally come together near the end of her life as I cried over the miracle of their love, even as I mourned the impossibility of it for myself. My only comfort was that even though Fosca and I were so alike inside, at least I could fake being someone else and live with that compromise.

Outside the Waterloo station that evening, I followed the directions on the card I found at the phone booth earlier that day and took stone steps that led down to a glossy black door, framed by a brick arch underneath the train tracks. There was no obvious place to ring, but I spied a gray button set discreetly on the door-frame and pressed. A buzzer sounded. I opened the door. There was a man collecting money right inside. I paid him, and he motioned me to a curtained area, which I shifted aside with one hand to walk through.

There were rubber mats on the floor and long benches on one side of the room. On the other two sides were lockers. There was a pile of towels on one of the benches. I was the only one there and had not been given instructions, but I figured I should take off my clothes, which I did slowly, then took a towel and wrapped it around my waist. I took my pile of clothes to the lockers, metallic gray with orange nubs sticking out that held keys with elastics attached; I noted that there were at least a dozen nubs that had no keys and wondered if that was crowded or light for a Saturday night.

Even before I opened the metal door to the next room, I could feel vibration emanating from the other side. I turned the knob and found myself in a concrete space lit in stark pools of light, with several shower stalls on one side and the dark orange light of a sauna on the other, several naked figures inside who I only saw in the periphery of my vision. I hung up my towel on a hook and turned on the shower—too cold—yet I stepped under it anyway, eager to dull the pulse of my senses, as I suddenly became aware that the throbbing sounds in my head were not only from my heart but the insistent beat of techno music.

Alone when I entered the room, I realized there were several men who had come in, all of them middle-aged, two paunchy and pale while one was dark and hairy. I imagined instant lives for these men, how maybe one of the pale ones was a postman and the dark one, handsome in his solidity even though the hair cover on his chest did not immediately pull me, was a married businessman from India who dallied on work trips. Then I realized they must have come to see the new meat up for offer, and from their languorous movements, their bodies like gentle waves, I could tell they liked what they saw, even if I couldn't quite believe it.

I walked past them to an area that seemed purgatorial, toilets on one side and sinks with mirrors on the other, lit in fluorescent. Yet I noticed as I reached the end of that area and nodded at a man with a newsboy cap on, sitting on a stool and monitoring the proceedings, that the room on the other side must be much bigger, because the sound coming from it was reverberant compared to the cramped thuds on my side. I was too far inside my head to notice until I got there that I was actually on a balcony and that a whole other floor lay before me, so the room was double the height of the others, which somehow made it feel airy despite being underground. The monitor instructed me to keep my towel on when walking to and fro, as I looked down to find more men swimming naked in a pool and lounging at a jacuzzi.

I associated locker rooms with being the short, skinny runt in a litter of men, but in that English bath, it became apparent that I, improbably, was one of the prized, as I sucked in my stomach to show off my nearly washboard abs. I quickly scanned the area to see if there was anyone promising and was disappointed to find none, though I was hopeful that they would reveal themselves as I got closer. There was a steam room by the pool, and I opened the door to clouds of smoke that revealed a clutch of men, connected and breathing heavily, which I decided was not my scene, or at least not yet.

So I, a bit theatrically, remembering my childhood status as the only blond kid in a land of dark-haired people, settled my towel on a lounge chair and stretched for a while before diving into the water. As my head bobbed up to the surface, aware that many eyes were trained on me, I realized how much I'd missed being the automatic center of attention. I hadn't felt like that in years, since I got to the States and was one fair-skinned blond boy among many. I swam back and forth and tried to enjoy the feeling of the water, imagined myself as a slippery grouper that none of these men could catch.

I emerged from the pool and stepped into the sunken hot tub, where I sat among pink-skinned men with ordinary faces, aware that mine did stand out among them, as I inwardly admired my sharp cheekbones that made me, in the image of myself I saw in the eyes of those men, seem foreign and exotic.

"Finnish?" one of the men a few feet from me asked. I shook

my head then said American, and the man smiled in relief as he tried to chat me up, what brought me to England and all that. I imagined what Gavin would do, that boy with heavy-lidded eyes who had expounded on glory holes in English seminar long ago.

"I'm a student on holiday," I said.

"Do you like London?"

"It's fine."

As if finished with him, I stretched out my body and leaned back, spread my arms around the lip of that circular hole in the ground, then closed my eyes. Maybe this was all I needed. Maybe this was worth the ten pounds, this feeling of being wanted even if I didn't want back. I smiled at the sudden thought that this was all economic, except the trade was not in money but in desire. Aware of my stock's value, I was unwilling to involve myself with anyone who was not of comparable wealth. This was not the system I grew up with, the one that prized qualities like kindness and loyalty above all else, that didn't think of desire the same as capital. But this was something I didn't need to worry too much about, when I was the one who led the market.

There was a pleasant thrum in the periphery of my vision when I opened my eyes, a slim shape that emerged from the pool and came to join me in the hot tub. There was confidence in his expression from the moment I could fully discern his face, eyes full of mischief and pleasant symmetry. He had clearly seen what was on offer in this place and judged himself a prize, just like I had done. Now that he was here with me, we could come together because we were worthy of each other.

I introduced myself, and he recognized my accent as American. His name was Danny.

"I'm from Liverpool," he said, pronouncing "pool" a millisecond longer than I expected as his intonation rose and his lips pursed. I resisted the urge to copy him.

"So what brings you here?" I asked.

"Same as everyone," he replied. "I'm new to blokes. I've a lass at home." He added that he worked in construction, which explained his tan complexion, his ease of movement with muscles developed doing manual labor, not sculpted at the gym like mine.

Danny's body angled toward me, inviting, but I had no idea how to make a move. I averted my glance, not wanting to seem too eager, and tried to focus on the feeling of the water as it surged around me, the sound of it suffusing my senses so the techno beat and humanity drifted away. But like a taut rubber band, my mind snapped back to Danny when his foot grazed my calf, an accident that wasn't quite. I shifted closer to him, and it wasn't long before his arm clasped my shoulder. I turned to see drops of water like dew on his elfin yet rugged face, like a fool in a Shakespeare play undressed to reveal himself as the hero—Touchstone turned Orlando. It felt silly to think of Shakespeare as his mouth met mine, and his kiss felt so pure in all that water around us, which made it feel easier to engage in unclean acts. I reached down to touch him, and he was already hard beneath the surface of the water. I stared into his light eyes, not the blue of an artificial pool but the aqua of the sea, and watched him exert control over his desire as I stroked, which I couldn't do when he touched me, the shock of my want too unbearable as my back arched and my eyes went blind from the glare of the lights in the ceiling.

He smiled when I opened my eyes again to reveal a gap in his teeth, which only made him more adorable. I was partly draped on top of him then, so he extricated himself and patted me on the head before he got out of the tub. I willed my eyes not to follow him, figuring he wanted the fun of being chased or the feeling that I was still the worthy catch and not the overeager young man who would surrender at his whim. Such excitement, as I turned onto my stomach and set my chin on the lip of the tub, to both pursue and be pursued, never really knowing which was which.

It was only then that I noticed the audience for our act, how the other men had given us room in the tub but had been at the pool, on the lounge chairs, as I got out to look for Danny. I expected to find him in the steam room, where we could continue our encounter, but couldn't make out his figure in the clouds of smoke. So I walked upstairs to see if he was in the sauna.

"Good show," the monitor told me as I passed his post. "Might wanna be more discreet."

I nodded then, embarrassed, remembering his first instruction about keeping my towel around my waist. I wondered whether this was why Danny left abruptly, at the knowledge that I wasn't playing by rules I didn't understand in the first place. As I got to the sauna and didn't find him there, I became convinced that I'd once again managed to fuck things up. I decided to clear my head in the shower, try to get over losing the only man there I wanted. There were going to be other occasions, other times. Yet I was also aware that the experience would have been significant, for reasons I couldn't entirely name.

I got out of the shower and took another towel to dry off, then tried to find a receptacle for my old one. I padded over to the toilet and sink area, put the old towel in a bin, and looked in the mirror to find Danny behind me. I turned around, and he took my hand, pulled me into a bathroom stall, and leaned me against one wall as we kissed and I found myself licking his neck, his chest, his nipples, with a rapaciousness I didn't know was in me, while he put his hand on my flank and firmly guided my body. His cock in my mouth unleashed a desire in me I didn't think existed, a want that rose from his casual, effortless masculinity. I stopped him when he made a move for my cock, asked him to kiss me while I jerked myself off until I came. I didn't know why I didn't want to see his mouth on that body part, but I didn't. There was something about it that would ruin the moment.

"Let's go to your flat?" he asked.

"I'm at a hostel. It's not private."

"My bird's at home. But she's at her job tomorrow."

We agreed to meet in front of the sauna the next day. In the locker area, I asked him if I should get his contact information in case something came up. Danny found a piece of scrap paper in his bag and scrawled a number on it, then pecked me on the lips before he walked out in his rain jacket and jeans.

I took the train to Waterloo station the next morning and walked across the bridge down to the sauna entrance. When Danny was fifteen minutes late, I began to pace back and forth so it didn't seem like I was lurking. I wanted to call him but was afraid we would miss each other, but after forty minutes, I finally decided to look for a pay phone. I asked a passerby for help, and she told me the closest one was next to the Thames near the National Theatre.

I dialed the number Danny gave me once I got to the red phone booth that overlooked the river and watched pedestrians cross the

Waterloo Bridge in the distance while I waited for someone to pick up. After several rings, a woman's voice on an answering machine came on.

"This is London Travel. Please leave a message at the sound of the tone."

I called the number again and got the same response. Then again. And again. It was starting to rain when I got out of the booth and walked back to the Tube.

Though I got other men to sleep with me over the next few weeks, I found myself dreaming of Danny as I lay on the top bunk of my hostel bed, the ceiling so close I could touch it, wishing that the white blankness was Danny's body. Something about him being new to blokes resonated with me, and how he guided my body like he was used to being in charge in a way I wasn't used to when I slept with other men, a way that I liked. I was convinced I wouldn't find that again.

11.

I broke up with Thomas a week after I got back to the States. We saw a movie one night and I refused to give him my hand. He started crying on our walk back to the Kendall T station, through the tall concrete configuration of biotech buildings on the edge of MIT's campus. He accused me of having changed, that it was more important for me to be cool than to have someone in my life who loved me. He wasn't wrong, but I didn't tell him that, and said instead that I didn't think we were right for each other.

A month later, after we'd stopped speaking, I got an envelope in the mail with a photocopy of the back of a postcard I'd sent him from London, the most saccharine one about how much I loved him and how I wished he was there with me, written at the height of my guilt about fucking other men. Thomas had underlined the purplest phrases and scrawled, "Is this what you mean by love???" at the bottom in a childish hand. I was tempted to call him and apologize but didn't want to get caught up in the relationship again, so my newfound nonchalance took hold as I sighed in exasperation at lunch with friends over how childish this display of emotion was.

I didn't have time to dwell on my breakup anyway, as I grew

regretful in my senior year over having wasted so much time on my dating life and how I would graduate without having made the most out of my Harvard experience. In particular, over the years when I'd read so much feminist and queer theory full of activist rebellion, I never did manage to be a political voice on campus, and I promised myself that I would get more involved. I also knew whose orbit I once again needed to cross: Josh Oppenheimer.

I first heard about Josh on my initial Harvard visit, the spring of my senior year in high school after I got accepted. My host started talking about this brilliant queer performance artist who lived in his entryway and was doing a show the following night in a drained swimming pool. When he invited me to come along, I was too intrigued to resist.

But once I found myself crowded around the far end of the pool at Adams House, I couldn't really follow what the piece was about. I only witnessed the teetering danger of Josh potentially falling into the pool as he pontificated at the edge, bald-headed in a white minimalist tube of a gown that made him both androgynous and alien. His pronouncements had an air of importance, the youthful conviction that his words had never been said before. Even the moments when he had to get into the pool using the rungs of a ladder, an awkward maneuver at best, were imbued with a certain delicacy of purpose, lit as he was by those clip lights you get at the hardware store. As he declaimed, and asserted, and pronounced, in ways that resisted my attempts to comprehend, I did understand that if this was something I could do at Harvard—witness and celebrate the illegible yet ardent manifesto of a gowned man in a drained swimming pool—then maybe I could blend right in.

But instead of following Josh's focused example, I'd spent so much of my time at school craving boys, too many hours cruising for them on- and offline. I heard of a kiss-in he and some friends were planning for Ralph Reed, the head of the Christian Coalition, who was coming to Harvard that fall; I decided to join.

Josh explained the details of the action at a meeting, though the logic remained unclear to me. We were to dress conservatively and pretend to be homophobes by holding up signs borrowed from Fred Phelps and the Westboro Baptist Church, like GOD HATES FAGS and NO RIGHTS FOR SODOMITES. The signs were meant to expose Ralph Reed's hypocrisy and Harvard's disingenuousness for inviting him. Though Reed seemed benign and respectable, he still reeked of the same homophobia as Phelps and his cronies. This logic made sense in a somersaulting kind of way, though I still wondered why we couldn't just kiss as we were and send a less confusing message.

Though I got on board in the end and put on the black wool suit I wore to interviews, procured at Filene's Basement with extra money from the Winter Coat Fund, which gave every Harvard freshman from west of the Mississippi three hundred dollars to buy warm clothes. The suit was an armor I didn't want, that cover of respectability and dominance as a man. I couldn't handle the idea of wearing a tie, so I settled for a linen shirt with a mandarin collar, unclassic but respectable.

I got to the auditorium early and made my way to the queer section in the center near the back. The group wasn't big, maybe twenty kids or so. I was chatting with one of them when Josh appeared in the periphery of my vision wearing a white dress, and I hadn't quite absorbed his outfit before he asked, "Would you be my kiss-in partner?"

That was when I noticed he was not only wearing white but that his head was covered in a wimple, and I recognized the familiar crisp fabric of a nun's habit from my dozen years in Catholic school. I had no idea why he asked me, the two of us having never hung out as friends over four years, but I nodded yes. Maybe it was as simple as me having the right look, a studious blond man in conservative clothes. I sat next to him as Ralph Reed's talk began, though there were still murmurs among us about who was ready to take action and who wasn't, who was risking arrest and negative backlash, or some sort of permanent smirch on some record, official or otherwise.

I had my doubts as Reed started his speech. I still wasn't quite getting the point of all the theatricality, as I held a sign that read DYKES WILL BURN IN HELL. Was this all a manifestation of Josh's ego? Judging by the absence of the more mainstream queers among us, the gay guys with their tight shirts and muscles, there didn't seem to be full consensus that this was a good idea.

Yet I also didn't have much to lose. I was already queer, albino, poor. I had no reputation to protect, no parental expectation to live up to. Something told me it was worth the risk, that whatever it was on the other side of Josh's parted lips would have meaning.

We stood up to begin the kiss-in at the start of the Q&A. I felt Josh tug at my jacket, a gesture that betrayed our lack of intimacy even as we were about to perform an intimate act in public. There was something unremittingly attractive in Josh's subversion, something that drew me to his face surrounded by cloth, the memory of my years among the nuns. So that by the time Josh's forehead nearly brushed the rims of my glasses as his lips touched mine, I felt ready.

Am I kissing a man? That was a question I found myself asking in the ensuing confusion like drowning, as my fear merged with the audience's agitation. *Am I even a man?* I had never kissed a girl before, and Josh was the closest by far. But the feeling of plugged ears under the sea prevented me from quite understanding what was happening, punctuated by moments when my consciousness bobbed for air even when my lips didn't catch a breath.

In one of those moments of clarity, Josh's kiss shook me into the awareness that I was not quite a man. I wanted to be in his nun's habit and not my suit, because a dress to me meant a release from the shackles of forced masculinity, a giving up that I felt somewhere between and within my heart, my gut, and my groin. It took Josh's kiss for me to admit to myself that I desired to be taken, not that only men take and women receive but that I could never be just a taker and never be just a taker as a man. I tensed then, gripped his lips with the confident force of learning who I was between tongues.

Even when the guards tried to break us apart, our tensed arms held on to each other. Our legs splayed as those guards pulled our feet from under us, and still we didn't let go. Those guards had to carry us out of the room, entwined and horizontal. Finally, as I lay on top of him on the pavement outside, Josh opened his oracular eyes and we broke apart. By then, I knew that my fascination with women, from their art to their plight, wasn't just a part of me I could parcel off, but that womanhood itself might be the vessel that best contained my being.

———

Since I was newly single, it became habit again to go to Liquid every Saturday night and enjoy the freedom from prescribed norms that space had to offer. Though I was content to wear preppy if muscle-flattering clothes in my daily life, Liquid was the place where I didn't have to worry about looking too garish or feminine, as its name signaled a melting of boundaries that evolved into the event's unique vibe, goths and kinksters cavorting with the Harvard and MIT crowd, where gender and sexuality were indeterminate. But having shed my ill-advised relationship with Thomas, I still dressed myself in a way that was attractive to gay men. So on one particular night in early November, when I paired a white baby-doll tee with lime-green bell-bottoms, procured for cheap in the women's section of Urban Outfitters' basement, it was intentional that the shirt was short enough to reveal a band of my flat stomach, the pants stretchy so they would flatter the butt I'd shaped with thousands of squats.

Both the dance floors—one that played alternative and the other pop—were sparse at ten o'clock, which I enjoyed as much as when it got packed, because I liked dancing where there was space and had come to love getting parties started.

Liquid exposed me to a part of myself I only discovered in college, incongruous even to my own self-understanding, that I was a natural dancer. This certainly wasn't true when I was a nerdy kid, but after Mama started sending me off to lessons while I was a child star, I found myself really enjoying them and continued to take a mix of ballet, jazz, and modern dance throughout high school and college. I was never the best dancer in class—I always fell behind learning choreography because I couldn't see well enough—but the practice of constantly having to imagine movement translated to a gift for improvisation, a key component of good club dancing, whether finding syncopations in the subtleties of Duran Duran or moving different parts of my body independently when I danced to one of the Jacksons.

As I strode to the middle of the pop floor when Janet Jackson's "Miss You Much" came on, someone whose choreography I enjoyed riffing to—sexy smoothness punctuated with abrupt stops— I experienced a moment of astonishment over how utterly confident and unselfconscious I'd become, in a space where so many people felt awkward. So much of this had to do with how I molded myself to any environment, but also how my physical being could be perceived in a vast array of ways. In the darkness of this club, it was virtually impossible to perceive me as a poor albino immigrant who'd only been in the country for six years. Rather, what people saw was a young, attractive white man, and this awareness scaffolded my confidence.

I went up to the bar and ordered myself a club soda, then ambled over to the alternative side, where Pet Shop Boys was playing. I looked out onto the crowd clad mostly in black, as Kit came out of the darkness to stand next to me.

"See anyone you like?"

"Not yet," I replied. "You?"

"There's that new MIT professor Rafe, but he rejected me already." Kit motioned with his head in a direction. "He's that stocky guy in the purple button-down. Only the British can get away with wearing that outfit to a club."

"Maybe I should check him out."

"I'll introduce you," he said. I always appreciated how my friend wasn't possessive about his crushes.

We meandered our way to the dance floor, where Kit said hi to Rafe, then introduced me as someone he knew from Harvard.

"Why are you wearing a Hoover shirt?" he asked, noticing the circle with the familiar lettering of the vacuum cleaner logo.

"It says Hooker, actually," I replied, and enjoyed his look of mild shock before he laughed.

The three of us danced for a while, but Kit wandered off eventually. Though Rafe moved well enough to the beat, he did have the air of feeling out of place, his body self-conscious and hesitant. I could also tell that he liked the way I danced, as I got closer and noticed him steal glances in my direction. It was amusing to have the social upper hand, especially with a professor.

"So what do you teach?" I asked between songs as I assessed his square, open face, which managed to feel both rugged and kind.

"Philosophy. You?"

"I don't teach anything, but I study English."

"You're not a grad student?"

"I'm a senior."

I sensed his body tighten, but this New Order song I loved started up and I ignored his hesitation, started to dance closer, swaying and singing along to "Every time I see you falling, I get down on my knees and pray" while I placed a hand firmly on his back. From this distance, I could see the progression of his thoughts, the panic and the urge to excuse himself, then the decision to stay because he was too polite but also maybe tempted. His loss of composure pleased me, as I made it a game to find creative and not too lascivious ways to put my body in contact with his, my shoulder

grazing his chest, my hip meeting his thigh, in small enough in-
crements that we soon fell into a wordless understanding that we
were dancing together, and our bodies touched because we were
attracted, without anything getting too wild.

I spotted a few other friends and drifted away, but kept tabs on
him out of the corner of my eye, returning to his orbit, sometimes
alone, sometimes with other people, throughout the night. I knew
what it was like to feel ill at ease in a new place, so I wanted to make
sure he didn't have to dance alone for too long. He seemed a little
delighted, a little awestruck, each time I appeared, and I found his
why-me expression endearing.

At the end of the night, I invited him to join me in my after-
clubbing ritual with the Harvard crew, slices at Hi-Fi Pizza around
the corner before walking or cabbing home, depending on the
weather and the state of our bank accounts. Rafe and I sat against
the wall in front of a long table with Kit and a few friends. In the
bright light, I could see the early wrinkles around his eyes, the
flecks of gray at his temple, and guessed he was around a decade
older, which I didn't mind, but I could sense discomfort in the stiff
way he held himself even though it was obvious he liked me. I
wanted to give him a clear but discreet sign that I really did like
him back, so I extended my hand on the bench and touched my
pinky finger against his. He didn't move his hand, and that was how
we stayed for the rest of the meal, until we headed off in opposite
directions, with plans to hang out in the near future.

Between end-of-semester craziness and holiday travel, Rafe
and I didn't manage to get together until shortly after winter

break. On a Friday in January, at a Thai restaurant near MIT, which tried to compensate for its industrial setting with saturated yellow walls and paintings of the Buddha, he informed me that even though I was pronouncing his name correctly, it was actually spelled Ralph.

"Of course, because you're English," I said. "Like Ralph Denham from Woolf's *Night and Day*."

He grinned. "I usually say Ralph Fiennes."

I told him about D. A. Miller teaching his students how to pronounce E. M. Forster's *Maurice* so we wouldn't embarrass ourselves. But since then, I'd discovered a bunch of other British words whose pronunciations were odd, like Bee-chum for Beauchamp, or wes-cot for waistcoat, which I didn't know was a vest until I saw the BBC adaptation of *Pride and Prejudice*.

"And a vest for us is what you call a T-shirt," he said. "Also my old Oxford college sounds like maudlin but is actually spelled like Magdalen. It's all to keep the riffraff out, you see; the more bizarre the pronunciation, the easier it is to tell if someone doesn't belong."

"You mean riffraff like me."

"Oh no, I-I don't mean—" Ralph stammered. "I detest Oxford snobbishness myself."

"I'm just teasing you."

He looked down at his curry with that timid expression I found so endearing. I asked him what Oxford was like, and he described individual tutorials, wearing gowns to meals, and the deer park at his college. He asked me about Harvard, and I described the naked pool parties at Adams, which were alas a thing of the past, but the queer rebelliousness lived on. And as we continued to discuss our interests, my fondness for women's literature and his for German opera, I was struck by how he had an instinctive ability to interact with me like a peer, even though he was so much more learned and accomplished, someone who had been part of the scholarly world, I was sure, his entire life. I mentioned I'd developed a recent interest in evolutionary biology.

"You know, I'm actually descended from Darwin," he said, and I could sense regret right after he spoke those words, like it was a breach of decorum to mention his lineage. I couldn't help but interpret this uncharacteristic revelation as first-date jitters, his eagerness to impress getting in the way of his typical restraint.

"You can't say something like that without giving me more details."

"My last name is Wedgwood, and Darwin married a Wedgwood, though his mother was also a Wedgwood. So actually," he said, now grinning, "I'm descended from Darwin twice over."

"So you're a product of inbreeding," I replied. "We're not so different after all. A geneticist once told me the reason I'm albino is probably because my parents have a common ancestor." I started, so I figured I might as well finish. "People think I'm white but I'm actually Filipino. I lived in the Philippines until I was fifteen."

"I lived in Malaysia for two years when I was twelve."

We moved on to less personal topics as we shared a mango-and-coconut dessert, like the differences between Southeast Asian cultures, and comparing Bahasa with Tagalog words. I carefully observed if something had changed after I told him I wasn't white, but I didn't notice anything.

Afterward, we walked through a maze of concrete buildings to Kendall Square Cinema, a new theater that specialized in indie movies, to watch Kenneth Branagh's *Hamlet*, a play I'd read for at least half a dozen classes by then, though I didn't feel a strong connection to it compared to other Shakespeare tragedies, maybe because Hamlet's tragic flaw is his indecisiveness, whereas I was prone to making decisions too fast rather than not. So the figure I'd always gravitated toward was Ophelia, whose only fault was loving a man who turned out to be disloyal.

Since I made the first move last time, I decided to play it cool on this date, though my determination waned over that long, four-hour stretch when Ralph seemed entirely engrossed, and it didn't feel appropriate to focus on our romance during a Shakespeare tragedy. But late in the movie when Ophelia has drowned, and Gertrude describes her death to Laertes, the camera gets close to the queen's face while her description mesmerized me, of Ophelia singing a song near a brook and finding herself falling in, momentarily buoyed by her billowing dress, though that same dress eventually dragged her down into a muddy death.

Then, just a single, half-second shot of Ophelia in the water, drowned. My hand clutched Ralph's arm, where it remained for the rest of the movie.

It was ten by the time *Hamlet* finished, and as Ralph and I walked through the broad, quiet streets of Kendall Square on our way to the T, I didn't know what would happen next. I knew that Ralph lived in Beacon Hill, the opposite direction from Harvard, and as we walked through the revolving doors of a hotel to get to the subway stop, I noticed his body orient toward the side of the tracks that would take him across the river and away from me.

"Wanna get a drink in Harvard Square?" I asked.

Ralph turned his head as his gait slowed down. It was like I could see his mind while it tried to weigh the implications of a professor dating an undergrad, even if we were at different schools.

"All right," he replied finally, and as we boarded the T on the same side, I wasn't sure if he expected me to make good on the pretense of a drink when we got out. But I figured Café Pamplona was open late and across the street from my room, so I led him down Mass Ave toward Adams House after we got to Harvard Square.

Among the dim lights of closed shops, I could see the bright fluorescents of Harvard Book Store even from afar. Ralph checked his watch as we got closer; it was a quarter to eleven.

"Really, you have a bookstore open this late?" he asked.

"It's a big perk."

"Mind if we go in?"

I shook my head and mouthed "nope," before I followed him inside, and wondered whether he was trying to slow things down. I took him through the store and my various enthusiasms, telling the story of how I once went in and bought every single book George Eliot wrote after finishing *The Mill on the Floss*.

"Do you know where the foreign language section is?"

I led him to the far row of the store where there were several shelves of foreign books. Ralph found a volume of Goethe, which he opened then started reading in German before translating the verses into English, lines about ascending a mountain in winter. I became aware as I listened that I had been in an altered state the entire night, physically present yet giddy over the prospect of being with this enchanting man.

"My English doesn't do him justice," he said when he was done, "but I suppose it's not bad for a spontaneous translation."

"Could've been better," I joked as we walked out of the store and a clerk locked the door behind us. I took his hand and led him around the corner to Adams, made history and architecture small talk as we walked up to my suite on the second floor, opened the door to a long hallway that led to my room, one of the largest on campus. As I walked in, I could see lights from the café below, as well as the imposing brick facade of St. Paul's Church, a building I'd never entered even though it shared its name with my beloved school in the Philippines, because it represented a religion that told me something I could never believe, that it was wrong for me to love another man.

I led Ralph to the futon and sat next to him as a streetlamp outside gave the room a dark yellow cast, and a shadow from my window frame cut a line across his face.

"Would you mind turning on a light?" he asked.

I turned on a halogen and sat down again, undeterred, facing him with one knee on the futon so it would be easier for us to kiss, but I felt him squeeze my hand.

"I like you a lot, but only as a friend."

Ralph's words took me so aback that I almost blurted out, "I don't believe you," but managed to keep myself in check. I wondered how I could have gotten his signals so wrong. Maybe being in a dorm room unnerved him, seeing the most apparent signs that I was still an undergrad. So why did he let things go so far, then? Why did he even agree to come back with me to Harvard? I wanted to confront him but was afraid of losing my composure if I did, and betraying how much I wanted whatever was between us to work out. But no, Ralph would be just another one of those men who only wanted to be my friend, and badgering him would only sacrifice my dignity.

"I understand," I finally said, and filled five more minutes of time, until it seemed plausible to say I should go to bed, lead him out of my suite, and allow myself to feel drowned.

12.

Ralph and I continued to see each other at events, but I more or less accepted that he wasn't interested in me, even though I didn't really believe him. I had too many other things to worry about, like my senior thesis on the status of women authors in Renaissance literature. I was also in crisis over a creative writing class, where the professor refused to continue meeting with me when I objected to his criticism of a story based on my bathhouse trips in London. I should have probably incorporated more of his feedback, but instead I decided he was just a prude.

I already knew my grade was in peril, so I figured I might as well go out with guns blazing and write a story that was an amalgam of my experiences dressing as a woman, slathered with the queer theory I'd absorbed in my classes. My working title was "Fucking Foucault," and the story started off with a character—a queer albino Harvard student, obviously—who time-traveled in a velvet dress to rock Foucault's world. I found myself composing in free verse instead of prose, so the piece became a spoken-word poem and the main character morphed into an androgynous dancer; Foucault fell out of the picture. By the time I turned in the piece, it had become a script for a one-person show called *Dancing Deviant.*

I began spring semester senior year excited about the prospect of staging the piece, which I envisioned as a full-fledged multimedia performance. I also decided that I wanted to perform the show during Harvard's ARTS First Festival, a weekend in April when alumni descended on campus to celebrate the arts. Harvard funding was generous, and I'd directed several successful shows already, one of which received an award for best college production in the state, so I fully expected my proposal to be accepted. But when I went down to my mailbox a few weeks later and found a letter from the Office for the Arts, it was a form rejection that had a handwritten note on it from the program administrator, which read, "We decided that your proposal wasn't suitable for ARTS First's diverse audience." Thankfully, the queer alumni association decided to fund the show.

A reporter for the *Harvard Crimson* who happened to be in one of my classes heard me talking about how Harvard denied me funding for reasons of decency rather than the artistic merit of my work, which to me was the equivalent of censorship. She interviewed me and asked for press images. A few days later, Kit came to breakfast and slapped the morning's newspaper onto the table.

"Congratulations," he said. "You might be the first naked man on the front page of the *Harvard Crimson.*"

There I was above the fold, crouched in a low squat that covered the bits you couldn't show in a newspaper, along with an article that included a quote from an administrator who felt I should be arrested for public indecency, because my proposal included a section where I planned to penetrate myself with a vibrator, to demonstrate how my rectum is a suitable substitute for a vagina.

The *Crimson* article was the start of *Dancing Deviant* becoming a campus sensation when it ran the last two weekends of spring semester senior year, my Harvard swan song. The *Lampoon* even put out a fake issue of the *Crimson* that featured me on the front page, which to many was an even brighter mark of fame than the real article. As a result, the underground theater at Adams, where the performance took place, nothing more than a basement room painted black that normally seated thirty people, found itself needing to accommodate more than twice that number, as I added more shows to keep up with demand.

Audiences lapped at my feet, some sitting on the floor so close to me they could reach out and touch my knees. The show was so popular that it became a badge of honor to have gone, even for people who weren't queer, especially when rumors started floating around that the climax of the show was me doing a backflip and impaling myself onto a Barbie doll.

One night, ten minutes before the show started, I lay inside a trunk in the middle of the stage, curled up in a ball, unbeknownst to the audience. I enjoyed squeezing into improbably tight spaces, testing the capabilities of my body. It was halfway through my run, and I'd done the show a few times by then, that tight squeeze having become oddly comforting, the smell of wood and the hint of light that shone through a crack at the top of the trunk. It reminded me of those nights in high school when I slept under a table in a classroom. I was taking French at the local community college to strengthen my university applications, even though the bus had stopped running by the time I got out at ten. Mama had agreed to pick me up, but she was too addicted to blackjack by then and ended up thirty minutes late, then an hour, and then didn't show up at all. But I refused to withdraw. Instead, I slept under the oak table where the college newspaper staff held our editorial meetings. I was news editor at the community college while also editor in chief of my high school newspaper. The windows in that room rested up high and only let in slivers of incandescent light, like the light from that crack in the trunk. That was how this tiny space became one of comfort and put me in the right frame of mind for my daring performance that pushed the limits of my being.

I was not comfortable that night, however, when I noticed that the buzz from the audience was several rungs lower in pitch than I was used to. I'd heard a rumor that the football team was planning to come, but I didn't believe they'd actually show up until those low voices reached my ears. There must have been a whole horde of them to affect the din of that crowd, as I tried to pick out their conversation. I couldn't tell if it was my brain or their mouths that formed the word "faggot," which transmitted a rush of danger into my system as the house lights dimmed, my signal to begin the show.

I emerged from the trunk, as blinding stage lights suffused the darkness within seconds, but not fast enough for me to unsee an entire row, maybe two, of broad-shouldered men, peering at me from across that imaginary border between performer and audience. I suddenly wondered if this was a boundary the young men knew to respect.

"Man and woman are not created equal," I began, these words taking on a different meaning in front of these straight, strong, virile men, whose superior bodies were designed for the collisions of sport. I estimated twenty of them based on their outlines, could only see shadows between my pool of light and their darkness, yet somehow perceived lines of bared teeth ready at any moment to laugh, hurl insults, devour.

There was an instant, just a sliver of time, when I felt fear and my voice nearly faltered, as I declaimed about the ability of creativity and technology to surmount gender inequality, how we needed to take shame out of sex and the body to make this possible. In that moment, I heard naiveté in my words, absurdity in trying to redefine my gender, while these normal men who performed their sport in front of thousands looked on. But I knew so well how it was only my conviction that could withstand them, just like my conviction that I needed to be seen as white to be worthy, seen as a woman to escape those men who would have beaten me up had they realized they desired a man. Trained to survive, there was no need for me to turn on the switch of bravado that I prayed would render those young men mute, because my mind and body knew how to work on their own. They had no words for me when I began to undress. By the time I stood before them naked, I could tell that I would, by the end of the night, earn not just their silence but their respect.

"This is the story of my body," I concluded as that first monologue came to an end. "I hope that you can one day tell yours." For the rest of the night, I described how my body, and the self that came with it, was so different from other bodies, especially after I realized that I could easily be perceived as a woman if I didn't have a penis, and more than that, I grew not to care whether I was a man or a woman, that I could be both or neither. But having been born with a penis, I imagined my rectum as my substitute vagina, a body part that gave me access to some of the womanhood I did not experience in my daily life. It's through this creativity that I combatted the embedded inequalities between men and women. I ended the show by inviting members of the audience to address the inequalities of gender through fucking, as I brought out a chrome vibrator to emphasize how technology can augment our body's destiny. I sat on the trunk from which I had emerged and began to penetrate myself as the lights dimmed, so the act was invisible to the audience even though I performed it for real, a shocking spectacle out of context but also the show's only fitting conclusion.

I graduated shortly after *Dancing Deviant*'s run and froze the experience with those football players in my mind until I came back to Cambridge twenty years later for reunion. In a marble-lined reception room at the Barker Center, a building that was only being built while our class was at Harvard, a large, grinning blond man came up to me and introduced himself as Tom.

"You're the *Dancing Deviant* guy, aren't you?" he asked.

"Girl now," I replied, "but yes, I am."

"Can I introduce you to some friends? We all saw your performance."

I followed him to a group of seven or eight similarly large, similarly broad men, some of whom still possessed muscled physiques, others rounder. These men took turns thanking me for doing my show, telling me how much it helped them be more tolerant of queer people, how it opened their minds. Later, one of those men took me aside and told me how his younger brother came out to him a few years after graduation, which was a huge crisis for his conservative black family.

"I don't know how I could have gotten through it if I hadn't seen your show," he said through near-tears and a quaver in his voice. I was not just speaking for myself then, but for this man's brother, and this man himself, who, as a black man at Harvard, must have also struggled to belong. His vulnerability cut through time and paired with the strength I mustered to get through that performance he saw, to assert not just my reality but one of the many possible worlds for those of us who lived outside society's expectations.

My preoccupation with Ralph continued amid this hubbub, as I managed to attend these monthly social hours some graduate students organized for Harvard and MIT affiliates, knowing he would likely be there. While the two of us made polite conversation, I did find some humor in thinking our situation Austenesque, the way we made small talk as if we were just casual acquaintances, even when we meant so much more to each other, except that social convention prevented us from being together. Though after I made plans to do an art internship at the Getty in Los Angeles for the summer, and maybe move to New York after that, I figured it was just as well that the two of us didn't become entangled.

I'd also started going out with an Irish MIT postdoc named David, red-haired and uncomplicated, someone I could just hop into bed with and hop out without getting tied up in knots. The Wednesday between the two-weekend run of *Dancing Deviant* in early May, I managed to get myself out to the last MIT–Harvard gathering at Napoleon's, a gay piano bar in downtown Boston. As I came in, David and Ralph happened to be sitting next to each other on barstools, so I decided to stand between them.

"I had to ditch my paper on *Henry VIII* to get here," I said.

"Now that's a fascinating chapter in British history," Ralph replied, as he informed me about the beheading of Anne Boleyn, an event that does not appear in the play, and how Henry was responsible for the Protestant Reformation. I had the growing sense as he went on that Ralph was showing off, that he once again had shed his usual discretion for my benefit, and I couldn't help but be pleased because this meant that he still liked me. I listened with rapt attention as Ralph told stories about Henry's subsequent wives, how he ended the succession of kings when he couldn't sire a legitimate male child, so England wound up with Elizabeth the First as queen. Ralph's erudition continued to enrapture me, the range of topics he could talk about and how he made me feel like all this knowledge was within my grasp, as he spoke with no trace of superiority or condescension.

"The history of Ireland is a history of blood," David interjected.

"Oh yes, I'm sorry I forgot about how Henry VIII conquered Ireland," Ralph replied.

"Of course you would," David said, and the contrite look on Ralph's face endeared him to me even more. Even though I recognized David's peevishness as jealousy and felt bad about it, I couldn't help but feel tickled at the idea that the rhetorical battle between these two men was for my benefit. David excused himself as Ralph and I ended up talking for most of the evening.

At the end of the night and with wine-stained lips, Ralph asked me which way I was going, and I told him I planned to catch the Charles Street stop on the T.

"I live on Charles Street. I'll join you."

As we began walking, I wanted to be sure I knew what would happen, but I had been sure before and it didn't turn out the way I planned. So I just followed Ralph's leather dress shoes through the dark paths of the Boston Public Garden, so romantic at night with its footbridge over a large pond, and up one side of the Commons until we reached the top of his street with its iron lamps out of the nineteenth century. I had the sudden sensation of walking with a gentleman friend in a bygone era, when us being seen alone together would itself have seemed intimate to an observer.

"Do you wanna come up?" he asked when we got to his apartment, which was on the second floor above a leather goods store.

I nodded and followed him up the stairs to his tiny one-bedroom with redbrick walls on two sides, where he took my hand and led me to his bed, where we finally kissed for the first time.

"It took you long enough," I said. As we struggled out of our clothes, I decided to tell him something else, something I usually didn't tell people until it was too late. "Just so you know, I don't really like anal sex." I omitted the part about not having had anal sex at all.

"It's all right," Ralph replied. "We'll do it like the Greeks."

He got on top of me then, and we stared into each other's eyes as we rubbed our bodies against each other. I hadn't known this was how the Greeks did it. I felt comforted to learn that sex between men like this not only had a precedent but had been how men had sex at the dawn of Western civilization. In the throes of passion, I imagined myself as an athletic Greek youth, learning what I needed to know from an older man.

I reserved Ralph a ticket for *Dancing Deviant* the following Saturday, a bit apprehensive about what he would think of me after he saw it, especially the part about feeling like I was between genders. But because that was our last night, the show was severely overbooked and my box office manager had let go of the ticket I reserved for Ralph by the time he got there five minutes late. He never did get to see my gender manifesto in person.

The week after was graduation, so I didn't get to see Ralph because both Mama and Papa decided to come to town; I chose to be normal for once and not stop them. Though I still couldn't help but be embarrassed about having immigrant parents, who sat wide-eyed in our dining hall while I didn't bother to introduce them to anyone, and they were too shy about their English to introduce themselves, which was just as well. Though late that afternoon, after the marching and the receiving of diplomas, as my parents sat on my futon while I finished packing, I decided to stop avoiding what I had kept from my family. While I led this radical queer life in college, I also hadn't managed to come out to them.

"We're going to the lesbian and gay dinner," I said.

Mama met my eyes with a look of incomprehension. She knew what I meant, but it was more convenient for her to hide behind our cultural divide than express her thoughts.

"I'm proud of you," Papa said as he patted me on the shoulder on our way out. I didn't know that I wanted his approval until I felt my throat catch before I thanked him. Both my parents were impassive as they sat through dinner at the Lowell House Dining Hall, even at the mention of my performance piece, which the Harvard Gay and Lesbian Caucus helped fund. I could tell that people were confused I showed up with two Asian guests because they thought I was white, but they were too polite to ask questions, and I refused to clear up any misunderstandings. It was a relief when my parents left after the dinner and I could call Ralph.

"My flight is tomorrow," I said.

"Do you want to sleep over?"

Instead of spending my last night as a Harvard student on campus, I decided to go to Ralph's apartment and sleep with him one last time. He made me eggs the following morning, and I couldn't help but sigh at the sight of him in his sleeveless undershirt, my gentleman unclothed, the part of those Victorian novels I never got to experience vicariously. When it was time for me to go, he helped me with my suitcase as we walked to the Charles Street station together.

"Let's keep in touch," he said as the train doors opened and he kissed me goodbye. My only association with that phrase, "keep in touch," was its frequent appearance in my high school yearbook, then never hearing from my friends again, so I thought of it as just a polite way of seeing me off. But when I arrived at a Getty-affiliated performance space in Santa Monica, where I would be an intern for three months, the administrator told me that Ralph had left a message. That message turned into late-night phone calls that lasted for hours, which turned into a two-week visit full of beach bike rides and happiness, which led to my decision to go back to Boston after the summer and live with that English gentleman whose name rhymes with "safe." When Ralph announced four months later that the Beacon Hill apartment was too small and we should move, I began to peruse the rental classifieds, which was when he told me that he wanted to buy an apartment together because it felt right, for our lives to merge permanently, indefinitely, and I understood that the reason he was so hesitant to be with me in the first place was because he knew that once he did make that decision, he would want to be with me for good.

PART THREE

LADY WEDGWOOD

2000–2002

13.

I returned to the Philippines for the millennium, December 1999. My flight landed at the Ninoy Aquino International Airport near midnight, the coolest time of the coolest month. Even so, I bristled at the switch between the hermetic, air-conditioned confines of the arrivals area and the humid, cloying outdoor space where hordes of people waited to meet arriving passengers. Apart from the mingled sweat, there was that vague yet persistent odor of Manila I never noticed until I returned after a decade, and have since recognized as the faint rot of open sewage and never-collected trash.

It was Nanay Coro's voice I picked out among the relatives who called my name, and my grandmother greeted me with a gush of tears, lamenting that I had not seen my grandfather before he died. As we hugged, I wished I'd kept in better touch, but I was too busy earning the life she wanted for me, too focused on notches of achievement instead of sentimental letters or expensive calls.

We began the two-hour drive home to Talacsan, me wide-eyed with jet lag and nostalgia while my relatives in the back of the van, various family members from three generations, died down and slept after a while, until it was only me and the silent driver who were awake. I kept going through the feeble exercise of matching reality with memory, patterns of light as we passed through the city on our way to the province, which in my jet lag and poor vision I didn't fully recognize as real until we got to the familiar open highway that led to Bulacan, which itself was just a long stretch of vague blankness, no lights to illuminate the endless succession of paddy fields and give them specificity.

Ten years were enough to erase whatever intuition I had of my place in this world, until our vehicle turned right and into our municipality of San Rafael. With only the van's headlights to guide me, I recognized the old pattern of native wooden houses interspersed with cement constructions painted pastel, the municipal center where the road split in two, as I asked the driver to take the path next to the Angat River, which I could only glean as a dark absence while lights from houses dotted its banks. How strange it was, to think of this as the boundary of my knowledge as a child, when I had nearly circumnavigated the world since, crossing the Pacific to get here, and the Atlantic to get to England, a place I'd visited many times instead of returning home. Eventually, the roads met again and we came to the uphill rise that brought back a feeling of hope, because it led to our house next to the town chapel, and the memory of those years—really, until I moved in with Ralph—when this was the only place where I felt truly loved.

The car drove past the assemblage of bamboo and thatch my family lived in until I was twelve, and I suddenly felt the gulf between the child I was and the adult I had become. I excavated the precious memory of me lying on our bamboo-slat floor on idle afternoons, peeking through the spaces between to spy the sacks of rice beneath us, tracing lines with my finger and finding the spots where the slats were nailed to their underlying wooden supports. These were motions I'd performed out of habit for years, ones that started before I ever had any inkling of future wonders: a child star career, a life in America, Harvard, coming out, a relationship with a lovely man from a distinguished family.

Yet that home had become distant too, even for my own relatives in the Philippines, abandoned in favor of a house that mimicked the West with its marble floors, its chintzy chandeliers, its beds. It was at this house that the van stopped, and where my grandmother led me to my old corner room overlooking the poultry farm, the mango orchard, and the rest of our land, invisible at night, as I settled for staring at the blank ceiling until sleep began to take over, only for my eyes to pop awake with the realization that in that memory of my early childhood, I'd forgotten that my skin was white.

One of my aunts invited me to visit her at her new house in the Cainta district of Manila, three hours away at the eastern edge of the sprawling, badly planned metropolis. Nanay Coro and I made the trip together a few days after I arrived. The two of us had gotten more used to each other by then, though she had a lot more to adjust to, since she was the same doting woman who favored me over everyone else, just sadder because her beloved husband was dead.

Whereas I must have been alien to my grandmother, as I paraded around in my linen pants and designer sunglasses, an impeccable New-England-by-way-of-Hollywood accent to match.

This was typical of immigrants returning home, showing off prosperous lives while hiding the effort and sacrifice, making ourselves appear more moneyed, more accomplished than we actually were. Except I actually was moneyed and accomplished, my bank account full of my partner's inherited wealth, my Harvard degree an unquestionable reality, though there were times when the memory of that experience didn't feel real even to me.

Nanay Coro couldn't help but treat me like the child she remembered, maybe because she couldn't understand the person I had actually become. My grandmother humored childhood whims I no longer had, like my dislike of both vegetables and soup, so all my meals were a spoiled Filipino brat's fantasy—fried chicken, fried pork, fried beef—cured or seasoned with salt and served alongside rice and ketchup. I indulged her by not mentioning that the adult me preferred more complicated dishes, but I was indulging myself too by recalling the simplicity of my life before I was wrested from my grandmother. That simplicity itself was a luxury I no longer had, as someone who had to flit back and forth between vastly different realities of being, a Filipino who was also American, brown inside but white outside, deeply in love with a man I hadn't managed to tell my Philippine family about. I had asked Ralph to stay behind at the last minute because it felt too overwhelming to come out to my family and bring a white man home at the same time.

"How is life in America?" my grandmother asked as we sat in crawling Manila traffic, having left the house too late in the afternoon and found that the Christmas season extended our trip by several hours. The equatorial sun had shifted from day to night by then, so much sooner than in America. Among all my close relatives, Nanay Coro spoke the least English, so I had to recover my tongue as I tried to wander through a life I'd never thought of in Tagalog before.

"There is snow in Boston, like shaved ice except softer, and this makes it very cold."

"I live in a kind of house called a brownstone, because the outside of it is made with stone that is brown."

"I make drawings on the computer at a school called MIT, to show people how the human eye works."

As I rendered these scenes for my grandmother in my first language, it occurred to me that I was also translating them for myself, integrating the person I had become with the person I had been before I left, the gulf not so vast that there was no way to travel between the two languages and cultures I knew best.

"Is there someone you love?" she asked, though the verb form she used, "minamahal," with the prefix "mina-" instead of just the simple verb "mahal," in a language where verbs not only coded for time but subtle shades of feeling, to me sounded more like "Is there someone you are loving?" more active and ardent.

"There is," I replied. "We live together."

I muddled through a picture of my life with Ralph, his kindness and his strength, how he was a professor but also did most of the cooking because he enjoyed it. I knew that my string of sentences would end with me telling my grandmother that I lived with a man, but the convenience of genderless pronouns in Tagalog allowed me to defer that confession.

"Actually, the two of you remind me of each other, both smart and nice," I said, and I could tell even in the dark that my grandmother was smiling.

"Next time, you bring *him*," Nanay Coro said in careful English, and I was surprised to find myself unfazed by her knowledge and the deliberate switch to a language she barely spoke, just to tell me she knew without needing to discuss it at length. I realized then that I never really doubted her acceptance, but I was so afraid to tell her because it would mean that I could never again be perfect in her eyes, someone she and my family could unquestionably be proud of. Getting to my aunt's house with the knowledge that this part of me was no longer a secret between us, I felt more complete than I had in a long time.

I woke up in my old room several days later, Christmas Eve, after once again traveling back to Bulacan late at night to avoid traffic. The combination of jet lag and the constant din of Manila—from barking dogs to school kids on vacation singing karaoke through the night—meant that I hadn't been sleeping well in my aunt's house, so I was pleased to find my mind clear, after sleeping for most of the four-hour car ride and another several hours after that.

Staring at the white ceiling of my old room—stained slightly brown like a faint Rorschach test, probably from a roof leak—I thought about how I'd picked up a prepaid calling card and called Ralph from my aunt's house the night before, stretching the cord of her kitchen rotary phone into the bathroom for privacy. He was in England with his family, seven hours behind me. I told him about the conversation in the car with my grandmother and how she told me to bring him the next time I came.

"Sounds wonderful," he said. I thought it was wonderful too, except it also wasn't.

A memory emerged out of that faint blotch on the ceiling, the sight of water while I crossed the Charles River by train on my way to work the previous fall. I was unusually happy on that particular ride. At twenty-three, I had found the love of my life, my soul mate, who wrested me from poverty and gave me a comfortable life. I'd also graduated from the best school and had a promising future ahead of me. I asked myself how I could possibly be any happier, when a voice inside of me said: *You might be happier as a woman.*

It had been two years since I declared to packed audiences that I belonged to both genders, yet I had spent those years as a white gay man. This wasn't something I had intended, more a product of me falling into Ralph's world than anything else. His friends became my friends, and even though Ralph got close to all kinds of people, the fact that our close friends tended to be educated and wealthy meant they were predominantly white, especially the gay men—Chris and Joe, Charles and Bob, David, Tom, and any number of guys with one- or two-syllable Anglo names.

I became one of them. There was a restaurant a few minutes' walk from our apartment, Club Café, a concrete structure lit in tasteful pale blue neon, where all the affluent gays went for brunch. So that was also where Ralph and I imbibed the surrounding white gay culture as we helped ourselves to pancakes and eggs at the fancy brunch buffet, a mixture of professional gays in button-down shirts, along with the older campy types who looked like they worshipped Maria Callas, and the muscle queens in tight spandex tops, sleeveless in the summer, a gay uniform I learned to adopt.

I may have been a slight, inferior albino creature in college, but I grew to feel prized at Club Café, among strangers who had yet to discover that my blond exotic looks were not Scandinavian or Russian. I was also at my buffest then, working with a personal trainer to develop my naturally slim frame to one that at least approached the muscly twinks from those Eastern European porn videos, so popular in the late '90s.

"Lucky," I heard men comment. "Good job." This was not just at Club Café but at other gay establishments in Boston, at Napoleon's piano bar, for instance, or even just walking around our neighborhood. At first I thought the comments were meant for me, that they were telling me I snagged myself a good one. Ralph pointed out that he was the one they were congratulating, and I realized the power my blond youth held in that world, even if it came with the assumption that Ralph went for me because of my looks and I because of his money.

I got so used to that lifestyle—condo ownership, dinner parties, frequent trips to Europe—that I didn't even notice how I slotted into a particular kind of existence, a settled gay coupledom that Ralph sought, and it felt so right being with him that for several years, it didn't occur to me to ask whether that was what I wanted. Sitting on the train on that mundane fall day, I dismissed the idea of my womanhood as a passing notion too, an absurd thing to want in the midst of my intense happiness, compared to the havoc it would wreak if I even entertained the idea of transition, a word whose meaning I didn't really have a frame of reference for, never having met an openly trans woman in person. I ejected it from my mind, only for the quotidian memory to be excavated in my teenage bedroom halfway around the world, after my mind once again wandered toward the territory of hesitation, why I still found it hard to see the man I thought of as my soul mate being part of this world I grew up in.

Then another memory, the summer before that train ride, having lunch al fresco in a swanky restaurant in London's Soho district with a lesbian barrister friend of Ralph's named Karen. She wore a brown tweed suit jacket and had close-cropped blond hair set against a symmetrical face, which made her look altogether handsome and distinguished, but in a softer way than had she been a man.

She and Ralph knew each other through their work advocating for gay marriage, as they exchanged information about the issue between America and England. I was used to this, absorbing conversation as Ralph talked to various older, learned friends, whether about arcane issues in philosophy or matters of queer-related public policy. Though I wasn't paying that much attention—the details of lobbying the House of Lords weren't particularly interesting to me, and I had more reservations about gay marriage than Ralph, or presumably his friend. I believed in lasting unions, even believed that Ralph and I should be married if the option were available, but I was also concerned about how marriage could compromise the countercultural force of queer life. Though this wasn't an opinion I felt like expressing in front of a human rights lawyer and my partner, who had lectured and published on the topic.

"You know why I'm fighting for gay marriage in England?" Karen asked as she turned to me. "So you can someday be Lady Wedgwood."

It wasn't the first time I'd heard this; our art historian friend Tom, who followed British aristocracy, had made the same joke a couple of times to embarrass Ralph, who was self-conscious about being next in line for the title of baronet once his father died. He was to be called Sir Ralph Wedgwood according to his future position in British society as one rung above a knight, a detail he omitted about himself until after we'd been living together for six months. As a left-leaning liberal ethicist, Ralph found the idea of inheriting titles distasteful, so I tried not to get too worked up about the baronet thing myself, even though I'd been schooled in British literature and found it exciting to be partnered with a man some minor Austen character would want to marry for his title.

But this specific conversation affected me somehow, even for just the few minutes between when Karen made her comment and the rest of lunch. Vivid scenes flooded my mind, a mosaic of beautiful white women, from Gwyneth Paltrow's blond and vivacious Emma, to the gender-shifting Viola in *Twelfth Night*. Of course, my mind dwelled on Orlando from Virginia Woolf's novel of the same name, a nobleman who wakes up one day and discovers that he has become a woman, and from that point on is known as Lady Orlando. Even though it was just a joke, how women who are married to baronets get the title of Lady, and so a man who marries a baronet should be called Lady too, my mind led me to the possibility of literally transforming into a woman.

I didn't actively dislike being a man. It was more that for so much of my life, I lived vicariously through women, who were always the central characters in my favorite stories, searching for and finally finding the love of men. It was thrilling to imagine myself living these fantasies, whether in rom-coms or Shakespeare, but especially from great novels set in England. But whenever I finished those books, I had to live with the disappointment that while women in real life had the chance to experience some version of these stories, my pleasure in them was always destined to be indirect, so that one moment when a virtual stranger called me a Lady gave me an outsized amount of joy.

I dismissed this idea as a possible reality shortly after lunch was over and dismissed it again in my humid childhood bedroom in Talacsan. No point dwelling in idle fantasy—of course Ralph, the real, living person I loved as the man I was, would be with me the next time I returned home.

The day after Christmas, an exhausting family holiday involving visits with innumerable relatives and family friends, I decided to make good on a plan I had begun talking about the day I arrived, to gather old school friends for a night in Manila. It felt momentous to hire a van myself and leave my grandmother behind, my first act of true adulthood back home.

I'd asked my family and neighbors to spread the word, hoping the information would reach my school friends before I dropped by. There were no landlines in our town, let alone internet, and only the richest households owned gigantic satellite phones that cost a fortune to use. I spent the money to call Ralph Christmas Day on a weak signal, just long enough to say I wished we were together even when I was the reason we were apart.

"Many of our friends work abroad or live in Manila now," my friend Dek said as we got on our way; he was the only close friend from my class who also came from my village. Our friend Ramil, whose parents ran a convenience store next to school, was indeed gone; his mom said he was working in Singapore. At least my cousins Leslie and Brian were home in Pantubig, three villages over; they were technically uncles but were close to my age. We also picked up Hershey Rodriguez, who I wasn't that fond of because she always insisted on getting in everyone's business, but she was on the way and we knew would be eager to be part of the excursion.

"You know Samuel and Rosanna are together now," Hershey said when she got in the van. Rosanna was a meek and unassuming girl in our class. She was not the woman I would have thought of for Samuel, not just because she didn't stand out in any way but because I wouldn't have pegged her to go for someone so rakish, though maybe she too discovered immense kindness beneath his rugged athleticism.

Samuel was already on the list of friends Dek and I had planned to invite, and I tried to be casual when we talked about him. Though my family knew about me, my friends did not, and I wasn't planning to tell them. It felt too at odds with the image I'd cultivated, of a serious, accomplished person, not a bakla who worked in hair salons and florist shops.

Hershey provided more updates about our old classmates, and I enjoyed hearing about how everyone did after I left. Not only had the top two students from our class gotten into the country's most prestigious school, UP Diliman, which was no surprise, but Samuel had too. This made me wish we could have celebrated our college acceptances together, even though we were half a world apart.

As we reached Samuel's house, I wanted so badly to consign my love for him to the realm of teenage fantasy, yet I found it impossible to separate those old feelings from the picture of him in my head, ten years older than the boy I had known. Even with the intervening time and the dozen men I'd been with—all of them white—it felt as if there would always be a compartment in my heart reserved for my old friend, my secret love.

In my reverie, I found myself unprepared to encounter the sudden familiarity of the hunter green gate to his house, timeworn yet still bright. I got out of the van and yelled, "Tao po!" as I peeked through the bars above the metal gate, which the top of my head hadn't even reached before I left.

I expected a servant to come out and wasn't prepared for Samuel himself in a tank top and basketball shorts, the same lanky frame, just an elongated version of the boy I remembered. He even had the same bowl cut and shy smile I'd seen him offer when he encountered new people, even though I wasn't a new person.

"I heard you were in town," he said as he came to the gate.

"I'm taking everyone out in Manila, my treat," I said, and then, remembering: "Bring Rosanna."

"We already have plans with her family tonight," he replied. To cover for my disappointment, I asked him how his life had been since I left. He told me about UP and how impressed he was that I'd gotten into Harvard, how he was now a junior manager for a corporation in Manila, in a distant tone like we hadn't spent countless hours together, as if he wasn't my closest friend before I left.

"Why don't we get together while I'm here?" I asked.

"I'm going back to Manila tomorrow."

I was about to offer to meet him in Manila when, seeing that he was already at his door and wanted to go back to the safety of his house, I realized he wanted to finish this interaction as soon as possible. He hadn't even opened the gate, hadn't even touched, let alone hugged me. It was how I knew he recognized who I was and found me pitiful, even disgusting, that he disavowed whatever we were to each other, our friendship, my love.

In the fifteen steps between the gate and our van, I composed myself and informed everyone that Samuel couldn't come, maintained that composure as we picked up a few more friends, through the entire ride in Manila, during dinner at Barrio Fiesta, during dancing at a club called Euphoria, and during the long ride back to the province, arriving in my old room after two in the morning, where I finally eased my grip but couldn't even cry, because there was nothing to cry about. I didn't know how to be heartbroken about a love that existed a decade ago, that I made no effort to maintain when I left, and turned out not to be real. But I did know that I needed to get out of that house, so I woke up the next morning and told my grandmother that I was going back to Manila and checking into a hotel.

That room where I was supposed to choose a man reminded me of the open pen at the farm where we kept all the pigs. One of the walls only went up a few inches above my waist, as a dozen young men sat on the other side, nearly close enough to touch. Many of them perked up with open smiles, convincing enough under dim fluorescent light. Maybe I was the best they could expect—a young, slim American.

I scanned the room for a face I would like, some clear way to distinguish these young men from one another, all with the same build and around the same height, their skin different variations of brown. A couple had mustaches, a few had curly hair, but no one stood out at first glance until I noticed him in the corner, dark and shy, maybe new, not as confident as the others, in a country where dark people were meant to be ugly, a city where people from the province were made fun of. I pointed at him, and the man in charge asked if I was sure; I nodded yes.

I paid the man two hundred pesos, half the amount it said online; the other half I'd give to the shy guy once we were done, for a total of about ten dollars.

"Boy," he said in a near-whisper when I asked for his name.

I decided to be American that night, no Tagalog, maybe because I thought of this, the buying of a body, as something only my American self would consider. I also wanted to feel like myself, and I didn't know how to do that as a Filipino person who left an anak araw and came back as simply American. No one even recognized me from my TV actor days, and I found myself unable to undo whatever American body language I'd learned that made me invisible as Filipino. If I did speak Tagalog, then I would have to explain myself at length, so it was better just to be American and nothing else.

After a twenty-minute cab ride from the Malate red-light district to my hotel in Makati, Boy and I found ourselves in my room on an upper floor, a narrow window overlooking the street our only sign of the outside world. It was a hotel one could find in any developing country, designed to look fancy even though everything was fake, from the faux-leather headboard to the Formica tabletops.

"Very nice," Boy said, wide-eyed, when I turned on a lamp. This confirmed my suspicion he was either new or didn't get picked that often.

I couldn't place his accent, only that it was from one of the thousands of small islands in the middle of the country, maybe a fishing village he'd left because he could not afford a boat of his own. I wondered how he ended up in this room, but I couldn't extract this information unless I switched to Tagalog, nor, I reminded myself, did I want to know Boy as a person. I just wanted him as a body, as a fuck, to see what it was like.

I told Boy to undress, and when he stood before me at the foot of the bed, I finally saw a Filipino man naked for the first time. I motioned for him to kneel in front of me as I unbuttoned my jeans. I didn't have to tell him what to do next.

But as I stroked his coarse, straight hair, I found myself imagining him in his village, swimming with his friends, wrestling on the shore. I closed my eyes and tried to concentrate on just the pleasure, but I couldn't imagine his mouth without his face, his body, his life. I was one of his friends on the beach, who he unexpectedly ended up on top of, and no one could tell who started, what look or touch began it all, but we found ourselves kissing. I turned off the light and undressed myself, motioned for him to lie next to me in bed, then put my hand against his lower back to guide him on top of my body.

We rubbed against each other while my hands explored whatever parts of him I could reach, as he explored mine. I became the boy I was before I left, made true those fantasies of youth I never got to fulfill with Samuel. I kissed him like he wanted me to, as our surroundings fell away and we were just two boys from the country who had never been taught what it meant to be together, that boys could do things like this, be this to each other. As our hands and our breaths became one, there grew no distinction between giving pleasure to the other and giving pleasure to ourselves.

I opened my eyes after we came and met Boy's too-wide smile. Even in the darkness, the only light coming from the narrow window that overlooked the street, his face reminded me that while I only felt like a village boy, he was a true village boy who'd just been with a rich white man, who might take a shine to him and take him back to America, lead him away from his life. Whatever lay beyond our initial transaction could not surmount the difference between how he saw me and how I longed to see myself.

I wanted to tell him I wasn't American, but I couldn't because I *was* American. I would never again be that provincial Filipino boy who stayed close to home. I could never unknow my years in America and the sacrifices I'd made to belong there, to have the accent, the mannerisms, the ways of being of my new country. Even if I did convince Boy with my fluent Tagalog that I started life as a kid from a Philippine province like him, my skin and hair would still distort his perception. I wanted more than ever to be with Samuel, because out of everyone I'd ever loved, even my own grandmother, he was the only one who didn't care at all that my skin was light and knew me as the person I really was, the person I was meant to be, a kid from a rural hamlet in a poor country who should have been brown but turned out white. No one else could ever know me the way Samuel did, not even Ralph, who up until I came home I considered the love of my life, and probably still would as soon as I landed in the U.S., because I'd covered up that kid for so long that I also hid him from myself, buried him beneath so much education and pretense that there was no hope of ever finding him again, and the best I could do was love and be loved as a ghost of myself.

I dressed quickly and took a thousand-peso bill from my wallet, set it down on the nightstand, and turned the lamp back on.

"Thank you very much," Boy said, visibly pleased when he picked up the money. He noticed a piece of paper next to where the bill had lain and picked it up too.

"It's just a friend's business card," I said as I snatched it from him. I wondered if he was less innocent than he seemed, if he was capable of keeping the card and threatening to expose me for money.

I led him to the door and told him I had New Year's Eve plans the following night, but I might drop by in a few days, even though by "might" I meant "won't." I didn't know if he understood everything I said, but there was still hope in his face when I closed the door, and I regretted having given him so much of myself.

I journeyed back to Bulacan the next day, but the combination of gridlocked traffic and a late start meant that I was still on the road by the time the new millennium came, as the commotion of fireworks escorted me to Talacsan. I had missed my family's celebration and Ralph's call by the time I got back. He was logical when we talked later that night—I didn't tell him about Boy, though we'd already agreed from the start we could sleep with other people, a modern relationship—and said there was no need to be sentimental about missing midnight, since there were twenty-four of them.

It was true that his midnight hadn't even arrived, but I did feel the loss of not having been there with my family at the turn of the millennium, not being on the phone with Ralph as it happened. I wanted that feeling of belonging to the exact time and place, though I'd spent an entire life never feeling that way and had learned to adapt. Even just once, it would have been terrific.

14.

I came back to the U.S., to Boston, the South End. I woke up in the airy brownstone apartment I shared with Ralph, grabbed a lemon scone at a café called the Garden of Eden, took the T across the bridge to Kendall Square. I'd fallen into a technical assistant job at a cognitive science lab at MIT, where I designed figures for scientific papers. I returned to dinner with Ralph at night, at home or at a restaurant, and either read afterward or occasionally went to a movie or the theater.

This routine shifted steadily over the following months, after I started a color darkroom class two evenings a week. My plan after graduation was to become a fiction writer, and I submitted stories about immigrant life to literary journals while also working on an autobiographical novel. I even applied to writing programs, which, like the literary journals, all rejected me. I had started college in a state of wonder, but with no frame of reference except for the countless speeches about Harvard students being the best of the best, I found myself overconfident when I got out, and thought I could be a professional author with one fiction class as training, where I fought with the professor the whole time. When that didn't pan out, I looked around for something else to do and settled on photography. I'd taken a beginning class at Harvard and enjoyed using my camera to bring the world closer to me, to be able to see details up close in a photograph that I couldn't see in real life.

I would have chosen somewhere less vocational than the New England School of Photography, which was geared toward commercial shooters, except I enrolled late and it was the only school with open slots I could find. We were to bring a processed roll of something we shot to our first class, where we got a crash course in color printing.

That was how I first got to know the other students, when their prints came out of the photo processor, a giant machine that emitted a steady hum and smelled sweetly of chemicals, like the printing presses I'd been around as a kid. I'd taken pictures of my inline skating club and started on a print of a guy who knelt awkwardly as he posed for me with his rollerblades on. I saw images of a mountain landscape, a bank lobby interior, a street performer, the kinds of photographs I expected. Except there was one print that kept catching my eye as it went through various versions, lighter and darker, redder and pinker. It was of two bald mannequin heads against a red background, with blank eyes that gave me the uncanny feeling they were decapitated. I leaned closer while another print of the image came out of the processor, and I noticed that the skin on those heads was crinkled, not like the smooth plastic I expected.

"I make them out of papier-mâché," a girl said as she pulled the print out of the machine. Her hair was a vibrant red that verged on artificial, cut in a bob with bangs straight across her forehead, which might have felt severe except for the large eyes and plump face that made her look like a more childlike, happier version of the dolls she created.

After the instructor evaluated our photographs at the next class, he gave us a ten-minute summary of his life, from his Ohio upbringing to his marriage to a woman who wanted to return to her home city of Boston, which was how he had ended up working as a portrait photographer and teaching at the school the past twenty years. When it was the red-haired girl's turn, she introduced herself as Lenora Mayer, a painter who had graduated from RISD the previous year and had since gotten more interested in photography because of how it rode that fine line between make-believe and reality. She grew up with hippie artist parents, her father a gentile and her mother a Jew, a culture that she deeply identified with, in Minneapolis of all places. She now lived in an artist loft in South Boston, a former shoe factory that was falling apart.

Because everyone else's introductions seemed so honest, I started from the beginning when it was my turn, how I grew up in the Philippines then moved to California at fifteen, and went to Harvard after that. I even added that no, my parents weren't missionaries or in the military. I was actually albino, which meant that I didn't see that great, but I enjoyed the challenge of doing things I wasn't supposed to, like rollerblading and taking pictures, sometimes even at the same time. Lenora turned around from a few rows away to watch me, and I could tell from the way she nodded and laughed that we were going to be friends.

We started working on enlargers next to each other and set ourselves apart as the two artists in the group with that overconfidence of young graduates from elite schools—cringeworthy in retrospect—in contrast to the other students, who were hobbyists or budding commercial photographers. That was when I became privy to Lenora's process, the way she did so much by feel, while my head was full of numbers and procedures—the right f-stop to get optimal exposure, how many points of magenta to add so a subject's skin looked natural.

"Don't forget it's art," she often told me when I showed her a print that was technically perfect but refused to give off that magic feeling of something you wanted to look at for more than half a second. I found that so thrilling about her, how she always put feeling before thought. Sometimes her prints came out so underexposed they were practically white, but she presented them for critique anyway because she found them visually interesting. Or she intentionally printed the frame where the main subject was out of focus, just to see if it would look cool. This loose approach extended to the rest of her life, from the illegal loft she lived in, where the toilet was in the kitchen, to the very fact that she spent four years perfecting her painting technique, only to end up working in photography and papier-mâché.

Lenora and her world were the opposite of Ralph's world of academics and rich gay men, or the sterile, deliberate environment of my MIT lab. She was everything I was missing from my life, which blossomed when she started introducing me to her school friends and artist neighbors, who ended up being my friends too. Over time, Lenora and I started seeing each other multiple times a week, whether in the darkroom or her loft or the various openings and parties she invited me to. We were each other's first post-college friends, and we adored each other in quantifiable and unquantifiable ways, how my logical and her emotional natures were complements, how we bonded through our ingrained eccentricities, she a gentile-passing Jew from the Midwest, me an Anglo-passing Asian from the Philippines, and how we were simply at a point in our lives when we each needed a best friend.

At the end of that spring class, and as I began to take my shift to photography more seriously, I decided to rent space in a photo studio a few blocks away from Lenora's loft, clean and polished in contrast to her dilapidated digs, and even bought a professional lighting setup. I'd been taking pictures for work at MIT and wanted to experiment with the aesthetic of scientific photography for fine arts purposes. I did this one series where I spread various white substances—tapioca, yogurt, cottage cheese—onto plexiglass and photographed them with a macro lens, to explore different varieties of white, my first, awkwardly literal foray into conceptual art, the incredibly white photographer taking pictures of sour cream. The first set of prints didn't look great, so I abandoned the concept, since I was the type of person who insisted on being precocious and didn't stick with ideas for long if they didn't work the first time.

Lenora, on the other hand, had no reservations about trying out version after version of the same idea, constructing elaborate backgrounds for the papier-mâché heads that she also kept remaking, photographing them from an inordinate array of angles, learning how to control the features of her camera as she went along. She started to spend more time in my studio to do her setups, because she could control the light better with my professional equipment, rather than the clip lights she used at home.

That was how Lenora met the other new friend in my life, a new graduate student from MIT named Richard Russell, who I'd met the previous August when he started out in my lab, and came over to my cubicle on his first day.

"I heard you're the artist in the group," he said.

Richard's attention caught me by surprise. Everyone in MIT's cognitive science department was cordial, but I was used to being in the background there, as a lowly technical assistant who had no plans to be a career scientist. As nice as people were, it was always implied that my work was less of a priority than theirs, so it was jarring—though pleasant—to meet someone at MIT who sought after my talents.

"I do photography," I replied.

"Then you're the person I'm looking for."

It turned out Richard had been taking black-and-white pictures with an old Nikon F1 but had no idea how to print them. I started bringing him to the darkroom I rented in Jamaica Plain and showing him the ropes; then he became another beneficiary of my studio rental, since my setup came with a black-and-white darkroom so he could print at my space whenever I wasn't using it.

I was attracted to Richard the way I was attracted to pretty much any good-looking straight man who crossed my path, a dynamic I'd gotten used to over the years, to "look but don't touch," as my straight Mormon friend Chris once told me in undergrad, comparing himself to a painting in a museum. It helped our friendship that Richard wasn't Hollywood attractive—Ralph compared his looks to a golden retriever after they met the first time —and I knew what he meant since Richard had a slack face and sleepy eyes, though his jaw was well-defined. He also wore wire-rimmed glasses that gave his slim but muscular frame a nerdy slant, a combination I couldn't figure out until he mentioned that he had taken a year off during college to sail with the merchant marines, which explained his overdeveloped forearms. He was one of those people who was aware he was attractive to some extent but was too deep in thought to care much about it.

It was inevitable that Lenora and Richard would run into each other in my studio, on a Saturday afternoon in spring when she was shooting and he was coming in to print. Seeing the two of them awkwardly shake hands, a feeling of satisfaction welled up in me, because they somehow represented two ends of a mind spectrum that felt uniquely my own, Lenora the emotional artist and Richard the analytical scientist. I loved that I was friends with both of them, that I understood their motivations and interests in ways they each would find difficult in the other. This was the better side of being me, how even if I didn't fully belong anywhere, part of me belonged to so many places, because I'd grown accustomed to always being in between.

Richard and I grew closer the more we both immersed ourselves in art, and he got me into the habit of taking walks together around the MIT campus, where we enthused about our latest artist finds. There was one day when we walked to the lunch truck and back, with him talking the whole time about a documentary he had watched about Andy Goldsworthy, an artist who rearranged natural elements like rocks along a riverbank or twigs in a forest to create exquisite, ephemeral artwork. As Richard went on, I couldn't help but reflect on how multifaceted he was, logical yet artistic, both rugged and sensitive, an in-between like me.

One of our frequent walks together was to ZONA, the photo lab close to MIT where we got our film processed, a walk that included a long pathway with an open field on one side, a line of trees and benches on the other. We made a habit of sitting on one of those benches to extend our conversations, especially after seeing movies together at Kendall Square Cinema, since that path lay in between the turn he took to walk to his apartment a few blocks away and my turn toward the T station to get home to Boston and my life with Ralph.

One evening in May, Richard and I decided to catch the photo lab right as it was about to close, so he ended up inviting me to dinner at his house. Over time, the distance between us when we walked grew smaller and smaller, so that by then, my shoulder intermittently bumped his upper arm as we ambled to his place in silence, unusual for us, but I sensed that he was not in the mood to talk.

Richard also seemed subdued over the dinner he heated up, lentil soup over rice, spare and simple the way he was. Afterward, we sat next to each other on his living room futon, him with one knee up while I'd taken off my shoes and sat cross-legged, so close to him that I could feel his breath when he sighed. We'd neglected to turn on the halogen lamp and neither of us seemed inclined to stand up, so when I turned my torso in Richard's direction, half of his face was shrouded in darkness, the other half dim and pale from the light of a streetlamp outside.

"I'm thinking of leaving science," he said.

He might have been talking about his career, but I knew that for Richard, expressing doubt about science, so much that he wanted to quit, might have been the most intimate thing he could tell another person.

"What would you want to do instead?"

"Maybe I'll be an artist like you."

He told me he'd been making abstract paintings in his basement, and they weren't that great but they made him happy, allowed him to express more of himself than the confined lab he
inhabited, performing experiments that were not even his idea. He
envied the freedom Lenora and I had to let our passions take us
wherever we wanted and bring our entire selves into our work.
While I tried to focus on his words, I also wanted to hold him
because I knew that his steadfast nature meant he could only reveal this part of himself to someone he trusted, which meant that
he felt closer to me than I ever dared to think.

"Everyone has doubts," I said, and told him how I wondered all
the time if I only quit writing because it was too hard to sit in a
room all day, needing to use all your energy to fill pages with
words, only to find that those words weren't any good. At least with
art there was always busywork that made it easier to deflect this
feeling, how all your effort would probably amount to nothing.

"You're not always going to just execute other people's ideas," I
concluded.

"You're right," he said. "Thank you."

For what? I wanted to ask, not because I didn't know but because I wanted him to say the words. For listening. For our friendship. For our closeness.

I longed to kiss him then, but instead I told him it was getting
late, then we both stood up and hugged for a while. I could have
tried to kiss his cheek or brush my hand against his face, to give
Richard some indication of the feelings for him I was discovering,
but I could sense he wasn't attracted to men. I didn't want to compromise what we had, and it would have been an emotional betrayal to Ralph anyway, even when we'd agreed we could sleep with

other people. So I allowed myself that one satisfying hug, before my walk back to the subway and life with my partner at home.

But later, when I was in my studio, I allowed myself to do something I had wanted to do for a long time. I went into the darkroom and found the work shirt Richard wore when he printed there, with the merchant marine logo in blue where his heart was when he wore it. I held the shirt to my nose, smelled his skin beneath the vinegar scent of fixer, the chemical that prevented photographs from fading. His odor as it reached my mind blended with the memory of my childhood and Samuel, rugged and sensitive, in-between, kindred yet thwarted. These were patterns I was destined to repeat, stories of love I told myself at night like those novels I'd read over and over, even though real love like when my partner looks at me with intense adoration, looks at me like we're destined to be together always, this real love can coexist with the impossible love in my fantasies, where I am a woman who enraptures a man because he finds me enticing and beautiful.

Later still, in Lenora's bed on one of our sleepovers, also in the dark except for a desk lamp on her bedside table.

"I can't help it. I have feelings for Richard," I said.

"But what about Ralph?"

"I mean, what about Ralph?" I echoed. Whatever I felt about Richard was just what I felt about him, as a lyric from Sondheim fluttered through my mind—"I do not hope for what I cannot have / I do not cling to things I cannot keep"—lines by my beloved Fosca from her song about reading, where she explains why she loves to read about beautiful men falling in love with beautiful women but she would never dare imagine this would happen to her in life, because she is so ugly. I was ugly too, because I was a man.

"Richard's too much of a scientist for me," Lenora said. "I wouldn't date him, especially now that I know how you feel."

My younger brother visited me in Boston for the first and only time, the summer of 2000. He went by his first name, Ramon, to the outside world by then, while my father, the previous Ramon, started calling himself Ray. But he was still Tonton to me, Tony when I talked about him with American friends, diminutives of his middle name, Antonio. Now seventeen, he had come to live with Papa after he had trouble getting clean in California.

I hadn't seen Tony in a couple of years, and I wasn't prepared for the young man who towered over me and wore a dagger tattoo on his upper arm, which I noticed as he got out of the Peter Pan bus in South Station, wearing a wifebeater shirt, baggy jeans, and a Yankees baseball cap turned backward.

"It's been a looong tiiime," he said as I hugged him, his LA Latino intonation so much more pronounced than I remembered. But as I released him from my embrace, I noticed he had the same delicate features, high cheekbones, full lips, and a chin that came almost to a point. I wondered how I could have ever thought of him as ugly.

"Welcome to Boston," I said, not really knowing how to talk to my brother. "Anything in particular you wanna do?"

He shrugged and stuck out his bottom lip. "I dunno, maybe a Red Sox game?"

The following morning, we took the Green Line with Ralph out to Fenway Park and braved the crowds to see our home team play against the Phillies. We must have made a curious trio, an older man with two younger ones, one white and one brown. I couldn't follow the ball from our last-minute seats in the grandstand, though I clapped and cheered when Tony did, nodded when he pointed out a good hitter or how many runs the Red Sox needed to come back—being in Boston, he left his Yankees cap at home and used the hood of his black sweatshirt to cover his head in the heat, then let the rest of it drape down his back. He turned to me with a toothy smile when Boston scored a home run, his face incandescent with a happiness that exceeded the moment and reached all the way back to his rural childhood playing kick the can and climbing trees with other boys. If I had improved my lot by coming to America, Tony would have certainly been better off had he stayed at home.

As we walked among the crowd after the game, I noticed how the nearly all-white bystanders around us glared at my brother with his shaved head, baggy clothes, and brown skin, like he had already done something wrong just by being there, as they parted to give him a wide berth. It was paradoxical how the two of us shared so many genes yet moved through the world so differently, how our places could have been switched had he only been born with my genetic anomaly, one that was supposed to disable me yet had clearly conferred on me advantages Tony never had.

My brother took a nap on our living room couch when we got back, and I couldn't help but watch him as he slept on his stomach, a pillow on his head to keep the late-afternoon sun out of his eyes. He'd been diagnosed with schizophrenia the year before, and I'd heard stories of him coming home late at night in a panic, banging on doors, convinced that someone was about to murder him. But I never witnessed any of this, not even in the couple of visits I made to New York after he started using; Papa thought that Tony wanted to be on his best behavior whenever I was around. Maybe the childhood he spent under my thumb had kept my brother deferent, and I wondered whether I should offer to let him live with me. But I dismissed this idea as soon as I thought it, terrified of failing at taking care of another person the way my parents did with both of us.

I was expecting Tony to stay at least another day, but he decided to go back on the bus as soon as he woke up; old friends of his in the city had Saturday night plans. I offered to ride the subway with him, but he insisted that he knew the way and that we'd see each other the next time I was in New York. I didn't consider until years later that he must have left early to look for drugs.

Ralph and I spent the rest of the summer in Europe, first in England and then France. I woke up to the charm of his family home in Surrey, a three-story stone structure that had once been a paper mill, next to a river that reminded me of *The Mill on the Floss*. As I looked out the window of Ralph's childhood room, the expanse of rolling green outside reminded me that the house was situated at the bottom of Box Hill, precisely where *Emma*, the first Austen novel I ever read, was set. When I walked around outside, it really did feel like I was in one of those novels, where English gentlemen came upon and wooed their brides-to-be, down to a bench in Ralph's family garden that was braided out of live vines, their roots still planted in the ground, which didn't feature in any Austen novel but could easily have.

Being there reminded me that my relationship with Ralph was

at the aftermath of courtship, the settled bond between two like minds. If it didn't have that dynamic of a man chasing after a woman, then so much the better, because the world needed fewer regressive stereotypes, romantic as they were. We habitually took the train to London and spent afternoons poring through used books at Skoob, evenings in the theater at the Old Vic or Donmar Warehouse, walks on the bank of the Thames.

We were also there so that Ralph could be the best man for his good friend Alex Bird, someone he'd known since they were students at Westminster, the boarding school attached to the abbey. So there was a whole slew of events for that occasion, receptions and lunches where I met various friends and old relatives, before the ceremony itself, where Ralph wore a tuxedo with a pink vest—or a waistcoat, as the English called it—while I wore dark gray tails and an ascot, his choice of color and my neckwear our own signals that we were different from the other men around.

I was just "American" to these people in polite British society, my origins invisible. The huge store of literature and movies in my head had no template for "Filipino immigrant in England" but was full of examples of Americans abroad, from Henry James to *An American in Paris*, and it was from that collection that I procured pointers about how to behave. Ralph sometimes pointed out that I was from the Philippines, and someone would talk about a nurse or maid, marveling how "they" were so sweet or helpful, as people assumed my parents were Americans who had been stationed in that country, despite my partner's careful explanations. This was more alienating than being assumed American, how they separated me from my own people while talking to me about them, unable to see this blond Harvard graduate and professor's partner as someone who could be from the same world as the people who tidied their house or cleaned their bedpans.

At the rehearsal dinner, a cousin of Alex's, a woman with frosted-blond hair who was just shy of beautiful, just shy of young, talked to me at length about her indispensable Filipino live-in nanny. "She speaks such wonderful English and is so dedicated to my baby," she said. "I don't know what my family would do without her." I wanted to reply, *How do you think her own family does without her?*, but didn't because I somehow became unfailingly polite among these fancy English people, domesticated in my own way. At least I had a camera with me and took photographs of her and other people I met in those rooms, tried to capture the absurdity of their mild pomp on film.

After the wedding, Ralph and I spent a week in Paris together, stayed at an all-white hotel in Montparnasse, the better to appreciate the ornamental bevels and curves of everything, which made me wish I'd taken an architecture class, a gaping hole in my humanistic education. I did redeem myself in my own mind when we saw *Raymonda* at the Paris Opera Ballet, which Rudolf Nureyev had choreographed and whose ballet career I'd read about, from his brilliance in Nijinsky's *L'après-midi d'un faune* to his defection from the Soviet Union, to his eventual death from AIDS. That Nureyev was a gay man gave me a sense of belonging amid the grandness of that sumptuous world. I was too intimidated to speak French though, but Ralph did, and being associated with him made me feel learned and cosmopolitan too.

After Paris, we traveled south by train to join Alex and his bride, Lucy, at the tail end of their honeymoon in Agde, a village near the Spanish border in the Montpellier region, where Alex's parents owned a charming vacation home made of stone, painted white, with cathedral-style windows and wooden shutters. Joining the newlyweds were their good friends Ned and Sandra, who had the sweetest toddler named Arthur. Over that week, we whiled away the time with day-trips to the countryside, procured wine from the local vineyards that was cheaper than bottled water, and made dinner together accompanied by lively conversation.

Our last afternoon in Agde, I set up my tripod and the seven of us took a group picture by the pool beside the house. I felt like shooting in black and white that day, and I made prints in my studio when I got back. There we all were, our feet dipped in the water, looking happy and relaxed, Ralph's arm around my shoulder and my hand reaching up to touch his. I felt so close to him then, and we were such a handsome couple, Ralph dignified and gentlemanly while I was slim and bright-eyed, no sign of trouble, except maybe that I'd let my hair grow so it was at the bottom of my nape, as if those dead cells were aware of the crisis to come.

My return to the States coincided with the start of the fall semester, and my friendships picked up pretty much where they'd left off, except I added a couple of new classes at the Museum of Fine Arts to my schedule. Lenora and I saw less of each other, especially after she picked up her own lighting equipment so she didn't need my studio anymore. I didn't see too much of Richard either; his research led him to work at a different lab in another building. Though I didn't mind that my friendships became less intense; it gave me more time to work and prepare to apply to art schools the following year.

I expected my feelings for Richard to subside, especially after the previous, happy summer with Ralph. I caught my friend up on one of our walks together, the wonderful time Ralph and I had in Paris, how our relationship was as strong and supportive as ever. All of this was true, but there continued to be an intimacy between me and Richard that went beyond what we talked about and extended to the ways we interacted, how we found ourselves alone on benches, or talking about our hopes as we sat on the grass, or even in his room, in his bed a few times. Maybe this was something all men needed to some degree, intimate friendships with those whom they could share their deepest thoughts, but American society frowned upon such closeness. I allowed my relationship with Richard to develop even though there were times when it felt unbearable to me.

One of my first class assignments that semester was to take a self-portrait, and I set up a tripod in my living room on an early fall day. My hair had gotten long, so I decided to tie part of it back, let the rest fall to my shoulders, and then set the timer. I sat on my couch, rested my hands on the arm, and turned my head toward one of the bay windows. When I presented the image in class, the other students talked about how androgynous it was, the interplay between the sunny window against my only slightly darker outline, how my face was delicate even though I had strong features. I found myself inspired to play with my gender again. After several years of button-downs and slacks, I returned to the aisles of Allston Beat, the garment district, and Filene's Basement, adding translucent, tight, and shiny fabrics to my wardrobe. Ralph didn't seem too intimidated. "I see you're experimenting again," he said when I modeled some of my new outfits for him.

One weekend in October, Ralph was out of town for a conference, so I decided to have a last-minute gender-bending party at our apartment, which felt oddly clandestine because it was the first time my new artist life would spill over into the quiet space I shared with my partner. I replaced our regular bulbs with red lights and picked up some movie posters to put up on the walls—*Rocky Horror, Ma Vie en Rose, The Crying Game*—then put together a mix CD with Boy George, Annie Lennox, and the Pet Shop Boys.

With the combination of snow arriving early that year, the short notice, and the intimidating theme, especially for my MIT friends, only about seven people came to the party, all artists except Richard, who I pestered until he reassured me he would be there even though there was no way I could get him into a dress. He borrowed spandex pants and a shiny gold lamé blouse from me instead, too tight for him to button so he wore it open and, as I suspected, he had a six-pack without even trying. I hadn't seen Richard and Lenora together since the summer, so it was fun to talk and dance, while I took pictures to show for class. For once, I didn't have that nagging feeling that Ralph was waiting for me at home while I was out having fun. People ended up sleeping over that night, a couple of friends on the couch, Lenora next to me on my bed, Richard next to her.

My phone rang while I was working in the lab the following Monday afternoon, and when I saw on caller ID that it was Richard, I figured he just wanted to do lunch.

"Hi, I already ate," I answered.

"There's something I want to talk to you about."

My hand quivered at the dread of what I knew he was about to say, even though the conscious part of my brain still denied it.

"Lenora and I started seeing each other," he continued, and, as if to absolve her: "I was the one who initiated."

An image flashed in my head of the two of them leaving my party together, and my mind picked up from after they were out of my sight, how they probably had brunch somewhere and wanted to continue their bed-sharing from the night before, so they went to the closest apartment—Lenora's—with its red-and-orange flower-print sheets and raw wood floor I knew so well. Then they took off each other's clothes, not the party ones, the ones they changed into before they left, button-down for Richard and that geometric shift for her, and I didn't want to imagine their naked bodies but I did, Lenora getting to experience what I'd fantasized about for months, even though she had expressly said she wouldn't see him because of how I felt, even though that meant she'd considered it, which should have been a sign.

"I need time to think," I told Richard before I hung up.

Instead of doing work, I spent the rest of the afternoon drafting letters with pen and scrap paper for both Richard and Lenora. To him the focus was feeling cut out of the friendship I had built with both of them, how they would leave me out of their intimacy. I was harsher with Lenora, reminding her that she was doing what she explicitly said she wouldn't do, that she was selfish and inconsiderate, that I didn't know if our friendship could recover. I took the train home and started recopying the letters onto stationery, intending to mail them as soon as I was done, when Ralph returned to our apartment.

"Lenora and Richard got together," I told him when he asked what I was doing.

"And you're upset?"

"I'm telling them how I feel," I replied, "about my two best friends cutting me out after Lenora specifically said she wouldn't date him."

"That's not a promise she should have made."

Ralph tried to reason with me. It was impossible for people to control who they fell for, and it wasn't like Richard and I were in a relationship, so there was no real betrayal. I explained that I had introduced them, how I would see so much less of them now that they were together. He said that shouldn't matter, that I should be happy two people I adore had found each other, and it was selfish of me to only focus on my own happiness.

"You don't understand. They're totally wrong for each other."

I saw Ralph's expression freeze, the color drain from his face. "Oh my God you're in love with him."

"I am not in love with him!" I shouted as I stood up and went into the bedroom, slamming the door behind me.

Later, after I cried and, finding myself exhausted, slept for a while, Ralph came into the room and lay in bed with me. As we cuddled, I explained that I really wasn't in love with Richard because it was still him, my partner, who I was in love with. There was no question in my mind that being with Ralph was the best thing that ever happened to me. In his arms, I understood how lucky I was to have him, and regardless of how close Richard and I were, it was unfair of me to limit his or Lenora's chance of finding the same kind of happiness I had with Ralph. After my rush of emotion, I agreed with my partner that I shouldn't send the letters, that I just needed time to adjust to the situation. I had no doubt I loved Ralph, but as I drifted off to sleep, I did wonder if it was possible to be in love with two people.

But even later, past midnight, after I found my eyes open, staring at our high ceiling, barely visible in the dark, I had the sudden realization that in my fantasies of Richard, I had a woman's body when he kissed and made love to me. I'd fantasized about being a woman in bed before, after I'd read books or watched movies where I found myself attracted to the male protagonist, so I didn't notice the moment when, for the first time, I fantasized about being a woman with a man who was real.

I wasn't in love with two people. I was in love *as* two people.

15.

I grew to accept the idea that I loved Ralph and Richard as different people, one as the person I was and the other as the person I could be but wasn't, a twin spirit who lived inside me but had no permanent physical form. I searched for a metaphor that could describe this feeling, and the only one that came close was that story of a man who comes into the hospital complaining of horrible stomach pains, only for doctors to find that there was a hibernating fetus in his stomach, a twin that had suddenly started growing after he had somehow absorbed it in their mother's womb. I read about that story in a Filipino tabloid when I was a kid, and it became one of those curious oddities that lodged itself in my mind. But once I began to consider that there were two spirits living inside me, I wondered if that man with the twin in his belly had any inkling that another spirit lived within him, and what precipitating force awakened this dormant being, what nourishment, that it suddenly decided to grow and threaten the man's life.

Around the same time, I was walking into the Museum School when a student from one of my classes called me over. She was talking to a girl I'd seen around who had an indie rock aesthetic—short black hair artfully chopped up, a cropped leather jacket, and dark eye makeup. It was only when I stood in front of the girl that I noticed she was flat-chested under her fuchsia top.

"Marc, this is Ben," my classmate said with a grin as I tried to contain my surprise.

"I thought you were a girl," I admitted to him.

"I know," he replied. "Everybody does."

Ben turned out to be a performance art major, and I explained how I'd been exploring gender through photography that semester. He asked if I could take pictures of him, and we agreed to meet in my studio the following week.

Once we parted ways, I asked my classmate if Ben always looked that way and she said yes, pretty much, a piece of knowledge I wrestled with. I didn't even know the possibility of Ben existed, someone who challenged the boundary between perception and reality in terms of gender. That dormant memory awakened in me, of walking down the street late at night in a black velvet dress, of being approached by men in a car and pretending to be, no, being a woman to escape. I'd dressed up as a girl, played a girl, been mistaken for a girl since, but Ben gave off the aura of a young woman in public, all the time, a possibility I never considered until I met him.

I knew about transgender women like Christine Jorgensen and Renée Richards, had even seen that trans *Playboy* model interviewed on a talk show, maybe on *Donahue*. But I didn't recognize myself in those women because, apart from being white, they all seemed to deny their past in a way that didn't resonate with me. Meeting Ben was the first time I considered the possibility of exploring what it meant to be perceived as a woman without needing to be one, to embody womanhood without needing to relinquish manhood.

Ben buzzed my studio the following Thursday night.

"Did you get here okay?"

"It was fine," he replied. "I can always take care of myself." I heard a hint of Southern in his husky twang, which made me think of him as a modern version of Blanche DuBois from *A Streetcar Named Desire*.

"I hope no one bothered you," I said as I asked him to stand on a spot while I set up my camera. South Boston was not the safest part of town, and there were a couple of Irish bars between my studio and the T station.

"I got bothered just how I wanted."

I asked him whether he told guys who hit on him that he was a boy, which seemed strange to say, as I looked through my view-finder and was reminded of his impossibly slim, almost prepubescent figure, his doe eyes, his full lips, all enhanced with a healthy dose of makeup.

"I don't pretend to be anything I'm not."

I set up a bright yellow backdrop and began to photograph him; the background complemented the large pink flower he wore in his hair, which in turn matched his bright pink lipstick. Ben told me how men approached him on the street all the time, and he always introduced himself as Ben. If he thought a guy was cute, Ben would invite him to do something together.

"It's fun to turn them," he said into my lens. "You should try it sometime."

Thankfully, I had a medium-format camera where I looked down at the viewfinder to take the picture, so Ben couldn't see my face as I clicked the shutter, which triggered the flash of my studio strobes. If he did, he might have noted the evolution of emotions there as we continued our studio session, him striking pose after pose, while my mind flashed to that Halloween weekend five years before and those men in the car. What Ben conjured was a possibility I had not considered, that I could have approached them, introduced myself, and made them realize I was not the girl they thought I was, but instead of beating me up, they could have still wanted me.

"I've been mistaken for a girl before," I told him when I finished our session and looked up at his face.

"I'm not surprised."

He asked me if someone had taught me how to put on makeup, and I shook my head.

"Wait here."

He left my studio and came back a few minutes later with some foundation that matched my skin, from the CVS on the ground floor of my building. We squeezed into my utilitarian bathroom with its tiny rectangular mirror, and he showed me how to spread the liquid all over my face. He then applied darker powder under my cheeks, my jaw, my forehead, as he explained that this made my face look thinner. Already, I found myself overwhelmed with instructions, so he showed me how to dab eyeshadow just with my pinky finger and how to put on lip gloss, as he puckered and toyed with the wand.

The most I'd ever done was put on lipstick and mascara. But as I watched my face change in Ben's hands, when he drew in my otherwise pale, bleach-blond eyebrows, curled my eyelashes, swept on some blush, I realized that I could be even more feminine and beautiful than I imagined. For the first time since those glimpses in college years before, I saw a physical manifestation of that woman's spirit who lived inside of me, suddenly more powerful because of Ben's makeup.

Seeing that beguiling face, with its sharp, high cheekbones and full lips, the striking contrast between my blue eyes and their almond shape, I realized how much I could actually resemble that archetype of innocent blond beauty I'd read about for so many years, yet also harbor an undefinable, alluring quality due to the mystery of my Asian features set against the fairest skin. A plan also began to form in my mind, a sequence of steps that, if my hunch was correct, could lead to a love that up to that point I had thought impossible.

Maybe I would have been more cautious had I not spent my childhood standing out from everyone else, but after a trip to the makeup store and a few more tutorials, I went into my boss's office one Friday afternoon in late October. I told him I was exploring gender as a project for photography class, and part of my experiment was to dress as a woman all the time. The professor I worked for, Ted Adelson, was a logical man who regularly conducted experiments himself, so he just nodded and wished me luck.

I left his office for the weekend wearing black jeans and a button-down shirt. I dressed for work the following Monday—thankfully, Ralph had already gone to his office—in full makeup and a gray tweed coat I'd bought from a fancy Cambridge shop, fitted on top and flared with several pleats at the bottom, unquestionably feminine. The coat fit me except I had to wear just a blouse underneath, red with a mandala-like pattern, since my shoulders were too broad. I also wore a loose hunter green velvet skirt that reached a couple of inches past my knees, a silhouette I would later learn from a magazine was A-line, my boots knee-high, new terms for someone who learned about womanhood from novels and not *Vogue*.

It was the first time I'd dressed up in women's clothes during the day, except within the safe confines of my undergrad dorm. I half-expected someone to yell, "That's a man!" five minutes after I left my apartment, and I would have aborted the whole experiment. Instead, a woman on the subway complimented my coat. When I entered a crowded bus after work to get to my Museum School art class, a man stood up to offer me a seat and flashed a smile in my direction while I took out a book to avoid his direct gaze.

It shouldn't have surprised me that people thought I was a woman even on that first day; people had been mistaking me for a woman ever since I first wore women's clothes, in large part because they also mistook me for white. Had I still lived in the Philippines where it was obvious to people I was albino, at least before I left, an observer would have noticed that my features were too strong, my shoulders too broad, to be a woman's. Had I been brown and not white, my facial structure and build would have been consistent with an Asian man living in America. But instead, I was read not just as a woman but as a young, attractive blond woman from the start. It turned out my only impediment to manifesting the womanhood that lived inside me was not other people's perceptions but my perception of myself.

Later that night, as I walked the three blocks to the train that would take me home, a man on a bicycle slowed down as he rode past me.

"You're the woman of my dreams!" he yelled, then stopped, and walked his bike as he matched my stride. "Can I get your digits before I end up in an accident?"

I couldn't help but smile, which egged him on even more, but I continued to look ahead without saying anything while he kept asking for my number. He sounded casual, unthreatening if over-eager, with a pronounced Boston accent and wearing some type of sports jersey, I spied out of the corner of my eye. I heard Ben's voice in my head and wanted to be bold like him, introduce myself with a boy's name. But I was not Ben and kept walking until my stop on the aboveground Green Line, as the guy peeled away and shouted, "Your loss!" which left me wondering whether that might be true.

Several men on the street gave me compliments over the next few days, which left me pleased that passing myself off as a woman wasn't nearly as hard as I thought. I saw Richard at the lab, Lenora in the darkroom, and they both told me I looked good. I was still racked with jealousy but simulated a kind of disappointed equanimity, normal for someone who was adjusting to their new situation. But I was relieved that Richard didn't seem perturbed when he saw me, even though we only interacted briefly at a lab meeting.

I came home Friday for dinner and a movie with Ralph on our usual date night, ready to leave as soon as I got home.

"Aren't you going to change?" he asked. I was wearing a stretchy black turtleneck and a long tan skirt.

"Don't you think I look beautiful?" I asked as I twirled around.

"Your face looks strange in makeup."

He'd seen me in makeup before, but I didn't want to argue, so I looked inside my closet to change. I took out a bright purple button-down, and as I went inside the bathroom to take off my makeup, I found myself staring in the mirror for at least a minute and thinking I didn't want to go back to how I usually looked, until I finally turned on the faucet to wash my face.

I wore women's clothes over the next few weeks but found myself needing to get more out of this experiment after I took pictures in front of mirrors all over town. I wanted to probe how other people felt about me as a woman, especially men who were attracted to me. But I wasn't as brave as Ben or as immune to rejection, so I figured the best way for me to find men to go out with as a woman was to look online. This was 2000, when there were no dating apps, not even social media, and I wasn't aware of any chat rooms that catered to men looking to hook up with cross-dressers. But I'd heard that people connected through AOL, so I started an account. AOL ran an online bulletin board with a personals section, and there were other ads of the type I wanted to post.

I'd never placed an online ad before and didn't know what to expect, but I figured there was no harm since my account was anonymous. I found myself typing a single line:

"Cute transvestite, 25, blond/blue, 5'6", 120 lbs., looking for some fun."

There was no way to include a picture with my ad, so I hit submit, turned off my computer, then took a cab home from my studio that night. I didn't have a computer in my apartment, so the next time I checked AOL was when I got to work the following morning, hoping to have at least a few responses to choose from.

At first I thought there was a glitch, when the first set of messages downloaded and the subject lines filled the whole screen. But then another page downloaded, then another, then another. After my email finally stopped downloading, I counted nearly two hundred messages in all, and more kept coming as I began to read.

There were a bunch of single-line emails with a dick pic attached, but also earnest messages that launched into full descriptions of these men's lives, often either prefaced or followed by something along the lines of "I've never done this before but I've been dreaming about it" or, for the veterans, a promise to "treat you like a lady." Nearly all of them asked for a picture and either promised one of their own in exchange or apologized that they couldn't send one out of discretion.

I eliminated the ones who didn't want to send photos since they probably wouldn't agree to be part of my project. I had no idea how to sift through the rest, so I wrote quick, single-line responses to the ones on the first screen who I deemed acceptable and attached a picture of myself that I asked a bystander to take after a night at the club: me leaning against a black wall in high-waisted jeans and a spandex tank top, my arms gathered languidly above my head, the very epitome of cool chick.

Early that evening, I waited until after everyone had left the lab to check email again, where I found dozens more new messages and mused to myself how I was so hard up for sex at eighteen, when I could have easily just put on makeup and slept with as many guys as I wanted. I had to mute the sound on my computer because the

"You've got mail!" announcement kept going off every five minutes when it checked for new messages. In the middle of this chaos, a message popped up on my screen: "I've been waiting for you."

I didn't realize that anyone I responded to could chat with me; I matched the username on the chat window with a message I'd gotten from a guy named Bill, a construction worker in Needham, thirty minutes south of Boston.

"You're very pretty," he continued as he asked me about my life. I told him I was an art student, and the idea of me as a college co-ed made him even more excited. He wanted to meet up that night.

Bill sent over a couple of pictures of himself, a thin man in his forties, with a mustache and a backward baseball cap. Not really my type, but he did have attractively tanned skin, which confirmed his profession and activated my straight, working-class fantasies. He asked me for a naked picture, but I told him I didn't do that, and it turned out I didn't have to. He offered to pick me up, so I gave him my apartment address and told him to meet me in an hour and a half.

"Also I bring my camera with me everywhere," I wrote. "I hope you don't mind if I take pictures."

"As long as you don't mind I have a wife and kids," he replied. It turned out his wife, Barbara, was visiting his in-laws and brought along their two children.

That was how I wound up in a car with a stranger, who drove me to an anonymous house in the suburbs. We stepped out of a dark garage and into an eat-in kitchen, fluorescent-lit, the floor lined with linoleum, a circular wooden table in the middle with a glass top, family pictures sandwiched in between.

Bill closed the door and kissed me for the first time, his tongue meaty and probing, his breath with a trace of cigarettes as his mustache—surprisingly soft—tickled my face. He asked if I minded not going into the bedroom, and I shook my head; it was sweet that as excited as he was, even he had compunctions. One last request: he didn't have time to bathe before he picked me up, so he told me to make myself comfortable in the living room while he hopped in the shower.

That was when I ended up alone in Bill's living room. I took off my clothes down to my black panties and a negligee top, sheer except for a row of three black velvet hearts that ran across the chest, covering my nipples until I raised my arms. I picked up my camera and stood in front of a large gold-framed mirror hung on one of the walls, with fading family pictures wedged between the glass and the frame.

I looked through the viewfinder and took pictures of myself, making sure to keep those family photographs in the frame—a kid's birthday party, Bill and Barbara sitting on a boat, even one from their wedding, which looked like it had happened in the '70s, Bill with a full head of dark wavy hair while Barbara, a pretty brunette, wore a long-sleeved white gown whose train extended several rungs below the top of the church steps they were standing on. I felt a pang then, my conscience, but the collective voices of my photo professors drowned it out, with stories of how Diane Arbus woke subjects up at sunrise to get them at their most vulnerable, how Nan Goldin took out the doors to her bathroom so she could take pictures of people having sex or doing drugs, and how the French artist Sophie Calle even worked as a maid at a hotel just to take pictures of guests' private belongings. Art had a looser set of ethics than life, which gave me permission to take advantage of this moment to highlight the contrast between this man's family, the sanctity of his marriage, the place of his wife, and what the two of us were about to do, who I was about to be.

Bill emerged from the bedroom naked except for that backward baseball cap, which must be covering a balding head, and I found his self-consciousness endearing. He turned off the overhead light, and under the lone lamp next to his brown corduroy sofa, he took off my clothes and beheld my body with wonder in his face. I felt beautiful then, just as I was, as he proceeded to take my penis into his mouth. That duality didn't intimidate me, but I did close my eyes to feel instead of see, no images in my mind except for the dark ache of pleasure. When we reversed positions and he closed his eyes, I wondered what images of me blurred together in his mind.

Bill let me take pictures after as he lay sideways on his own couch, relaxed and trusting. I wondered how aware he was that his naked image, his languid eyes alluding to the aftermath of coitus, could someday end up in a gallery or a magazine. Maybe he figured he was far enough away from my world that no eyes he cared about would ever see him exhibited.

"You're the perfect first experience," he said as he dropped me off outside my apartment. "You're you, but you're also more beautiful than any woman I've been with."

I spent hours turning Bill's words over in my mind, as I continued to have more dalliances with a seemingly endless stream of men I met online, who became both the subjects of my photographs and instruments through which to gauge my womanhood. If I were more beautiful than any woman he'd ever been with, I wondered if this made me a woman in his mind. Where did my manhood end and my womanhood begin? These were questions that drove my subsequent dates, where I compulsively took pictures of myself and those men, but also asked bystanders to take pictures of us together, as I began to insist that I needed to see guys in public, so I could figure out whether I looked like any woman in pictures with them. I also asked the men themselves to take pictures of me, asked them to pose me how they wanted so I could understand the angles and mannerisms they found desirable. Though we chatted online, Bill and I never did get together again after his wife came back into town.

I kept the sordid details of these excursions from Ralph, but he was aware of their outlines and noticed the ramp-up in the sexiness of my outfits. While he tolerated seeing me in makeup and women's clothes, and we even went out in public that way, he wanted me to appear as a man if we were seeing people he knew. I agreed to lay off the makeup when we went to Ovid, New York, an upstate town where Ralph's grad school friend Chris lived with his partner, Joe, in a big farmhouse, along with several polydactyl cats who jumped and clung to the screen door whenever they wanted to get back in the house. It was a wonderfully cozy time, the landscape white as far as the eye could see, hearty dinner by the fire with chosen family. I was once again reminded of what that quiet, settled life could be like, and how a part of me wanted that with Ralph.

But my fantasies began to fill again as we made our way back to Boston, not just the men but the new choices, the daily mundane discoveries, whether conversations in women's rooms or taking dance classes as a woman and not being criticized for being too feminine, then going to the bars at night and getting drinks for free. It was as if an entire world that had been kept from me was suddenly available, and all I needed to do was modify how I looked.

Though what I couldn't explain, even to myself, was how

increasingly intolerable I found the idea of presenting myself as a man, which began to feel like withholding the best parts of me. Not only was I uglier as a man, but I was also more nerdy and a lot less fun. Being a woman gave me access to an entire gamut of behaviors I never knew were inside me, from my breezy manner to the way I toyed with men who underestimated me, baited them by pretending I was just a dumb blonde and then asking them leading questions about French literature or evolutionary biology.

The week after we got back from Thanksgiving, the graduate students in Ralph's department organized a holiday party in someone's apartment, and the two of us planned to go.

"I hope you dress appropriately," Ralph told me over the phone before he got home.

I knew what he meant—dress as a man—but I hoped to mollify him by wearing something elegant, a black silk blouse and pencil skirt with a rose tastefully embroidered near the hem. I wore my long hair down with just eyeliner and red lipstick that had a golden sheen.

Ralph didn't say anything when he got home from work and asked if I was ready to go. We started down the brick sidewalk of Dartmouth Street that led to the Back Bay T station, but he was walking too fast, and I asked him to slow down because I was wearing heels.

"I don't understand why you had to dress like that," he said ahead of me.

"You really need to be more tolerant," I replied as I tried to catch him, when, without warning, he wheeled around to face me, his face ugly and gnarled in the near-darkness of early evening.

"This is a fucking curse!" he shouted.

I'd never seen Ralph angry; we'd never fought before. His voice, the expression on his face, left me so shocked I couldn't move. The stripped branches of the trees above us suddenly felt like arms that threatened to strangle me.

"Oh my God, I'm sorry," he said. He regained his composure and took my hand; it was only then that I could take a breath.

I tried to mentally prepare myself for our next public outing with his friends, and even told him I would dress as a boy. Another childhood schoolmate of his, the tenor Ian Bostridge, was making his Carnegie Hall debut, and Ian wanted us to join some of his friends for dinner at a restaurant afterward. Ralph reasoned that since we'd met Ian and his wife, Lucasta, in London, it would be too confusing for them to see me as a girl. I also didn't want anything to distract Ian from his big night.

We took the train to New York, me in makeup and a black blouse with a pattern of tiny pink roses, a string of raw pearls around my neck. Traveling with Ralph that way felt like our compromise, that I could dress how I wanted until it was time to see Ian in concert. I tried to register the world through his eyes as we got our train tickets, had lunch at a restaurant near Lincoln Center, checked in to our room, service people treating us in subtle and not-so-subtle ways like a straight couple, whether in solicitous smiles we hadn't gotten before or Ralph automatically receiving the check. This must have been such an affront to his sense of identity, what he'd had to overcome to come out in the '80s as someone from a well-known English family, only to be mistaken for straight when he was with his partner and feel as if he was back in the closet again. Though he also had to deal with always wondering if people perceived me as a cross-dresser, which came with its own complications. As much as Ralph tried to be tolerant of all queer people, he had still been raised in respectable British society, and a man flaunting his love of cross-dressing must have violated his sense of propriety. But it also began to dawn on me that, just as other people treated me like a totally different person when they perceived me as a woman, Ralph too began to think of me that way the more feminine I became, and that meant he didn't see the person he fell in love with when he looked at me.

I tried to keep all this in mind as I faced the mirror to take off my makeup, an hour and a half before Ian's concert. It seemed like a simple thing to do, as I held a wet wipe in my hand. I'd had no compunctions about going out into the world as a man just three months before. Yet facing that mirror felt like one of those fairy tales where an innocent girl is awakened to her captivating beauty. Once that power had been uncovered, it seemed cruel to lock it up against my will.

"Can't I just keep a little bit of makeup on?" I asked from the bathroom.

"You promised," Ralph replied, somehow both plaintive and stern, and I found myself coming back to the bedroom to face him.

"But why is this so important to you?"

"Why is it so important to *you*?"

"I don't know," I said as I shook my head and began to cry. "It just is."

I went back to the mirror and began to take off my makeup, at first slowly and then faster and faster, taking hard, scratching swipes, only vaguely aware that I was hurting myself, the pain in my eye as I gouged against its socket a relief compared to the much greater pain, from somewhere much deeper than my skin. I didn't notice I was sobbing, almost moaning, until Ralph came into the bathroom and took the wipe away from my hand, hugged me close, and didn't let go until my sobs diminished, then stopped.

"I won't ask you to take off your makeup again," he said.

I loved him then more than ever, more than I was capable of loving anyone, but I couldn't be the man he needed me to be.

16.

Ralph's words stayed with me, that whatever I was going through was a curse. Certainly, I didn't always feel that the woman's voice inside of me was benevolent. Released after a lifetime of hibernation, she could be selfish and rapacious, able to justify any action through the sheer enormity of her desires. I often felt as if I was in a trance, heeding no call except that beguiling woman who stared at me from the other side of the mirror whenever I put on makeup, my transformation something out of alchemy, the stuff of myth. Maybe she was a siren, yet I was afraid to think of her that way because I knew that sirens led seafarers astray. Or maybe she was a goddess, because it did seem as if she demanded daily offerings in the form of cosmetic ornamentation, the glint of jewelry, the luster and color of clothes, amassed through the generous resources of a partner who despised her. She also required constant confirmation of her beauty, through the parade of men she dallied with online and the ones she enticed at clubs but never went home with, so they wouldn't know that this spirit did not entirely match the earthly body she inhabited.

Whatever was left of me who was not her found myself helpless to counter her demands, as I continued to ignore Ralph's feelings—despite my love for him—just to heed her.

Ralph was not the only person whose emotions I cast aside. Once I started dressing as a woman, and as I confirmed my beauty through my encounters with men, I developed a plan to take Richard away from Lenora and make him mine. I convinced myself that Richard and I would make the better couple, because we had so much more in common, as logically driven spirits who yearned for creativity. I convinced myself that while Richard became attracted to Lenora because of her emotionally driven nature, there was no way their relationship could sustain itself in the long run. And besides, I reasoned, while I pored through images of myself, I was more beautiful than she would ever be.

This was how I was able to remain friends with Lenora, as we began to see each other again, through the conviction that Richard would be mine in the end. Lenora was unfailingly supportive as my appearance shifted, giving me pointers about how to live as a woman in the world, because while I passed almost all the time, there were still people who could detect that I wasn't like other girls.

I once went to a party with Lenora at an art school friend's loft, during that early period when I only started wearing women's clothes. We walked into a large, open room painted dark gray with a pool table in the middle and a few dozen people, skinny guys in skinny jeans and pretty girls who seemed to hover around them, as one of the guys who was Lenora's friend said hi to us. The party felt straight in a way that made me uneasy.

"Let's just stay for a little while," Lenora said.

I told her I'd circulate while she played a game of pool. I walked over to the kitchen, tried to join a couple of conversations that fizzled out, so I decided to go back to the living room to check on Lenora, but she found me first before I got there. Her brow was furrowed, her mouth clenched into a hard pout.

"We should go," she said.

Lenora didn't make eye contact with anyone as we walked through the now-crowded party. I spied her friend near the door as we left, but he only eyed me then turned back to his conversation and didn't acknowledge her at all, while I heard mumbles and whispers as we exited.

"What happened?" I asked when we got outside.

Lenora explained that as she was playing pool, her friend started asking about me. Apparently, I looked familiar from a party of hers he'd gone to, but I looked different then. Lenora said he must be confusing me with someone else as she signaled with her eyes for him to stop talking, but he wouldn't.

"I'll spare you the details, but he was a jerk," Lenora said. "We're not friends anymore."

Her loyalty touched me, the way she remained resolute in her friendship through the radical change in my appearance, when she must have known even before I said it out loud that this wasn't just an experiment, what was happening to me. When I got home from that party, it was Ralph who was waiting for me at home, who made good on his promise never to ask me to take off my makeup again.

Yet late at night, in the darkness of my fantasies, it was Richard's face I saw, and her voice that ruled, that woman inside me. Never mind that I had someone to love who loved me back, never mind that the man I coveted was with my best friend. *They shouldn't be together*, that voice commanded. But what about Ralph? *You can't be with him as the woman you're meant to be.* I tried to quiet that voice, but it only grew louder, like that dormant twin who, once awakened, needed to exert herself all the more, even if it threatened the life of her sibling and host. *You've had your chance to live in the world*, the beautiful woman inside me seemed to say. *Now it's my turn.*

No one was aware of these thoughts—not Ralph, or Lenora, or Richard. There were many moments when I doubted myself in Richard's presence, reasoned with the voice inside me. It was impossible that a straight man would fall for me, having known me for so long as a man, I told her.

But look how beautiful you are, the voice said. It was true that in the less than three months since I began to dress as a girl, men paid attention to me wherever I went. I couldn't be in public for long without being approached, and I allowed myself to flirt, to accept drinks, to dance with these men, but refused to go home with them because of what they would discover. It was during these moments of thwarted desire that I began to ask myself whether it would be better to have a vagina instead of a penis.

It would be better to have a vagina with Richard, I found myself thinking one day. I had been too delirious to think beyond figuring out how to be with him, how to share his bed. With Ralph there was always talk about the future, that we would get married once that institution became legal for us, that we might eventually settle in England. With Richard there was only the present, as if the fever of love allowed me to only see what was just ahead, with everything else enveloped in fog. But if I had a vagina, then Richard and I could have a real life together.

From the beginning, I searched for signs. Unlike some people at MIT, who were polite but shied away from me as soon as I changed, Richard did not keep his distance. If anything, he went out of his way to see more of me, dropped by at the lab more often just to say hi, invited me to gallery openings and grad student parties.

He came by the lab one afternoon in January, after he got back into town from winter break. I was about to leave to drop off some film at ZONA, the photo lab near his house, so he offered to walk with me as we took the elevator down the building and into the chilly dusk.

We'd taken this walk many times before, around the building to a paved path facing a green field, except this time I was in heeled leather boots instead of sneakers. Richard offered his arm and gave me support as we walked along. I realized that this physical connection was an extension of what was already a specific intimacy between us, one he didn't have with other men even before I started wearing women's clothes. We'd always confided in each other, hung out just the two of us. Without ever having any need for it, I'd always felt his protection, his greater physical strength. It wasn't just that I felt like a woman with Richard, it was that even before I did anything with my appearance, he treated me more like a woman friend than a male buddy.

Like we'd grown accustomed to, Richard and I stopped at the first bench to sit and talk, on the mouth of the path that led to the photo lab and his apartment. The bench looked out onto a field and then a building made of granite in strict parallel lines, unlike the two denuded oak trees that flanked us, their branches eerie and menacing. I suddenly recalled those trees from *Dead Poets Society*, the ones that Neil stared at as he contemplated a future he couldn't have. It was an omen I tried to shut out of my mind.

"How are things?" Richard asked.

"Not too bad," I replied. I told him the gender experiment was going well, that I was learning a lot about myself, while I wondered what Richard might be thinking as I spoke. Surely he must be aware of his involvement in this experiment, that so much of the reason I started to dress this way was to see how he would respond. But I also supposed that in his mind, I'd already been playing with gender before I started doing it all the time, that unless he was living my life, the distinction between what I was doing before compared to what he saw in front of him wasn't particularly great.

"It looks like I'll be dressing as a woman for a while," I said.

"I'll be sticking with what I'm doing for a while too." For a second I thought he meant his relationship with Lenora, before he continued: "I'm staying in science."

"I'm glad."

"It's cold," he said, as he crossed his arms and hugged himself, brushed his hands against his wool navy peacoat, the one he always wore in winter, which had a nautical air that reminded me of his sailor days. I expected him to stand up, but instead he unfolded his arms and turned toward me. I slid through the space between us and leaned my head against his shoulder, smelled his past in the wool of his coat, his present in the skin of his neck.

We stayed just like that, as darkness settled around us.

Olafur Eliasson was exactly the kind of artist Richard liked, someone who worked outdoors with elemental materials like earth and light. As soon as I heard he was having an exhibition at the Institute of Contemporary Art, I knew it was the right place and time.

I invited Richard to the opening reception when he visited me in the lab. I was afraid he would want to come with Lenora—she'd be interested in the show too—but he respected something unspoken, that I wasn't ready for all of us to hang out together. He agreed to pick me up at my studio early Saturday evening, where we would take a cab to the show.

For the rest of the week, the voice inside my head insisted that I had to be as beautiful as possible. I sifted through the racks at Filene's Basement after work one evening and found a shimmering gray velvet gown, spaghetti-strapped and encrusted with rhinestones. I also went online and found the most recent Best of Boston winners for best hair and best makeup, then booked appointments at two separate salons.

When I went in to get my hair done early Saturday afternoon, I told the stylist I wanted to look elegant, so she suggested keeping my length—my light blond hair had grown an inch below my shoulders— and just trimming the ends before doing it in an updo. After the trim, she spent the next hour teasing my hair to a volume I didn't think possible, curled it into ringlets, then scaffolded the hairdo with what seemed like an entire container of hairspray and at least a hundred bobby pins. This was followed by a trip to another salon, where I had my makeup done professionally for the first time. The makeup artist was not pleased with my bushy eyebrows and told me I should really wax them even though they were the lightest shade of blond. Nonetheless, she deigned to cover the errant hairs with powder and draw thin, defined lines with pencil before she sent me on my way.

Later that evening, Richard was shocked when I opened my studio door. He had come directly from the lab—scientists were prone to working even on Saturdays—and was wearing his standard button-down, corduroy pants, and hiking boots uniform, all green and brown as if he were in camouflage.

"I forgot to tell you I was dressing up," I said, and realizing I needed a plausible reason for being so fancy, "I figured it would be good to take pictures there."

Richard seemed to accept this explanation and picked up my camera bag.

"I'm your photographer for the night."

We hailed a cab to the ICA, which took up an entire historic building in downtown Boston, its exterior hard to make out because of my poor distance vision and the blinding lights shining through the gallery windows, the biggest rectangle of brightness at the end of some stone steps that led us to the door.

"May I take your coat, madam?" a solicitous attendant in a tuxedo shirt and bow tie asked as he greeted me, and the way he said "madam," combined with his awestruck, enthusiastic expression, confirmed what I already suspected when Richard showed up at my studio, that I had made a grave error. In my desire to make myself beautiful, I failed to account for the possibility of coming to this opening grossly overdressed, as the people around me wore cocktail attire while my gown and updo were fit for some gala, or maybe the Oscars. Worse, and what made me wince at the attendant's attention, was that the one type of person who would wear an embellished gown with thick makeup and the most theatrical hairstyle to an early-evening reception was a drag queen, a role I was even more appropriate for in my four-inch heels. This was supposed to be the occasion when I would show Richard I could be a beautiful woman, but instead my outfit exposed me as a man in women's clothes.

I wanted to turn around and tell Richard I suddenly didn't feel well so we should go. But he stood beside me as I spied his understanding face, his continued readiness to escort me through this misadventure. I'd been a performer my entire life, and this was just going to be another turn, as I felt myself put on the armor of confidence that had gotten me through the worst of times.

Somehow, what rang in my head as we crossed the main reception floor was one particular ballet teacher's instructions, to look out into the horizon as I danced, as if I were an ethereal creature who merely acquiesced to walk among mortals. I noticed stares and whispers from some guests holding champagne glasses, mostly women who looked either young professional or matronly. Among their faces, in which I noticed only looks of admiration and delight, I realized that if I remained insouciant, maybe it wouldn't be such a disaster after all, and that it might only be that knowing attendant who became aware of my secret. Besides, Richard was the perfect prop. Despite being underdressed, he still conveyed the aura of a masculine, handsome, and normal heterosexual man, so having him on my arm was like a stamp that authenticated my womanhood. I began to pay less attention to myself and more attention to the art.

Richard and I toured the exhibition for the next hour while he took pictures of me. It was a captivating environment to photograph in; so many of the pieces played with reflection and light, including an entire floor that reminded me of a dock, light reflecting against undulating water while viewers observed from a platform made of wooden planks. Richard and I spent a lot of time in a circular room with a rotating contraption in the middle that emitted a stream of light, which widened and narrowed, lengthened and contracted, as it continuously revolved around the space, white in the center while its wavelengths broke up into subtle rainbow colors at the edges. Richard told me to stand still as he posed me in profile to take a picture of me while the light sped through my face, and when he was done, I asked for the camera to take his. I took several frames trying to imagine the complement of the picture he had taken of me, Richard in profile except facing the other direction. He felt self-conscious after a few shots, so he turned to me and told me he was done, as I clicked my shutter one last time while he smiled.

I spied the attendant a couple of times during the reception, and once, when he offered me a glass of champagne, he had on such a conspiratorial look that I couldn't help but try to read his mind. He was queer, clearly, soft in both manner and body, his cheeks mildly flushed. It seemed like he got a vicarious thrill from this secret we shared, something the rest of the room didn't know about. I wondered whether he thought Richard knew, and if the attendant thought he didn't, whether that was part of the conspiracy in his mind, that we were toying with this straight man together. Because it seemed to me like that was how he saw me, someone pretending, maybe because he saw himself in me and, like I began with Ben, that was how his feeling of connection must have started. But even as I smiled back at that attendant, a nascent part of me already knew that the line between pretend and real had grown porous for me, especially with Richard by my side. The two of us planned to have dinner afterward, but I asked

Richard if it would be all right for us to go back to my studio first so I could take pictures there.

When we returned to the loft, I turned on the track lights that illuminated a brown leather couch and chair dividing the darkroom area and the shooting space. I sat on the couch and hoped Richard would sit next to me, but he sat on the chair instead, as we talked about the show, other exhibitions we'd recently seen, and art in general.

"The pictures are going to be beautiful," he said. It was the closest he'd come to complimenting how I looked, which gave me courage to say the hardest words.

"I wanted to be beautiful for you."

It took him a few seconds—too long—to respond. "I don't understand."

"I wanted you to see me as a woman because I love you."

His face expressed a mixture of emotions—puzzlement, concern, but not joy, and yet joy was not something I expected. I knew that it would take effort to get Richard to understand that we were meant to be together.

"You know I can't—"

"We're so much better for each other," I insisted. I went over the history of our friendship, how the two of us could talk about anything, how our emotional and intellectual sides were well balanced. What I left unspoken, what I'd tried to communicate through the effort I'd taken, was that I was more beautiful than Lenora, so he wouldn't have to feel like he would need to make that particular sacrifice to be with me. "I know you feel it too when we're alone together."

"You and Ralph seem so in love," he replied. "That's why I

thought it was safe. If I had known you'd have these feelings I would have never gotten this close. I'm not attracted to you that way."

"I don't believe you."

"I'm not attracted to men."

"I'll be a woman for you." It was the first time I'd considered permanently shifting genders out loud, but my words felt right. I explained to him, as well as I could, that being with him made me realize how much the woman in me needed to emerge, that my love for him brought her into being. The physical manifestation of that spirit was secondary. "I can take hormones and have surgery."

Richard silently absorbed everything I had to say, didn't betray any antipathy or disgust.

"I want to have children with my wife someday," he said.

I found myself with no response. It was the most obvious argument I should have prepared for, but hadn't. Maybe it was because I didn't have enough faith in myself, to allow my love and imagination to reach their full breadth. It would be more than a decade before I learned that among my own indigenous ancestors, select male-bodied people who lived their lives as women were held in high esteem and found themselves husbands, in domestic life treated identically as other women. Had I known this, maybe I would have advised Richard to use his imagination, to consider that we could adopt, tell him his desire for creativity should extend to the way he led his life.

"You should probably go," I said instead, and nodded when he asked if I'd be okay.

I didn't notice that I was weeping until he left. In my sadness, I turned to the only thing I've been able to depend on my entire life—my work. I set up my studio camera, put a stool in front of a cobalt blue backdrop, and took a roll of photographs while wondering, having now failed, whether this was the end of my experiment with gender.

I spent the next few days in a stupor of emotion, having no one to talk to about what happened between me and Richard. Apart from being brokenhearted, my actions were disloyal to Ralph and Lenora, my partner and my best friend, the only two people to whom I could have possibly confided something so shameful. Maybe I could have sought Ben out, but I knew he would have just told me to move on, as if it was the easiest thing in the world when, knowing myself and the permanence of my love for Samuel, I would always experience my feelings for Richard as a dull ache.

Though it wasn't just Richard; the whole idea of expressing my womanhood suddenly seemed both pointless and exhausting. I went back to work in women's clothes and makeup the following Monday, thankful that Richard and I no longer worked in the same lab, while I tried to figure out if I could make it through the world as a woman, knowing I was probably giving up on love, especially the kind I had with Ralph. Richard's rejection, and the need to evaluate my entire life it spurred on, allowed me to confront the real possibility that Ralph and I could not continue as a couple if my gender shift became in any way permanent, whether or not I started hormones or even had surgery, a move that would definitely end our relationship. Just like with Richard and his assertion that whoever he ended up with needed to beget children, I didn't really challenge Ralph's refusal to accept me as his lover when I presented myself as a woman. I couldn't picture myself as a woman with him either, my twin spirit unable to perceive him as the person my male self held so dear.

Thankfully, I had work to distract me and keep me company, even if that work also reminded me of the previous weekend's sorrow, as I went to the darkroom and began printing images from the opening after I left the lab the following Monday. Class wasn't until the following night, but I wanted to print around people I didn't know, and especially wanted to print away from Lenora.

My urge was to print an image from my studio after Richard had left, knowing it would probably be the most revealing. I looked through the contact sheet and passed over what I saw as insincere attempts to communicate my sadness—forced expressions, a hand on my face—and decided on the last image I shot that night, just me staring into the camera, my eyes wide and mouth slightly open, shoulders slumped, shocked and exhausted.

Unlike the black-and-white darkrooms bathed in red light from movies, color paper cannot be exposed to light at all, so color printing has to be done in total darkness. As I began the process of making the best print out of the negative that depicted my heartache, I found that lack of illumination soothing, the method of turning life into art a panacea for the disarray I was experiencing. The physical process of adjusting exposure and color knobs, of setting my easel and feeding my print into the giant processing machine, this all induced a meditative state that allowed me to contemplate my future, while the various imperfect versions of that print became my talisman.

There was a part of me that wanted this image to be the last I would take of myself as a woman, the conclusion of my experiment.

I didn't want to further jeopardize my relationship and, having lived for so long without needing to be a woman, I figured I could get used to once again wearing makeup and women's clothes only as a costume. Looking at that image, I saw how much work it took to express this womanhood, all that effort and ornamentation. As I contemplated my flat chest in the picture, I also wondered whether I wanted my body to change and how long that would take, having learned online that trans women—because that was what I would be, or maybe already was, a trans woman—needed to be in therapy for at least eighteen months before even being allowed to go on hormones, because psychiatrists classified what was happening to me as a mental illness that needed careful evaluation.

I wondered if it was an illness, since it did seem to run against my best interests. Wasn't that what sickness was? When a foreign entity invades your system so that you're worse off than you were before, even though it seemed impossible to evaluate my life according to two simple sides, better or worse. Nonetheless, it was hard to disagree that my life would be so much worse without Ralph, especially when I couldn't be with Richard.

These thoughts were circling my mind when I noticed my friend Max from photo class, waiting for a print to come out of the processor. I went over to say hi.

"I've been here for a while, but you didn't notice me," he said.

Max was a stout Italian man who was pursuing commercial photography as a post-retirement career. When I mentioned the week before that I was getting professionally done up for an event, he asked if he could stop by the salon and take pictures while I was getting my makeup done, since he wanted to build a fashion portfolio. I'd been so preoccupied with Richard that I'd forgotten.

"I got a great shot. I hope you like it."

He handed me the print after he pulled it out of the processor. He'd taken the picture in the giant mirror that spanned an entire wall of the salon, its edges out of frame, so it didn't seem like a mirror at first, except the back of my head was visible and out of focus on the bottom left edge of the vertical image. At the center was just half my face, and I was confused at first, until I realized I was looking at a second mirror in rapt concentration, and the border of that mirror covered the rest of my head, except outside the mirror frame were the top and side of my face, just the very edge, and my grand pile of blond curls. As if the intentional accident that brought these visual elements together wasn't enough, there in the far background, in the upper-left corner, was a famous makeup book called *Making Faces*, its cover a gorgeous woman's made-up features—her red lips, blue eyes, arched eyebrows, and rouged cheeks—the rest of her face entirely white, its edges out of the frame. It was as if the picture was inviting me to compare my features to that ideal woman on the cover.

"You can keep it," Max said as he walked away.

I went back to my private darkroom, closed the door, put away my photo paper, and turned on the overhead light so I could examine the photograph alone. That image felt like a Magritte painting, its surreal elements designed to reveal the viewer's unconscious. I remembered the moment the picture was taken, as I sat on a soft cushion in front of that mirror examining the details of my face and marveling how a professional had made it even more beautiful. But what my memory hadn't captured in living that moment, rather than looking at that single frame, was precisely how beautiful I was.

Because I was looking at one of the most beautiful faces I'd ever seen, even if I could only see half of her. That face belonged to me. From deep inside, her voice emerged again, to ask whether I was really willing to smother her, that beautiful woman, and let her die. She might be in pieces now, parts of her still unknown, the world she inhabited a confusing hall of mirrors. But it was up to me to cross that bridge of light and make her whole, with whatever I had, to endure any sacrifice so that her spirit could finally live in this world without condition.

I had a vision of my future then. I would call myself by a different name, one I have yet to determine. I would use chemicals to alter my body and eventually have surgery. I would endure the judgment of society, the loss of friends and loved ones. I would lose the person I love most, so I could love myself better. I would do whatever it took, so that I could finally see the whole of that most beautiful face.

17.

"This is how I came to love my vagina," I recited, pretending to read from the page even though I'd already memorized most of the monologue, but didn't want to seem overeager. My chair was too low, so my elbows felt unnatural against the gray laminate table, shiny compared to the dull, also-gray walls of that nondescript MIT seminar room, where I sat in front of half a dozen undergrad women in hoodies and nerd-joke shirts. Though nothing felt natural about auditioning for *The Vagina Monologues* without a vagina in October 2001, nine months after that ill-fated night with Richard that nonetheless led me here.

It was coincidence that they asked me to read the monologue I happened to have learned. "Because He Liked to Look at It" was about a woman who hated how her vagina looked until she found a guy who adored it. When I read the piece, I began to think of my own genitals not as a man's body part but as an unusual vagina that only needed to be appreciated.

"Why do you want to be in the show?" one of the producers asked after I finished reading.

I expected something more like "Thank you, we'll be in touch."

Taken aback, I contemplated an impersonal answer, something about the power of theatre or my belief in women's rights.

"I'm transgendered," I said instead. "I was raised as a boy, but I discovered that I'm actually a woman. Except I don't know exactly what that means. I figure doing the play would help me find out."

It was the first time I'd come out to a group of strangers. Walking across MIT's concrete-dominated campus back to my office, I realized this was something I would have to do over and over. Just as being me had always meant informing people I wasn't white, I would also need to tell them I didn't grow up a girl.

From the discussions I was having with other trans women online, I became aware that my position wasn't typical. In the most popular chat room for trans people, TGForum, passing was the ultimate goal, and as soon as passing was achieved, it was assumed that people wouldn't tell anyone they're trans. After all, if your goal was to be a woman, then it didn't matter how you got there.

This philosophy didn't sit well with me, and I told people in the chat room that I planned to be out even though I passed, because I wasn't ashamed of my history. A lot of the girls there took that as judgment of their choices, which left me isolated even among trans people. But I couldn't help feeling that withholding my history not only implied I was ashamed of it but also sacrificed too much of myself and my life. It was never a question for me that I would come out if I were to do *Vagina Monologues*, but I'd assumed I would do it if I were cast, focused as I'd been for so long on challenging people's assumptions, getting into spaces based on mistaken perceptions of me then using those occasions to rebel.

But auditioning was enough. Stage lights thrilled me the way they always did, but I was coming to realize that being trans—in a way that was even more magnified than anything I'd experienced before—felt as though I was onstage under glaring lights all the time. Every day, every moment I was in public felt as though I was under scrutiny, how any second someone would recognize I wasn't real and banish me. But one thing I knew well, had known my whole life, was that the key to playing a part convincingly was to believe in yourself, even if that belief was something you needed to fake. By the time I auditioned, I was well on my way to knowing I was a woman rather than just playing one, as Ralph and I had parted the previous June so I could figure out who I was without him, after many days of anguished tears on both sides. When those producers shone the light of their perceptions onto me, I refused to blink, even when I was not the kind of woman they were expecting.

This was the same confidence I armored myself with when a friend drove me to a DMV in Natick—the one I'd heard through the grapevine was liberal—and changed my name on my state ID, switched the letter of my gender to F. It was the same confidence that brought me to a well-known therapist in the field, Dr. David Seil, where I combined my impeccable appearance in a stately summer dress with insistent arguments against the standard procedure of therapy for at least eighteen months before hormones could be prescribed. I reminded this therapist that mainstream mental health professionals had also treated homosexuality as a disease until at least the '70s, that I had no prior history of mental illness, that denying me hormones amounted to saying that I was incapable of making sound decisions about my own body, despite graduating from an elite school and working for another. I did not expect him to acquiesce so easily, prescribe me hormones without requiring therapy, until I read his approval letter where he attested that I "appeared to be an attractive woman," and realized that without my impressive performance as my new gender, without the face and body that mimicked a blond white woman's, I could very well have been denied the right to choose the future of that body, regardless of my state of mind.

But in the months after I started taking hormones, I also had to wrestle with whether I wanted to have reassignment surgery, which felt drastic not because of the specific procedure but simply the prospect of a major operation, to change a body part I didn't have significant psychological issues with. It was clear to me that my concerns about my body didn't stem from some paralyzing dysphoria that only surgery could fix, but from the simple reality that my genitals were the main reason why other people judged me unacceptable and why the government refused to fully acknowledge my womanhood. Having surgery just to appease others felt too much like surrender, though there were times when surrender felt like the right thing to do.

I was in the lab one afternoon a few days later when one of the producers sent me an email informing me I'd been cast; my body's power to persuade had worked again. I figured if I had any doubts about a surgery that would sever my ties to my old gender irrevocably, being around women for several months would help me decide.

The first night of rehearsal, I walked from my office at the northeast side of campus, through the main building with its seemingly endless corridor, passing student upon student in unkempt jeans and hoodies. I'd worked at MIT for three years and hardly interacted with undergrads there, except for the couple of research assistants who came through our lab. As I found my way to the spacious rehearsal room with its shiny tile floors and MIT-gray walls, looking around at a group of young women who less than a year before belonged to a gender I wasn't a part of, I suddenly wondered what it would have been like to go through college as a woman and immediately felt as though I would have been less lonely and isolated.

Although the cast performed monologues and so didn't interact with one another during the play, the director, Ruth—who in her placid smile and always-ready hug managed to be motherly as a college sophomore—wanted the experience not just to be about putting on a performance but for this group of twenty MIT women to bond and share experiences together. So as we spent the next three hours discussing our motivations for being in the show, each cast member taking a turn to stand in front of our semicircle as we sat on the floor, it was clear that my sense of belonging would have come with challenges I didn't have to face as a young man. I learned about how difficult it was to grow up smart but for the world to see you as valuable only if you looked beautiful. I learned about trying to live up to an ideal of attractiveness but being beset with obstacles as soon as you approached it, how the prettier you are, the less you're taken seriously, how you become more vulnerable to harassment or rape. I suddenly flashed back to the summer I spent in England at nineteen and how much freedom I felt, how often I wandered out of clubs and onto the street in the wee hours, oblivious to danger. I realized how different that summer could have gone had I been a different gender, how I would have needed to be much more alert. My great adventure would have been compromised, and yet that compromise suddenly felt like an unavoidable part of life as a woman.

When someone in the group told the story of a friend being given the choice of whether to be raped or killed, I remembered when a group of men started running after me outside my studio in South Boston, after one of them approached me on the street then realized I might be a man. He threatened me because he had anticipated a chance to have sex and was denied. He wanted to exert his power over me whatever way he could. This was what I began to feel whenever a man approached me in public, and kept insisting when I wasn't interested, that the guy would try to overpower me if I found myself alone with him, only to be humiliated or worse if he found out I was trans. Hearing these stories in that rehearsal room that somehow felt more cramped than when I first entered, I came to know that what I went through as a trans woman was not fundamentally different from what they'd been going through their entire lives.

It was simple enough to absorb these lessons within the confines of that room, so much harder outside. The following weekend, I went out clubbing at Liquid with Lenora, who had recently broken up with Richard. She didn't seem to resent me for going behind her back, maybe because she still felt guilty for dating Richard in the first place, when she knew I had feelings for him. Now we were suddenly two single women out for a night on the town.

The great thing about Liquid, apart from the freedom I had to dress in whatever gender, was that all sexualities were welcome there. As I moved through my transition while clubbing almost every weekend, it was as if each pulse of Liquid's flashing disco lights shifted me away from the gay man I was when I first entered that club and toward a confident, glamorous type of womanhood, as I danced with Lenora that night in three-inch ornately strapped heels and a dress made of black lace, which stretched to fit my increasingly feminine frame.

We got on the alternative floor, and the familiar strains of New Order came on. In that black box populated by people and lights, I suddenly remembered what I thought I would never forget, that on a November night almost five years before, this was the place where Ralph and I met, him under a rose light and me a different person. I tried to dance to the words I serenaded him with long ago—"Every time I see you falling / I get down on my knees and pray"—but as I listened to the lyrics more carefully, I realized this was a song not of hope but of loss. "Why can't we be ourselves like we were yesterday?" the singer asked. "I don't think you're what you seem." As I glanced at the corner where Ralph and I first danced and spied the same flashing light without him under it, I found myself clamoring for something else to remember.

"I'm going to the other dance floor!" I shouted to Lenora, who waved me along as she closed her eyes to face the lights above her. There was a lounge area between the two floors, and after I swayed and bobbed to get there, I felt like I was in a sort of gender purgatory. Many of the regulars on the floor I came from knew me by sight, had seen the shifts in my appearance. Because of this, I could tell they still saw me as a cross-dressing man because their perception had been shaped by their memory. But among the familiar faces in the lounge were the occasionals who weren't part of this queer alternative scene, the kind who treated Liquid as a temporary stop on their tour of Boston nightlife. I could tell them apart as I ambled to the long bar along one side of the room, based simply on how they eyed me, looks of appraisal from women, smiles of appreciation from men as they reminded me of the paradox residing in my body. In less than a year, I had transformed from a short, ordinary man to an attractive, slim woman with light blond hair and unusual features. Yet the more beautiful I was perceived, the greater the danger if the wrong person were to find out I was trans.

"What are you having?" a voice behind me with a foreign accent asked, after his hand rested on the small of my back for an almost indiscernible moment.

"Fuzzy Navel," I replied, quickly shifting my plan to just grab water. I only ordered alcohol when men offered to buy me a drink, so I wouldn't seem like a prude.

I chuckled when he ordered for me, pronouncing the drink hesitantly as though his tongue had just woken up. As I gingerly sipped while he downed his rum and Coke, he introduced himself as Alex and told me he had just arrived in Boston to study medicine, after being in the Israeli army the past couple of years.

"I didn't think the girls here were so pretty," he said, "and then I saw you."

Maybe it was the accent, but this didn't sound like a line coming from Alex. Or maybe it was just that he was pretty himself in that stereotypical way I'd always thought unattainable, until I became a thin blond stereotype of my own, his angled, scruffy jawline balanced by languid eyes, his bulging forearms offering a preview of a muscular build under his black dress shirt with the sleeves rolled up.

"Drink your drink so we can dance," he said as he took my hand.

Though I usually took just a sip or two whenever guys bought me drinks, I quickly swallowed the rest of my Fuzzy Navel since Alex was watching, and I wanted to be that confident, carefree American girl for him. It was a good thing I'd tucked, less in preparation for dancing this close to someone but because men had already grabbed me without my permission, and I was afraid of what would happen if they touched the wrong place. Before that night, I was also too afraid to engage with men who didn't know I was trans, so I was content to dance around the ones who approached me at clubs, presenting myself as an alluring yet unattainable creature.

But as Christina Aguilera flirted in song and told a guy she just needed to be rubbed the right way, I found myself dancing close with Alex. With the help of vodka and darkness, I overcame the fear of up-close discovery and found myself with him for the better part of an hour, his hand traveling up and down my back, as we made two more trips to the bar for drinks, until the DJ announced last call. I was more relaxed than I'd ever been with a man who didn't know I was trans.

"My friend and me can drive you home," Alex said when last call was announced. And when I replied that I came with a friend too, he offered to also drive Lenora. I was excited by what this implied, wanted to extend the night for as long as possible, so I agreed. Just then, I saw Lenora's red hair out of the corner of my eye and told her the plan.

"I don't think that's a good idea," Lenora told me, the last strains of ABBA's "Dancing Queen" in the background. I told her she could get a cab if she liked, but I was getting a ride, and she reluctantly agreed to come.

After we got our coats, mine made of shiny white plastic to contrast with my black dress, Alex led us to the door as his friend drove to the club entrance and picked us up in a black SUV. Lenora sat in front as we drove through the winding streets of East Cambridge toward South Boston to her loft, where we planned to drop her off before going to my place. Alex put his hand on top of mine on the car's leather back seat, and I felt a twinge of what it would be like to be just a woman with a handsome, med-school-student boyfriend, away from the complications of who I was.

As a gas station came within sight, Alex asked his friend to stop because he was thirsty and wanted to grab something to drink. His friend parked in a dark spot at the side of the station, and Alex asked me to come with him to keep him company. Lenora turned around in her seat, and our eyes met. We were in the middle of nowhere late at night, and as I looked out onto the bright fluorescent lights of the gas station convenience store, I wondered if Alex suspected something.

But I had learned that acting out of the ordinary aroused even more suspicion, and not wanting to get out of the car when I had been so friendly just a moment before would certainly do that, so I allowed Alex to take my hand as we walked from the unlit parking lot toward the station's store. As I trailed slightly behind him, I saw the substance of his body as an outlined shadow against light and wondered about everything he was capable of, pleasure and violence. I imagined everything he might see under the glare of those store fluorescents, the protrusion of my Adam's apple, the prominence of my brow, the flatness of my chest. I imagined the expression that would dawn on his face and the thought of it was almost as painful as the possibility of a fist or the bottom of a shoe.

When we rounded the corner and out of our companions' sight, Alex stopped walking and turned to me, as light from the deserted gas pumps behind him haloed his dark hair. "I just want to be alone with you," he said, raspy and low. "Do you want to take me home?"

"Not tonight," I replied breezily to mask every fear, an important skill I had learned in my struggle for life.

Alex kissed me like it was his last chance, his tongue deep in my mouth, his body against mine, the buttons of his shirt rustling as they brushed against the plastic of my coat. His hand pressed against the small of my back, in that limbo between car and gas station, where I didn't know what was darkness and what was light, or which of them I actually wanted. He must have sensed my arousal because his hand reached under my coat and rested on my bottom. I was momentarily lost in his solidity, somewhere far away I'd never been, until the distant sensation of skin on a swath of my bare inner thigh brought me back to myself, and I realized that his hand was under my dress, inching between my legs. I pressed my hand inside the crook of his elbow to stop him.

It didn't last long, a few seconds at most. I felt him resist my pressure, his hand insistent. I saw my face bloodied in the dark, my body crumpled on the ground. I used all my strength to push his elbow so his hand would leave me, as surprise registered on his face from the power beneath my small frame, and I slid my body out of his grasp.

"I want you so much," he whispered like it was an apology,

before I turned around to walk back to the car, allowed Alex to talk and pretend we couldn't find anything we liked so came back empty-handed. Lying with Lenora in her futon later that night, where I decided to sleep instead of getting dropped off at home, she told me she'd been afraid Alex had found out I was trans, that he might have wanted to leave me stranded at the gas station, or something else she didn't want to think about. Lenora was relieved it had all turned out fine but agreed it was a good call for me to stay with her instead of driving alone with the two men.

"Yeah, I'm glad it worked out," I said, as I lay on my side away from her and clutched a pillow, too dumb to say anything else.

By the time I performed my monologue in front of a few hundred people for several nights in February 2002, I'd already decided to be a woman the rest of my life. The fact that I could experience these threats and hear terrible stories from other women only fortified my belief that I should be a woman myself, that if I could see how being a woman was not the objectively ideal gender and still want to be one, then I was meant to be a woman after all. Just as I'd done in the books, movies, and TV shows I'd read and seen throughout my life, I identified with the challenges women faced rather than the power of men and found myself experiencing regret over the ways I had taken advantage of being male, how I didn't do household chores like the women in my family, how I was consistently praised for being smart while girls were only expected to be beautiful. Just as I'd struggled with how my whiteness unfairly advantaged me, being among women gave me the means to comprehend my immense alienation from the advantages of manhood.

As for the question of reassignment surgery, I concluded that it would be worth doing not because I hated my penis or my mental health was compromised, but because I didn't have a strong commitment to having a penis in the first place, and it made me feel like a more complete woman to have a vagina, which alone was worth the risk. But I could not have had surgery so quickly, or possibly had it at all, had Ralph not given me the money, even when it meant letting go of the person he loved, in the gender I could no longer be.

One of the things I'd always loved about Ralph was his strong sense of ethics, independent of what served his own interests. From the time it became clear that we weren't getting back together, he grew concerned over how I was going to adjust to not having the financial resources we had as a couple, and whether it would be fair to give me some of his money, something he brought up over dinner a few weeks after our breakup.

It wasn't something I'd considered at all. Even though Ralph and I shared our finances while we were together, I didn't feel entitled to his inherited wealth, which was part of why I didn't want to be listed as a co-owner of our condo, even when Ralph asked if I wanted to be. But he made the point that had we been straight and married, I would have been entitled to half his money, and it became a thought experiment between us, if we would have gotten married had we been straight. So many things would have been different, but, given that we were not actually married, I had no real claim to Ralph's wealth, so I told him that he could make whatever decision he felt was right.

He finally decided to give me twelve thousand dollars in exchange for a set of large, framed pictures I'd taken of his family and friends. The pictures themselves weren't worth anywhere near that much, but it comforted Ralph to think that he was helping me out by buying some of my art, how this was the best way to honor the end of our relationship. Yet I wondered whether he knew—consciously or not—that this was almost exactly the amount I needed to have reassignment surgery in Thailand.

It certainly would have been tougher to make that decision had I moved through the world thinking of myself as just like anyone else, as normal. One of the big adjustments about being a trans person is standing out, being different from most anyone else. But having been white in a sea of brown people, a first-generation immigrant among native-borns, especially in the elite circles I operated in, I was so much less intimidated than other people would be about the prospect of being radically different.

It would have also been harder had I been closer to my family and sought their approval. But I was estranged from my mother and only had a tenuous relationship with my father, who I didn't talk to about my transition until I was supposed to come to New York for my sister's sweet sixteen party, the summer after I started living as a woman full-time. His reply on the phone when I told him I would come as a woman: "As long as you're beautiful." As for my family in the Philippines, they were so far away and I saw them so infrequently that I figured I would cross that bridge when I got there.

Though I did not anticipate how much the world had gotten smaller. Even though Talacsan did not have internet, the adjacent city of Baliwag did, and one of Nanay Coro's neighbors apparently frequented an internet café where he periodically looked me up online. That was where he discovered that I had changed my name and photograph on my MIT web site. I found this out on one of my visits to New York, where my father told me that my grandmother had been waiting at my aunt's house to speak to me on the phone.

"I do not understand," Nanay Coro said when I heard her frail, distressed voice on the line. "Why can't you just dress like a girl sometimes? Why do you have to change your name?"

I tried to explain that bakla did not exist in America, that it was a lot harder to just dress in women's clothes and wear makeup on the street, or to be feminine like my cousin Jembong or the hair-dressers at the salon. In America, doing that would get you beaten up or even killed. In America, I had to become a woman.

"I loved you so much," she said in English as she cried, and I wondered if I had misheard. But she said it again, "I loved you so much," her tense unmistakable. My grandmother only used English when she tried to span the gap from her world to mine, like when she told me to bring Ralph to the Philippines to demonstrate her support. Now the woman who promised me she would always love me was talking about that love as though it were in the past. The rejection rippled through me, and I had to get off the phone for fear that she would say something else we would both regret.

Though once I had time to think, I refused to believe that Nanay Coro no longer loved me. What she actually wanted to say was that she no longer recognized me, and I understood how she couldn't feel love for someone she did not comprehend. I determined that she would love me again someday once she came to know the woman I would become.

Another person I didn't entirely account for was Tony, who

called me from California one afternoon in March 2002, after I'd scheduled my reassignment surgery for that June, to tell me that he'd decided to go back to the Philippines and live there.

"Here I'm only your shadow," he said. "Back home I can be myself."

"Are you sure you wanna leave? You'll be the eldest son in three months," I joked.

"You really doing that? Papa's okay with it?"

"He's thinking of going with me to Thailand for the surgery."

"You can do whatever you want."

I heard resentment in his voice, over the freedom I had to be trusted to make my own decisions, when my family always expected my brother to make the wrong choices. He told me he didn't want to talk for a while, so he could be his own man, and I respected his wishes. Three years later, I got a call from my stepmother. Tony's heroin addiction had started during his first stint in juvenile detention and ended at a drug rehab facility in Manila, where my brother hanged himself with one of his bedsheets.

Lenora decided to have a going-away party for me at her place, the night before I left for Thailand—I would move directly to San Francisco for art school after my recovery. I'd left some books at the old apartment I shared with Ralph, who offered to drive with me to Lenora's after I picked them up.

Though the two of us had dinner at least once a month since we had broken up, I knew it might be the last time I would get to talk to Ralph alone before I moved, not only across the country but to a gender that would permanently separate us. A typical Englishman,

Ralph was not prone to talking about his feelings at length, so I figured I needed to be the one to draw them out, as we entered that largely desolate zone between our old apartment and Lenora's South Boston loft, plunged into darkness except for the car's headlights.

"I keep thinking about how strange it is that we love each other so much, but this one thing stands between us."

"It's a big thing, the biggest really," he replied. "When I look at you I feel as if the person I fell in love with died, and the person in front of me is very much like him, but isn't him." Maybe he felt the immensity of that ride too and was more forthcoming than he had ever been. "Are you sure you're ready?"

"I am." I looked down at my lap because I was about to say something hard. "But if there's a chance we can still be together, I'll call it off." Maybe that could be our compromise, that I wouldn't transition all the way if he could accept me as a woman.

"That wouldn't be fair to you," Ralph said, his eyes on the road. "You'll always wonder what your life could have become."

"I'll always love you, Ralph," I said as we reached Lenora's, and I could finally see his face, from his headlights' reflection when he parked the car in front of a brick wall. He turned off the ignition, and it was dark again.

"I don't think I'll ever love anyone as much as I loved you."

As we made our way from the parking lot to Lenora's building, I heard echoes of my grandmother in the words of my partner, the two people I loved most in the world, one I'd left for a life in America, the other I was about to leave so that I could be a woman. It hurt so much to know that the man I had been was dead to Ralph along with a love I thought would last our lifetimes, when to me that man I had been was still with him, just in a different form.

In their utter generosity, both Ralph and Nanay Coro let me go out of fairness to me, yet I wondered then why they didn't demand of me what was fair to them. At the same time, it was true that I would always wonder what it was like on the other side of gender, that the wondering would be even worse than staying where I was for this man I loved.

Ralph and I managed to walk into that goodbye party together. Richard was there, along with my two half sisters, who took the bus from New York, sixteen and fifteen at the time, pictures of innocent beauty. Papa and his wife had to work, so they couldn't come, and he ended up not being able to take the time off to be at the surgery with me, so I was going to Thailand by myself. I wanted to invite Ben to the party, but his phone was disconnected, and he didn't respond to my email; I hoped he was all right.

There were no speeches that night, no public goodbyes, just conversations among friends, which fortified me because I would have the actual experience alone, of becoming a woman, naked or dressed, legally and medically, in the eyes of the world. I boarded the plane to Thailand the next morning, and that flight became my bridge in a direction I wanted to travel, even when I wasn't sure what it would be like when I arrived.

The last time I came to Harvard, May 2018. The old Harvard Gay and Lesbian Caucus, now the Harvard Gender and Sexuality Caucus, had invited me to speak at their commencement dinner and receive an award. I'd boycotted that group for over a decade because it refused to change its name to incorporate trans people, and I was pleased to be invited to address it once the organization finally did, as someone who was in a position to affect the perspectives of others through my writing.

"It was at this dinner that I came out to my parents as a gay man," I told the gathered crowd in that grand dining hall. "So it pleases me to know that this organization has taken the first step in recognizing transgender alumni." I emphasized that there were many more steps to be made before we could feel like we fully belonged among them. I was pleased to see my old friend Kit Clark at the table closest to my podium, same as ever as he audibly shushed a white man next to him who was talking while I spoke.

But I also wished I could have seen other trans people in that room, or that I could have met any over dinner after that talk. In particular, I wished that Jamie Park could have been there, the college friend I sang *Miss Saigon* with all those years ago. She was now Eve but, because of her traditional Korean family, was still not publicly disclosed as trans. In a room of more than a hundred queer Harvard alumni, who in theory accepted trans people, I still found myself alone because of so many barriers that kept us from being in that room—the bullying in school, the lack of parental support, the social isolation, the discrimination at work, the judgment of the world. I worked hard to be able to count myself as a person who could be raised up as worthy of imparting wisdom to groups of people, but I could never forget how much passing has shielded me from the worst effects of being trans.

I woke up the following morning at a hotel near MIT that the alumni group had booked because there were no affordable rooms in Harvard Square. Improbably, my eleventh-floor room looked

out onto the path I habitually took with Richard during that fe-
verish time when I couldn't tell whether I was in love with him or
with the feeling of womanhood I got from him. I walked down the
path that morning, sat on the same bench Richard and I used to
sit on, though it was May and the oak trees above me were verdant,
the straight lines of the building behind it comforting instead of
cold. I last saw Richard a year before, when he came to New York
for a talk, and I caught up with him over dinner, where he told me
about his wife and kids, his professor job at a small liberal college
in Pennsylvania, a life I didn't want. Both of us had lost touch with
Lenora, who moved to New York for her art MFA the same year I
moved to San Francisco, and sent me an email a few months later
letting me know that what happened with Richard had not been
okay and she didn't want to be friends anymore. It took time, but
she did feel my betrayal after all.

As I left that bench, I wondered why becoming a woman had
seemed so urgent then, when it felt so mundane now, as I realized
that being a woman was less important to me than having experienced being a woman, that I'd grown much less precious about
how people gendered me, even though I still felt alienated from
the toxic parts of manhood. I returned to my hotel room to pick
up my bags, then got on the T to South Station and the train that
would take me home to Brooklyn, where my partner, Josh, and our
dog, Ronnie, were awaiting my return. It had been an unexpectedly long time away, when I agreed to take a last-minute trip for
work and had gone to LA right before coming to Harvard. I posted
online about being on the West Coast, and Ralph texted me to see
if I wanted to meet up; he had left MIT to teach at Oxford the same

year I left for art school, but had returned to the States to be a professor at USC a few years before.

Englishmen might have a reputation for avoiding feelings and awkward interactions, but it was Ralph who'd kept up with me over the nearly two decades since our breakup. He was the one who asked to have brunch in 2005 when I moved to New York, who I saw a couple of times when I was at Cornell for grad school and he gave talks in the area. He got me used to keeping in touch despite the challenges of distance and ambivalent feelings, something I hadn't been able to do with important people in my life up until then.

I'd seen his hair turn grayer over the years, the wrinkles around his kind eyes deepen, so those changes didn't feel surprising when I saw him at a café in West Hollywood on a too-sunny day. I asked after his family like usual, his mother, Sandra, his sisters, Frances and Julia. I used to ask about his dating life but stopped a few years earlier because he never mentioned anyone special, and I didn't want to think of him as lonely or unhappy. His father, Martin, had died a few years before, so he was now officially Sir Ralph Wedgwood, even though he refused to use the title. I grinned as I recalled that fleeting moment when I imagined myself a Lady, a fantasy I'd made my own and turned into real life.

He asked me how I was, and I felt words about to leave my mouth, my mind a split second too late to consider them.

"I just got engaged," I said.

It had happened a couple of nights before I left on the trip, when Josh got into bed and told me he thought it would be a good idea for us to get married. I wasn't prepared because the two of us had both started out four years earlier firmly believing that marriage was too confining an institution, even though I'd harbored a desire for a permanent relationship, having lived a life that was constantly in flux. Unbeknownst to me, Josh had grown to want that too. Because his proposal was so casual, no bended knee or a ring I wouldn't wear because I was too afraid to lose expensive jewelry, I didn't even register that night as a momentous life event until I said it out loud and saw the flitter of sadness on Ralph's face as his eyes closed for more than a blink.

"I'm happy for you," Ralph said when he opened his eyes again.

Someone observing us wouldn't find anything amiss, just two old friends catching up, but I could tell from the lingering pauses in the rest of our conversation that part of Ralph's mind was thinking of what I had just said. Maybe there were questions he wanted to ask, and maybe he too could tell I wasn't the same, because I also had questions I wanted answered. Like whether my transition mattered as much as he thought it would. Like whether he still saw Marc as dead, the person before him fundamentally different from the man he loved. Like whether he still thought of his love for me as something in the past. But those questions guaranteed answers I didn't want to hear, so I kept them to myself, brought them on the plane to the city where we fell in love, and kept them intact in this subway car, where I hoped they would dissipate when I got home and saw Josh's face.

As the train pulled out of the station, I suddenly remembered the question I asked myself one fall day riding down those same tracks nearly twenty years ago: *Could you be any happier?* Back then, an impossible answer occurred to me: *You might be happier as a woman.*

But I had made that impossible answer possible. I was a woman now, had been a woman approaching half my life, and because the train was leaving the station again, I couldn't help but ask myself the same question: *Could you be any happier?* As the train left its tunnel and began to hover over the Charles, I had to admit to myself that this was not a fair question to have asked all those years ago, even though I preferred being a woman over being a man, or that I was in a lasting relationship with someone who loved me for everything I was. By a certain measure, I was the happiest, the most content I'd ever been, but if I'd asked myself the same question at various points since my transition, my answer would have been: I was happier before, but maybe that's all right. I spent so much of that time believing that I had lost the love of my life only to suffer the harshest tragedies. I had a hunch that becoming a woman would end up being better and turned out to be right, but even if I wasn't, my journey across gender would have still been worthwhile.

I could have stayed a man, or at least presented myself as my version of one, and lived with Ralph in England as a professor's partner at Oxford, moved with him when he decided to go back to the States. I could have stayed in the Philippines and become a doctor. I could have gone back to the farm to live with my grandmother and manage her business. All of these, for me, could have been happy lives, and at each turn, my decision to leave made it impossible for me to return to where I'd been.

I closed my eyes as I crossed that bridge, because it hurt to know that had I been the person now that I was twenty years ago, I might have stayed in place and spared two shattered hearts, mine and that of the man I loved as a man. Had I been the person now that I was at fifteen, I would have insisted on not leaving Nanay Coro's side and prevented a different pair of heartbreaks. Yet maybe I needed to cross this many bridges to get to a state where even if there emerged other bridges I would want to traverse, I was finally satisfied with staying put, because I now know there's no such thing as the single best, the single fairest life.

ACKNOWLEDGMENTS

A book that spans much of my lifetime feels like it also requires a lifetime of thanks, but I will do my best with the space I have. The idea for this book came out of my writing about trans memoirs while on staff at *BuzzFeed News*. Thanks to Shannon Keating for the assignment and Isaac Fitzgerald for his early encouragement, along with lovely colleagues Azeen Ghorayshi, Eleanor Kincaid, Julia Furlan, Sandy Allen, Anne Helen Petersen, Sarah Karlan, and Karolina Waclawiak.

A fellowship from Jack Jones Literary Arts gave me the time and encouragement to keep going. Huge thanks to Kima Jones and LaToya Watkins for making this possible, along with the contribution of an anonymous donor. Enormous thanks to the OG Jack Jones crew, especially Kat Chow for her invaluable feedback and Jenna Wortham, my great supporter and friend in all ways possible; I'm so lucky to have gotten lost in the woods with you.

Thank you to my writing group for their valuable emotional and intellectual support: Lilly Dancyger, Nina St. Pierre, Voichita Nachescu, Zaina Arafat, Kaitlin Ugolik, and especially dear friends Lewis Wallace, Tim Manley, and Kaye Toal. A magical "Don't Write Alone" weekend from Catapult transformed my writing, thanks to Cal Morgan, Mira Jacob, Julie Buntin, and especially Porochista Khakpour, who took away a decade's worth of writing hurdles in a single hour; I'm so fortunate that you have since become my dear friend.

Much of this book was written while on self-imposed retreats in the Philippines and Guatemala. Thanks to the staff of Pyramid Guesthouse in Dumaguete, especially Leonor Cabigon, and thank you to the hotel staff at Laguna Lodge and La Fortuna in Atitlán, especially Jen Garcia, who kept me well-fed in both body and spirit.

Enormous thanks to my colleagues and former colleagues at *them* and Condé Nast for your friendship, insights, and snack breaks: J. P. Brammer, Cameron Bird, Kelly Bales, Aaamina Khan, Maria Tridas, James Clarizio, Tyler Ford, Sam Escobar, Samhita Mukhopadhyay, Chris Klimovski, Carolyn Kylstra, Michael Cuby, Lale Arikoglu, and especially my beloved favorite editor-turned-colleague Tyler Trykowski and dear Phillip Picardi, who has restored some of my faith in white male bosses, especially when they grow into friends.

Speaking of friends, many thanks to the emotional and intellectual support from mine—grad school pals Kristie Wang, Dana Koster, Will Cordeiro, Téa Obreht, Stephanie DeGooyer, Patrick Ayscue, Sarah Senk, and Michael Collis, along with great teachers Helena Maria Viramontes, Natalie Melas, Stephanie Vaughn, Shirley Samuels, Roland Greene, J. Robert Lennon, Alison Lurie, and Jonathan Monroe. Thanks to Harvard friends Lisa Gordon, Kit Gattis, Dana Gotlieb, Joseph Barretto, Lucia Brawley, and Alex Myers; MIT friends Richard Russell, Dav Clark, and Keith Thoresz; and art school friends Stephen Goldstine, Tanya Zimbardo, and Anna Maltz. Thanks to friends who don't belong to a definable category: Christina Newhard, Larilyn Sanchez, Julie Sionzon, Andrew Janke, Jess Dalton, Nick Rees, Vanessa Scott, Matthew Davidson, Arlene Bubbico, Rodger Garcia, and Diana Sahagun. Thanks and apologies to all the wonderful friends I've temporarily forgotten.

Thanks to the many editors who have immensely improved my work, especially Tennessee Jones, Megan Carpentier, Jacob Gross, Jess Zimmerman, Jen Parker, and Gabriel Arana, who convinced me to become a journalist in the first place. Huge thanks to my wonderful media and writer friends, including Hugh Ryan, Thomas Page-McBee, Raquel Willis, Elsz, Josh Allen, Geena Rocero, Fran Tirado, R. O. Kwon, Amanda Shapiro, Robert Moore, Hannah Giorgis, Kimberly Drew, Devin-Norelle, Drew Philp, Alex Chee, Esmé Wang, and Jacob Tobia. Particular thanks to early readers Peter Kispert, Matt Ortile, and Johnny Pizzolato, as well as wonderful blurbers Garrard Conley, Jenny Boylan, and Alex Marzano-Lesnevich. Enormous and special thanks to Jackson Howard, my sister in twinkness and book gossip; Amber Tamblyn, my sister in child-star-turned-author-slash-feminist fierceness; and Alok Vaid-Menon, my sister in deep gender, Cancer feelings, and bright colors.

Enormous thanks to family and friends who won't be able to read this but whose spirit I carry with me always: Socorro Talusan, Gaudencio Talusan, Ramon Antonio Talusan, and Joseph Hummel.

Almost finally, enormous thanks to the people who worked tirelessly to make this book the best it can be, especially my stellar editor who has never once asked for an explanatory comma, Elda Rotor, and my cool-as-a-cucumber agent Seth Fishman. Thanks also to the Viking dream team: Elizabeth Vogt in editorial; Maya Baran, Lindsay Prevette, and Sara Delozier in publicity; Nora Alice Demick and Mary Stone in marketing; Nayon Cho for her incandescent cover design; copy editor Andrea Monagle for being so patient with my ESL holdovers; and production editor Lavina Lee for being just as obsessed as me about getting details right.

Special thanks in his own paragraph to Ralph Wedgwood, for everything you've given me, including the permission to write this book entirely on my own terms.

Finally, thank you to my motley and improvised family: Juno and Joe Rosinsky, Clara de Jesus, Zeke Ramirez, Alberto Ramirez, Kris Sugatan, Jill Hanson, Ronnie Talusan Hanson, Cindy Sevilla, Monique Malvar, Lauren LaMance, Casey and Erik Crooks, Mark and Nanette Antonio, and Grace and Liza Talusan. Special and boundless thanks to Joe and Gloria Hanson for allowing me to partake of their unwavering parental love, and whose enormous generosity in all ways has made this book possible.